THE EDUCATION ACT AND YOUR CHILD

Felicity Taylor

Illustrations by Edward McLachlan

Longman Group UK Limited
Longman House
Burnt Mill, Harlow, Essex CM20 2JE, England
and Associated Companies throughout the World

First published 1990

Set in Linotron 202 10/12 pt Gill Sans by Best-set Typesetter Ltd

Produced by Longman Group (FE) Ltd
Printed in Hong Kong

British Library Cataloguing in Publication Data

Taylor, Felicity, *1934–*
  The Education Act and your child. –
[Successful parenting guides).
   1. Great Britain. Education. Law
   I. Title   II. Series
   344.1047

   ISBN 0-582-05079-0

Contents

Introduction

It was the bitter teachers' dispute that crystallised many parents' dissatisfaction with the way schools were run. A system that did not seem to know what the legal responsibilities of teachers were, nor how to keep schools open, was easily discredited. This was why the very wide-reaching reforms in the 1986 and 1988 education acts went through without much popular opposition. They may have been resisted by the people who ran education, but the public couldn't see much wrong with them.

The move was away from relying on heads and LEAs to do the right thing, towards setting out a legal framework and giving parents guaranteed rights over what goes on in schools. When people have rights, it creates a different climate. They have to be taken seriously and they can exert real power over what happens in schools. In the new Education Reform Act, parents have a substantial voice on the governing body, can make formal legal complaints about the curriculum in their school and can opt out of local authority control altogether.

This makes it even more important for parents and schools to work together. It is confusing for the child and frustrating for the teacher or parent if the school and the home seem to be pulling in different directions. They can support one another so much better when each understands what the other is trying to achieve, and what the obstacles are.

There is another important principle at stake too, that professionals should be accountable for the work they do. Schools are set up by our society to educate our children. As a society we have a right to know what they are doing, what their aims are, how they are working towards those aims, and what success they are having in reaching them. If they can explain and justify all that to a group representing parents and the public at large they should be on the right lines.

So it is essential for parents and other members of the public to be involved in schools. Schools need the perspective of the person in the street who is not a professional, but can bring a fresh eye to bear on what is going on in education. Schools also need a supporters' club who will champion their school, help it to get the resources it needs, celebrate its successes, criticise and commiserate with its failures. So does education.

FINDING A SCHOOL

Most parents want their children to go to a school near home, where they will do well, be happy and make good friends. It doesn't seem much to ask, and in fact many parents do find what they want in the school down the road. It's when the nearest school hasn't got a very good name, or when there is a choice of schools within easy reach, that parents begin to worry.

At one time these worries were not taken very seriously by the local education authorities (LEAs), who used to claim that all their schools provided a good education. That has changed now that parents have more legal rights to choose a school. What's more, it's now known from research[1] that parents are right to think some schools better than others at providing a good education.

Finding the right school for your child is important, so it is worth taking some trouble to see what your local schools are like, and which one you think would suit you and your child.

What you need to know

The law gives you the right to know a good deal about your local schools. The local education authority (LEA) must publish a booklet with the basic information about all the local schools, obtainable free from the Education Offices. Local voluntary schools (often run by the churches) must also publish information. This is often included in the LEA booklet. The booklet must explain the rules for deciding how children are given places in each school. Much other useful information is there too, about grants, special educational needs, travel to school etc.

Then each school has to produce its own prospectus, which sets out the aims of the

[1] *15,000 hours: secondary schools and their effect on children* Michael Rutter and others Open Books, 1979
School Matters: the junior years Peter Mortimore and others Open Books, 1988

school, what is taught there, and how it is taught. Parents must be told what kind of sex education and religious education is given in the school. The prospectus explains how the school is organised, gives school hours and holiday dates, sets out the policy for rules and good behaviour, lists what clubs and other activities are provided out of school and so forth. Secondary schools must also publish last year's exam results.

Each school also has to keep a stock of general information about education, that parents and other interested people can refer to if they wish. As well as the LEA and school prospectuses, the school must provide the syllabuses and schemes of work used in the school for each age group. You will be able to see for yourself what all the children should be taught and how the National Curriculum is organised. Information put out by the government, such as circulars and regulations about education, must also be there[2].

The LEA or the governors of the school can decide to have these documents translated into other languages than English if they wish.

You can learn a lot from all this information, not just the facts about the school, but also about how it chooses to talk to parents. It is a good sign if the material is clear, friendly and doesn't use educational jargon.

What to look for

However good the printed information is, there's no substitute for going to see the school yourself. You may be able to rule some schools out from the information you already have – for instance if they are single sex and you want a mixed school, or for religious reasons. But don't be in too much of a hurry to cross schools off your list, especially if you are rejecting them

[2] The Education (School Curriculum and Related Information) Regulations, 1989

because of local gossip. Have a look yourself first.

The school booklets should tell you how to arrange a visit. If not, ring up or write to the head and ask when you could come. It helps if you make a list of the things you think are important before you begin looking at the schools. You could also look through the prospectus and mark any points where you'd like more information, or anything you particularly want to look at. Don't expect to find a perfect school. Every school will have its own advantages and disadvantages. You will have to decide what matters most to you.

You might want to ask how large the classes are and whether very large classes get extra helpers. You're sure to want to know how parents are kept in touch with their children's progress and the part parents play in the life of the school. Exam and test results matter, but make sure you understand what they really show. For instance, a 100% pass rate doesn't mean a lot if only two pupils took the exam.

As you walk about the school, do you get the impression that there's a lot going on there? Noise isn't important, if it's a busy noise of

children working together, not just an undisciplined gabble. Notice the way children behave to one another and to the teachers. And notice the way the teachers behave to the children and to one another. The standard of behaviour can be formal or informal but you can still usually tell if everyone seems to be on good terms with one another.

A school may not be able to do much about its buildings and decoration, but it can do its best to keep them clean and tidy. Is work done by the children, (not the teachers) displayed in classrooms and corridors? And if so, does it look well-cared for? Or is it dog-eared and dusty, or even worse, disfigured by graffiti?

The more schools you visit, the more you'll be able to get a feel of what it would be like to be a pupil there and whether it's what you want for your child.

How to get a place

You've decided on the school, and how you want to make sure your child gets in. Although the law gives you the right to say which school you prefer, there is no absolute guarantee of a place there for your child. There are three good reasons in law for refusing you a place. These are: that the school is full; that it is a selective school and your child doesn't meet the standard required; that it is a church school with its own rules about admissions.

Most parents do get the school they choose, but there has to be some system for deciding which children get priority if a school can't take everyone who applies. The rules for settling this must be published in the school prospectus.

The rules will give criteria, in order of importance, which decide how places are offered. The first criterion often gives priority to children who have a brother or sister already in the school. The next priority, sometimes the first, will be for children living near the school.

Some LEAs draw up catchment areas round the school. A place at the school is guaranteed to every child living in the catchment if they want it. Voluntary church schools usually give first priority to children who are members of the church. Most schools will take medical or social reasons into account. You should ask your doctor or social worker to write a letter supporting your claim and send it in with the application form if this applies to you.

If you want a place at a popular school, it's important to make sure to mention any special reasons for your child to get a place there when you fill in the transfer form. Don't wait until you have been turned down before making them known.

When the school you want is a long way from home, and there are other suitable schools nearby, the LEA may not provide free transport to school. Some LEAs will only pay for travel in this case if it is to a church school. You can find out from the Education Offices what the rules are.

In any case, if you live a long way away from a popular school, and don't have priority for other reasons, there may not be much hope of getting in. Ask the head or the Education Offices about your chances. You can then decide whether to risk it, or to look for another school nearer home.

Open enrolment

The government has recently changed the rules about when a school is full, with the aim of giving parents more chance of a place at the school they want.

In theory schools are built to hold a certain number of children. This is calculated by 'forms of entry'. One form is counted as 30 pupils. The number of children depends on the number of forms of 30 pupils of the same age admitted each year. So a five form entry secondary school could take in 150 children each year and has room for 150 pupils in each year group. A two form entry primary school can take 60 children into the reception class, and the older classes.

Because of the fall in the birthrate there have not been enough children to fill all the existing schools. LEAs had to choose between three options. They could close schools altogether; they could amalgamate two or more schools; or they could reduce the size of schools by reducing the 'form entry'. LEAs used all three options. They didn't want to close every school surplus to requirements because they saw a chance to give schools extra space for new activities, like computers. They needed to keep some places in reserve in case numbers went up again. Also, closing schools is a messy and unpopular business.

So they gave each school a *designated* number which was published in the school prospectus, and were allowed to say that once that number was reached, the school was full. This meant that a very popular school could be turning pupils away although in theory there was physically room for them.

The government has now said that schools must go back to the *standard* number, usually the number that was admitted to the school in 1979, when school numbers were at or near their peak. Until that number is reached, the school isn't full.

It may therefore be easier to get a place in a popular school. There will also be much more competition between secondary schools to attract pupils since there are still not enough pupils to go round. (Primary schools are already seeing a rise in numbers, though not back to baby bulge levels.) Once Local Management of Schools (see chapter on School Finances) comes in, and schools get extra money for each extra pupil, there will be even more rivalry.

This could be a problem for parents. Many people choose a school because it is a small school. If schools have to cram in extra children, this may spoil the atmosphere that made the school popular.

Primary schools

When a child is to go into the reception class of a primary or first school, that is, the class for the youngest children of school age, parents need to find out well in advance what system the school has for taking in children of five and under. There are many different systems. Some schools draw up a list of rising fives – children who will be five by September or during the school year – in the spring term. These children are then given places for the beginning of the term in which they are five. Other schools offer places in September for all the rising fives, even those who will not be five until next summer.

When there are more children than places, the choice has to be made according to the rules published in the prospectus, and not on a first come first served basis. But it's still the case that you are more likely to get a place if you have put your child's name down before the list is drawn up. Latecomers may find that all the places have already been allocated.

Once a formal offer of a place has been made in writing, it can't be taken away. Don't rely on informal promises, as these can be misunderstood. Ask for a written offer of a place.

Secondary schools

You have the same rights to choose a secondary school, and the system has to follow the same legal rules. Schools must tell parents about the criteria used to allot places if there are too many applicants. The arrangements for moving on (transfer) to secondary school are often organised centrally by the Education Offices instead of by the headteacher. You should get a *secondary transfer* booklet from the LEA, probably in the autumn term before your child is to leave primary school, explaining the system and the forms you need to fill in.

Children with special needs

Parents of children with special needs may want to have them educated in a special school or in a *mainstream* school alongside other children. In practice they often find that they have fewer rights than other parents, because of lack of resources for meeting their children's needs. Even though the 1981 Education Act said that children with special needs should attend mainstream schools wherever possible if their parents wished, it may be a hard struggle to persuade the LEA to provide the extra support needed.

However, many more children with special needs are now successfully educated in mainstream schools in spite of all the difficulties.

When parents choose special education the LEA may be reluctant to accept the parent's choice of a special school, especially if it is one outside their own area for which they will have to pay. Although parents can appeal about choice of school, the decision of the appeals panel is not binding on the LEA if the child has a *statement* of educational need.

Appeals about choice of school

If the worst happens and you are told that you cannot have a place at the school of your choice, you do have the right of appeal. You should be told how to do this when you get the refusal.

Your appeal will be heard by an independent committee of local people with an interest in education. The Council on Tribunals has issued a code of practice which the committees have to follow. You should get reasonable notice of the date of the appeal and about a week beforehand you should receive details of the reasons why the school could not give you a place.

At the hearing, when you have a chance to state your reasons for wanting that school, make sure that this is as full as possible. Don't leave anything out that might help you. It helps if you take a friend along with you to give advice and support. The committee should provide an interpreter for parents whose first language is not English.

The LEA (or governors for a voluntary school) will put their case, and if they claim the school is full, they will have to produce evidence to prove that taking an extra child will damage the education of the other children. You will be able to question the evidence and the panel members will also ask questions.

Both sides will then withdraw and the committee will make their decision. Firstly, they have to decide whether the rules for allocating places were applied fairly in your case. If they think you were unfairly treated they will decide in your favour.

If they accept that the rules were applied fairly, and other people did have a better claim to a place than you, they then have to look at your reasons for wanting the place, and the school's reasons for refusing you. They must weigh one against the other and decide who has the better case. If they decide in your favour, the school has to give your child a place. This decision cannot be rejected by the LEA, except in the case of children with a statement of special needs.

So it is possible for the committee to overrule the LEA or the governors if they think you have a good enough case. Most appeals turn on one very difficult question: do the interests of one individual child outweigh the problems an extra child will cause to a school which is already full? It's often complicated by the fact that there may be a large number of appeals for a very popular school, so the panel also has to balance one child's needs against a number of others. About a quarter of appeals are successful. Appeals panels seem generally to favour cases based on medical or social needs, or where it seems that natural justice has been infringed.

Further appeals

If you are unsuccessful, there are various options open to you. You could appeal to the Secretary of State for Education on the grounds that the Appeals Committee acted unreasonably in refusing your appeal. Although the Secretary of State is reluctant to rule against a panel, this has occasionally worked.

You could apply to a court for judicial review if you feel that an important point of law is involved in the way they handled your case. This would be expensive, but at least one Law Centre has successfully done this for a client.

If you think that the way places were allocated amounts to maladministration, you can complain to the Local Ombudsman, but not if a voluntary school is involved, as they do not come under the Ombudsman's authority.

Waiting lists

Some schools keep waiting lists of disappointed applicants. Since the turnover of pupils is high, especially in urban areas, you may stand quite a good chance of a place if you are near the top. But if other parents are making formal appeals and get places in that way, you could lose out. It may be worth appealing even if you are high on the list.

Keeping your child at home until you get the place you want

If you are good at bluffing, this may be an option. But it can be very uncomfortable for you and for your child. Some LEAs have threatened to take children into care because they are not attending school. It's more likely to work if there are a number of parents campaigning together as they can support one another and the children.

You may be better off accepting an alternative place and badgering the LEA regularly for the place you really want. It's worth saying that parents who accept a temporary alternative often decide that it's not worth moving their child once they have settled into the new school.

The whole process of finding a school can be a very distressing time for parents and children, and you need to consider very carefully just what is to be gained by sticking out for a school. You have to be sure that the alternative school is as unsatisfactory as it may have seemed at first sight. The stress and disruption to family life can have a very bad effect on your child, especially if you have to give way in the end.

WHAT CHILDREN LEARN

What children learn in state schools is no longer left to teachers to decide. The government have taken a firm hand in it, and school governors and parents also have a say. Through the National Curriculum and national testing and assessment the government hopes to make sure that all children, whatever school they go to and wherever they live, get a good broad education, and that parents can know what their children should be doing at school.

The law says that the curriculum of every school must be balanced and broadly based. It must also promote the spiritual, moral, cultural, mental and physical development of all pupils, and must prepare them for the opportunities, responsibilities and experiences of adult life.

This means that schools must offer children all the areas of learning and experience that go to make up a balanced preparation for life – physical, moral, social and creative as well as language, maths, science and technology.[1] So sport, music, drama, art and design are just as important as the subjects usually thought of as academic.

The school curriculum isn't just a matter of what is listed on the school timetable, a set of subjects or activities taught in the classroom. Almost as important are the other things children absorb at school, in the playground, in clubs and after school activities, in the whole business of getting on with one another and with teachers. These all have an effect on what and how children learn. Parents and governors, as well as teachers, have a lot to contribute to these aspects of the life of the school.

The National Curriculum

The National Curriculum lays down the subjects that form the core and foundation of

[1] Curriculum Matters 2 The Curriculum from 5–16, HMI, 1985, £2

what every child should learn at a state school. It's not the whole curriculum, but it will probably take up about 70–80% of school time. The table below shows which subjects are compulsory for every schoolchild right through from 5 to 16, and which are optional. Of course most children were already doing most of this at school before. What is new is the rule that all primary schoolchildren should spend some time on science and technology. Older pupils will no longer be able to give up science or languages at the age of 14.

Independent schools do not have to teach the National Curriculum

---

THE NATIONAL CURRICULUM 5–16

Compulsory core subjects
English, Maths, Science

Compulsory foundation subjects
History, Geography, Technology, Modern Language (secondary only), Art, Music, PE

Optional subjects
More Science, second Modern Language, Classics, Home Economics, Business Studies, Drama, etc

Religious Education
For all pupils whose parents wish it

Cross-curricular themes
May be taught through other subjects
Examples: Health Education, Personal and Social Education, Careers.

Children will be able to take optional subjects such as an extra language but they won't be able to drop any of the core and foundation subjects before they are 16.

Many of the subjects and themes not on the compulsory list are taught across the curriculum as one of the cross-curricular themes. In other words, the topics they include are covered under other subjects. For example, environmental education could be found in geography, science and history. There are also many other themes that will be found in more than one subject. These are the links that bind the whole framework together. In the future, when all the National Curriculum is in place, pupils may be following a timetable that is based on studying themes rather than separate subjects.

The National Curriculum programmes for the three core subjects, English, Maths and Science, were the first to be brought into schools, because they are the most important. Technology came next, because the government believes that it is essential for more people to be educated in scientific and technical subjects. Every child will now begin to study technology as well as science in the primary school.

Programmes for the other subjects are being prepared, but in the meantime, the Secretary of State for Education and Science has ruled that all the compulsory subjects have to be taught to all pupils under 14 for a reasonable part of the school timetable.

The Secretary of State lays down what has to be taught in each subject. He is advised by the National Curriculum Council. To begin with a working party of specialists in a subject makes a report and proposals about what that subject should consist of. The National Curriculum Council consults schools, teachers and other educational bodies, including governor and parent organisations, about the proposals. It then makes recommendations to the Secretary of State. After more consultation the Secretary of State lays Orders for that subject before Parliament, with the dates from which they will take effect. When approved by Parliament, the Orders become law, and can only be changed by Parliament.

Once they know what the curriculum is, Local Education Authorities (LEAs) have to decide on a policy for providing it in their schools. They issue guidelines, which may say for example that the education puts a high value on preparing 'all children for life in our multi-cultural society, building on the strengths of cultural diversity'.

The school governors can make minor changes to the LEA guidelines for their own school, but they can't change them fundamentally. Finally, headteachers have to organise the way the curriculum is taught in their school. They must follow the guidelines and the National Curriculum, but it's their job to arrange how this is all put into practice in the classroom.

The National Curriculum should make it easier for parents to know what is going on in the classroom. It can help to make sure that all schoolchildren get the essential core of knowledge, skills and experience which will give them the chance to do their best. Of course we have to be careful that by setting up a national structure we don't spoil the richness and variety of education in our schools. But most parents will welcome a framework that lets them know what their child should be achieving at important stages in their school life.

How does it work

To make sense of the National Curriculum you have to learn some new jargon. The first change is that the years of compulsory school from 5–16 are now named Years 1 to 11, the sixth form being years 12 and 13. So a child in what used to be the fourth year juniors is now in year 6.

This change helps to show how education is a continuous process. There shouldn't be a big gap between primary and secondary school. When children change schools, having a continuous National Curriculum will make it easier for the new school to build on what the previous school has done.

The new system is based on *the ten levels of attainment*, through which children progress in their years at school. These levels do not match children's ages, as children develop at different rates. They indicate what children can be expected to know, understand and be able to do in different subjects at that level.

There are *four Key Stages* – Key Stage 1 at age 7. Key Stage 2 at age 11, Key Stage 3 at age 14 and Key Stage 4 at age 16. These are the ages at which national testing and assessment of all school children will take place.

Most children at Key Stage 1 could be somewhere between Levels 1 and 3, and some might be much higher. At Key Stage 2 the range might be between Levels 2 and 6. They may well be at different levels in different subjects.

How will children learn?

Each National Curriculum subject has a number of *profile components*, which are a way of dividing up the subject into manageable sections. Maths for example, has two:

> Knowledge, skills, understanding and use of *number*, *algebra* and *measures*;
> Knowledge, skills, understanding and use of *shape* and *space* and *data handling*.

For each profile component there will be a set of *attainment targets* (ATs) covering all the topics that pupils would be expected to learn during their time at school. For example, there are 14 ATs for Maths. Here are two examples:

> 'Estimate and approximate in number'
> (or in other words guess roughly what the right answer to a problem will be).

> 'Collect, record and process data'
> (or in other words, find the answer and write down how you found it).

At each Key Stage, children have to cover the set ATs. These are all compulsory, you can't choose which to do.

The ATs are divided up into a series of small steps. Each step is called a *statement of attainment* and matches one of the ten levels. The statement of attainment shows what level a child has reached in that AT. Take, for instance, a statement of attainment in 'Estimate and approximate in number' at Level 2 (age about 7). This says 'Make a sensible estimate of a number of objects up to 20'. To demonstrate that they could do this, children might be asked to guess the number of coats on the coat pegs.

Programmes of Study for each subject are specified, along with the ATs. These give teachers an idea of the work to be covered for each attainment target. Here are two examples from the Level 2 Maths Programme:

Understanding the meaning of 'half' and 'quarter'

Recognising squares, rectangles and other shapes and talking about them.

To sum up, each subject has profile components, each profile component has attainment targets, each attainment target has statements of attainment and teachers have programmes of study to help them plan the lessons.

You can see that although the content of the curriculum is laid down, there is still plenty of

17

scope for teachers to devise their own ways of teaching in the classroom.

Profile components, attainment targets, statements of attainment and programmes of study are all laid down in the Orders that go through Parliament. The National Curriculum Council also publishes notes and advice on the Orders, known as non-statutory guidance. Copies of these materials are sent to every school and are available for parents to consult in schools. Although it looks complicated at first, the system is easy to understand in practice. Parents can read the documents which will be available in the school and understand what their children are doing and how they may be abe to help them.

What do the subjects look like?

English

The English working party report stressed the need for children to be able to use language in speaking, writing and listening so as to give themselves power over their own lives. English has three profile components: *Speaking and listening*; *Reading*; *Writing*.

Speaking and listening
This is a part of English teaching that has sometimes been neglected in the past. Yet children must be able to communicate orally as well as in writing, and understand what is said to them if they are to make progress. There is just

one AT – *Understanding the spoken word and being able to express onself effectively*. At Level 3, when most children would be 8 or so, one statement of attainment expects a child to be able 'to relate real or imaginary events in a connected narrative' to the teacher or a group of children.

Reading

Reading also has one AT – the ability to read, understand and respond to all types of writing, and to use reading to learn. So a child at Level 3 could talk about a story, describing what had happened to the leading characters.

The programme of study for 7–11 year-olds provides for children to have the chance to use and choose from a wide range of stories, poetry, non-fiction, magazines. It includes listening to stories, writing their own and 'publishing' them, discussing what they read with the teacher and with the class, understanding the key points in a piece of writing and being able to sum them up.

Writing

Writing has three ATs – being able to communicate meaning in writing; spelling; handwriting. At Level 2 a child would be able: to produce independently short pieces of writing with complete sentences; to understand that spelling has patterns and begin to be able to discuss them; to use upper and lower case letters consistently, i.e. not mixed within words.

Because of the belief in the power of language, the National Curriculum stresses that children have the right to teaching in standard English. Otherwise they would be at a disadvantage in jobs and higher education. But schools are told that standard English should be taught in ways that do not denigrate the non-standard dialects spoken by many children. Schools should build on the knowledge of language that children whose first language is not English will already have. However, these children will be assessed in English and not in their home language.

Children should have opportunities to find out about the structure of language including grammar. They should begin to understand how much variety there is in spoken and written language, and how to use it. The words used to talk about language then become part of the child's experience of writing, reading and speaking, instead of 'parts of speech' that are learned by rote and often not understood.

In the programme of study for writing, the need for structure and clarity is stressed. Children should be encouraged to use different kinds of writing depending on the audience, the subject and the purpose. They should also begin to understand how writing differs from talking, and how people's spoken languages can differ.

Maths

The problem with maths, especially in the primary school, is that many of the teachers don't like or understand it, let alone the children. The people on the maths working party were enthusiasts, who wanted every child to have a chance to experience the excitement and satisfaction of maths. They hoped that by having mathematical concepts clearly set out in the National Curriculum, teachers could be liberated from a lot of their anxieties. And so could parents.

The first maths profile component is about understanding how to use numbers, algebra and measuring. There are 8 ATs in this component. One is *Understanding number and number notation* – what numbers represent and how they are written down, including decimals. By Level 6 children should be able to compare decimals and fractions and put decimals in order.

Another is *Recognise and use patterns, relationships and sequences and make generalizations*. Old-fashioned maths teaching sometimes used to frown on this, but it's an important part of maths to be able to estimate (guess) roughly what an answer should be. Then you can avoid embarrassing mistakes.

The programme of study in this at Level 2 includes exploring and using patterns for

numbers work, and practice in mental arithmetic is an important part of learning this. But there is no point in doing pencil and paper sums just for the sake of it, once the basic concepts are understood.

The guidance offered by the National Curriculum Council stresses the need for maths to be closely related to practical tasks that help children to understand how to use maths in everyday life. This helps them to develop their mathematical skills and gives an incentive to learn new ones.

Science

It is certainly a new thing for our schools to have to teach science to every child from 5 to 16. We had been one of the very few countries who have allowed children to give up science at a very early age. Perhaps we can now hope that more children will come to experience what the Science working party saw as so important: an exciting and active process, often fun; a sense of wonder and respect for the world in which we live; a preparation for the world of work and leisure, and a continuity and progress tied in to other subjects, not studied as though it had no meaning outside the lesson.

The big argument over science was about whether all children should have to take a science course up to age 16 which would take up about 20% of the timetable. The science working party wanted this because they felt it was necessary for a balanced scientific education and to make sure of having the scientifically skilled workforce that will be needed in the 21st century. It was also thought that fewer girls would specialise in science in the sixth form if they were able to substitute other courses for part of the science course lower down the school.

However, the Secretary of State felt that a science course which would take up only 12.5% of the timetable should be available for some pupils, who might want to specialise in other subjects. Pupils taking the shorter course would drop some of the attainment targets in

addition and subtraction. It gives as an example 'Continuing the pattern 5, 10, 15, 20 . . .'

The second component concentrates on shape and space and how to handle quantities of information (data). It has 6 ATs on topics like *Using shape and space in real life problems*, *Collect, record and process data*, using computers where this is appropriate. By Level 3 children should be able to set up and use their own simple database on a computer.

The arguments about whether children should use calculators and computers or work only with pencil and paper is really an artificial one. Children would not be able to use a calculator accurately without understanding the way

Key Stage 4. The understanding is that most pupils would take the broader course.

The Secretary of State decided that there should be two profile components for science – *Exploration of science* and *Knowledge and understanding of science.*

Exploration of science has one AT – *Communication and the application of knowledge and understanding.* Children should learn to plan and predict, to design and carry out their own investigations, to interpret the result and present them to others. For instance at Level 3 a child should be able to distinguish between a 'fair' and an 'unfair' test, and interpret simple diagrams and bar-charts.

The programme of study for Key Stage I says that children should be encouraged to develop skills by tackling problems asking questions and suggesting ideas of the 'how', 'describe which . . .' 'find a way to . . .' variety. These should involve, for example, sorting, grouping and describing objects and recording the differences.

The second profile component *Knowledge and understanding of science* has 17 ATs covering all the different aspects of scientific knowledge from *The variety of life* to *Earth and atmosphere* to *Energy, Light, Sound and Space.* These do not all have to be studied at all the Key Stages. There is a clear structure of progress through scientific knowledge beginning with very simple ideas and building on these for work at higher levels.

AT19 for example, *Earth and atmosphere,* begins at Level I with the simple statement that pupils should know that the weather changes and be able to describe changes in weather conditions. By level 9 they should be able to explain scientifically how changes in the atmosphere cause various kinds of weather.

Any parent, especially those with no scientific background, could learn a lot about how to help their child with science from looking at the statements of attainment and reading the programmes of study.

Technology

Technology in the National Curriculum has a much broader philosophy than the traditional Craft, Design and Technology (CDT) already taught in many secondary schools. In addition to art and design, business studies, craft, design and technology, home economics and information technology, other subjects could contribute too. Music and drama productions give opportunities for designing and making; Humanities can involve knowledge and evaluation of the achievement of others as well; knowledge of maths and science would be essential.

Technology as a National Curriculum subject is to do with generating ideas, making and doing. It can provide balance in a curriculum which could easily be dominated by academic subjects, by developing the practical and creative skills of pupils. The aim will be to help pupils learn to innovate, to find solutions to problems and equally important, be aware of and respond to the needs of employers in our rapidly changing inevitably technological society.

Science is concerned with finding out about the nature of the physical and biological world. It tests ideas about how the world works. Design and technology always has an end in view. It has to take account of deadlines, cash limits and environmental factors. It almost always involves value judgements – is this a more efficient (better designed) car than that one? The answer to such questions usually includes the element 'it depends what you want it for'.

Now that design and technology is to be for everyone, it is even more important for it to be broad, balanced and relevant, especially for girls. This is to be done by using different settings, home, school, the community, leisure. Boys and girls will not be able to succeed in the attainment targets if they only take part in a very narrow range of activities.

Many primary and secondary schools were already covering the topics that are now included in design and technology. However, without a proper framework it is difficult for pupils to build on their experiences and to make progress. The Design and Technology syllabus will provide a structure for teachers to plan activities, encouraging broader and more balanced work than in the past.

There are two profile components. The first is *Design and technological capability*. The use of the word 'capability' is intended to stress the practical nature of technology. *Design and technological capability* has four ATs. AT 3 for example, *Planning and making*, is defined as:

> 'Working to a scheme derived from their previously developed design, pupils should be able to identify, manage and use appropriate resources, including both knowledge and processes, in order to make an artefact or system.'

In other words they should design an object, plan how to construct it, choose what materials to use, and then make it.

At Level 2, for instance, children might "explain why they would want to make a bird-scarer, draw a picture showing how they will make a scarecrow and how it will scare birds away from crops".

By Level 10 this has developed into a full-scale project, in which they have explored ideas and existing models, identified ways of improving and refining their proposals, predicted possible outcomes, resolved conflicting demands and included their decisions in a coherent specification. This would be done by a presentation and exhibition which includes a comprehensive folio of drawings, sketches and models, evidence of working to a plan and a justification of all the decisions taken including fitness for purpose, experiments and trials.

The second profile component is *Information Technology capability* (IT). Although computers and word processors will be used for most aspects of design and technology, and in many other subjects, it is important to make sure that pupils develop their skills and knowledge of IT in a systematic way. There needs to be a structure to make sure that this happens.

The special IT profile component is about pupils being able to use IT to communicate and handle information in many forms. Even at Level 1 pupils should be able to use a keyboard or 'mouse' to construct a simple story on the screen perhaps using sounds and pictures as well as words. At Level 3 pupils should be able to use a computer to store, retrieve, change and use information. For instance they would be able to use suitable software to choose pictures from a stored set of standard pictures in order to illustrate a story, and change them where necessary.

By Level 9 they should be able to design a system that other people could use to help them in their business or other work. Don't forget that all pupils will be learning this, not just those with a particular interest in computers. At least the next generation will be able to appreciate what IT can do and what effect it can have on their lives.

National Assessment and Testing

Along with the National Curriculum there is a new system of assessment and testing for all schoolchildren at ages 7, 11, 14 and 16, based on the ATs and the ten levels of achievement.

Work records

The idea is to find out what children understand and can do, as well as what they know. The level a child has reached will be judged in two ways. Firstly, by the teacher in the classroom over a period of time. Teachers will be instructed how to do this. They will be expected to keep very careful records, and their results will be checked against other teachers and other schools.

The report on assessment and testing[2] (the TGAT Report) recommended that when testing primary school children the test could be presented in the form of a topic to work on. This would give the chance to test all sorts of qualities and attainments at the same time while children were working individually or in groups.

Standard Assessment Tests

Secondly, all children will take *Standard Assessment Tests* (SATs) at the four Key Stages. Teachers can choose from a bank of national SATs in each subject.

[2] Task Group on Assessment and Testing Report DES 1988, known as TGAT Report

When reporting on a child's progress, the teacher will look at how the child is doing in each AT, taking into account the classroom assessment and the SATs. These results will be used to decide what level the child has reached in the profile component. So the assessment won't be based on just one task or test, but on a whole range of different activities.

Profile of attainment

At the four Key Stages in a child's school life an individual *profile of attainment* will be drawn up. The profile will record the teacher's assessments and the SATs. It will be used not just to sum up how far a child has climbed up the ladder of attainment, but also to plan what extra help or extra stimulus might be needed.

What the system of ATs and levels should do is help schools and parents to focus on a child's progress. It will be much easier to see how each child is progressing from year to year by looking at the level of attainment reached.

There may be good reasons for a child's rate of progress, or lack of it. Once it is shown up in this way, it will be easier to see the kind of help and support a child is needing at different times.

The TGAT report puts a high value on teachers discussing individual progress with pupils. It is seen as a way of helping the child to build on strengths and combat weaknesses. Parents will be given all this information about their own children, so that they can work with the school. Otherwise it will be confidential.

Publication of results

The results of assessment at the Key Stages 2, 3, and 4 must be made public in the same way as schools have to publish GCSE results. In other words a summary of the whole year group's

profiles is made available, but not individual results. The results of testing at Key Stage 1 for seven-year-olds do not have to be published, though schools are encouraged by the Secretary of State to do so.

Schools are worried about the publication of results, as they fear it may lead to rivalry between schools which doesn't take into account the different backgrounds of different schools. On the other hand, the information from the summary of the whole year-group's profiles could help the school to spot trends in

different subjects. This could show up good ideas that other teachers could follow or the need for extra help. Comparisons with other schools may sometimes be uncomfortable, but there may be lessons to be learnt from what other schools are doing.

This is one of the reasons why the new system is welcomed by many parents and governors, because it provides a yardstick, however crude, for judging whether or not the school is meeting the needs of pupils. But it will be important to know why one school doesn't seem to be doing as well as others. It may be doing the best it can in the circumstances. The essential thing is to measure *progress*. Parents need to know the level of achievement when children enter the school, as well as when they leave, so that they can judge how far the children have improved on what they know, understand and can do during their time at school.

Records of achievement

Many schools are now providing their pupils with a record that isn't just a collection of marks and exam results. It is a continuous record covering all their activities and achievements in and out of school. It includes samples of their work. The pupils themselves help to draw up the record with their teachers. This is a way of involving them in what they are learning and the progress they are making.

There have been a number of trial schemes and these have been so successful that all schools are being recommended to follow suit, so that every school-leaver can take a valuable record of their progress with them when they leave school. Employers are supporting the scheme because it gives them a better idea of what they can expect from young employees.

Special needs and the National Curriculum

It is the intention of the government that as much as possible of the National Curriculum should be taught to children with special educational needs. They will also take part in the national testing and assessment system. There are special arrangements which will make it possible for children with physical disabilities to take a different standard test where this is necessary.

Parents may be worried that their children will suffer under the new system, because it won't meet their children's need for special help. On the other hand, the National Curriculum could give children with special needs an entitlement to a standard of education that hasn't always been provided for them in the past.

If children have severe learning difficulties, the head can exempt them from all or part of the National Curriculum. This exemption can also be given to children with a temporary learning difficulty, for instance after a long stay in hospital. The head must inform the parents, governors and LEA. If the parents are unhappy about the head's ruling they can appeal to the governors, and then to the LEA if they are not satisfied.

Sex education and other controversial topics

The 1986 Act gave the school governors the job of deciding whether or not the school should provide sex education and if so, how. (If a public exam syllabus requires some teaching about sex, governors have to allow this.) The Department of Education and Science advises[3]

[3] DES Circular 11/87, Sex education at school

governors that they should be strongly influenced by the view that schools ought to see that their pupils have some education about health and sexual matters.

The governors must make sure that any sex education given encourages pupils to 'have due regard to moral considerations and the value of family life'. They must make public details of any sex education provided, so that parents can find out what their children are being taught about sex. Governors can also decide whether or not parents may withdraw their child from sex education.

Most schools will take parents into their confidence about sex education, and give them the chance to discuss this with the teachers concerned and see any books or materials used for themselves. Parents are usually glad that the school is taking on this responsibility but if you have any worries about what is taught, or not taught, at your child's school you should take it up with the head and the governors.

Presenting a balanced view

There are similar rules about other sensitive topics. The governors must forbid any partisan political activities by primary school pupils in school, or outside school if a member of staff or someone concerned with the school has arranged for them to take part.

The governors must also see that when political and other controversial subjects are taught, the arguments are presented in a balanced way. This doesn't mean that controversy should be ignored altogether. Pupils should be helped to understand why different people hold different views. They should be taught to analyse these views and judge them critically. Respect for the rule of law and the rights of others, including the right to hold their own opinions should be encouraged.[4]

[4] DES Circular 7/87 Annex 11

The 1986 Act said that the local community and the local police have the right to comment on what is taught in the school, and the head must take their comments into account.

Religious education

Under the 1988 Act, governors must see that religious education is given to every pupil, including any sixth formers or nursery children. Note that the word is 'education', not instruction as it used to be under the 1944 Act. This RE must be in line with the religious traditions of this country which are in the main Christian. But it must also take account of the teaching and practices of other major religions. In county, special and voluntary controlled schools RE must be given according to the agreed syllabus drawn up by a local advisory committee (SACRE). This committee includes teachers and representatives of local religious groups. The agreed syllabus must not be denominational – typical of one particular faith.

In voluntary aided schools RE can be denominational so Roman Catholic schools for instance can teach Roman Catholic doctrine.

Every pupil must take part every day in an act of collective worship, also mainly Christian. This does not mean that every assembly has to be 100% Christian dogma. Matters of broad human interest and concern are acceptable and mixed faith assemblies are still possible. The main world religions have many moral values in common that all parents would want their children to follow.

The school can apply to the local SACRE for a dispensation because of the background and religious beliefs of a majority or a group of pupils. This will excuse them from providing worship with a mainly Christian character. They must still hold a daily act of worship but it needn't be Christian.

If a group of parents ask for a different kind of worship or religious teaching from the rest of the school to be provided for their children the school can help to arrange this.

Parents have the right to ask for their children to be withdrawn from religious education and worship. The request has to come from the parent, not the child. The churches hope that now that the emphasis is on education rather than indoctrination, parents will not feel the need to withdraw their children.

It may be difficult for schools to prevent discussion of religious issues coming up in other parts of the curriculum. The DES advises that if parents say that they want their child to be withdrawn from RE, the school must try to find out just what topics have to be avoided if possible. The school is not obliged to guarantee that the child will always be withdrawn from other lessons, only that a reasonable attempt will be made to meet the parent's wishes.

There are other practical problems such as the possibility of missing important notices if the child is not in assembly. Schools ought to make sure that children whose parents ask for their withdrawal are not made to feel uncomfortable, and that proper arrangements are made to look after them. If you are worried about this, talk to the head and the governors.

Individual teachers may not be penalised if they do not wish to teach RE or lead collective worship, unless they are employed specifically for this or work in aided schools.

Appeals and complaints

The new laws give parents many more legal rights to complain to the school or the LEA if they are worried about what their child is being taught. You should always give the head a chance to put things straight before making a formal complaint. You can also approach the governors, perhaps through the parent governors.

The head must see that information about the curriculum is made available to parents, according to the DES regulations. Parents can complain to the governors if this is not done, or if they think that the National Curriculum is not being properly provided in the school.

Parents who are not satisfied by the way the governors respond to their complaint can then go to an independent complaints committee set up by the LEA. Details about how to do this have to be in the school prospectus. The committee can hear complaints from parents against the governors about the way the school is offering the national curriculum, sex education, religious education, or collective worship. If it thinks the complaint is justified, it can direct the school to make changes.

There is an ultimate right of appeal to the Secretary of State if parents are still not satisfied.

YOUR CHILD'S TEACHER

You can't have a good school without good teachers. Parents know this very well. When they have the chance to see teachers at work they are usually full of admiration for their skills and dedication. 'I don't know how they do it' they say. Teachers have very little to fear and everything to gain from welcoming parents into school. The more parents know about their work, the more they value it and the more they can do to help.

It's because parents see that teachers are so important that they get very upset if their own child's teacher disappoints them. They know that a child gets just one chance at an education. Hopeless Mr X may only have their child's class for one year, but a year is a long time for a child to waste. There are not many poor teachers, but those there are do disproportionate damage to the profession's reputation.

Getting on with your child's teachers

You have to remember that heads and other teachers are no different from other people. Some are very good indeed at their jobs, a few are hopeless at them, but the great majority come somewhat in between. Just like parents, in fact. It's the same for schools as for children. Parents, teachers and governors have to build on the good things, and try to make up for those that are not so good.

There's no argument about the fact that a happy parent-teacher relationship does wonders for a child's education. But it is not always easy. Parents sometimes don't realise that a teacher is just as likely to feel insecure as a parent. Having parents in class can be very helpful for the teacher, who gets an extra pair of hands. All the same it's not very comfortable to have another adult looking over your shoulder while you are doing your job.

Teachers on their part don't realise that many

parents didn't enjoy their own schooldays, and feel very nervous, even resentful of teachers. This is especially true of headteachers. It is easy to make parents feel small without meaning to.

Just as you hope the teacher won't believe everything your children say about family life, it's best not to believe everything they say about what goes on at school. If something seems to have gone wrong, give the teacher the benefit of the doubt until you've checked what really happened.

Even with all the new laws, parents don't have any right to go into the classroom without being invited. It's up to the individual teacher to decide. If you offer to help, and this offer is accepted, you must be reliable. Better to say you'll come once a month, than promise to come every week and then find you can't

manage it. And try not to comment on what you see, at least until you have got to know the class and the teacher. It takes a bit of time to get used to modern ways of teaching.

Teachers will almost always appreciate it if you show a genuine interest in what they are doing. Their big complaint about parents is that they don't take enough interest in the school, or try to understand what is going on there.

What do teachers do?

For the first time ever, the 1987 Teachers' Pay and Conditions Act set out the details of what was expected of teachers, head teachers and deputy heads. Ordinary classroom teachers must work for 195 days a year, including five days for in-service training when the schools are closed. Over the 195 days they must work for a minimum of 1265 hours each year as directed by the head (this is known as directed time.) That's about 32 hours a week during term-time.

School hours alone don't account for this total. The law used to say that children under 8 must get at least 3 hours' teaching a day, including midmorning or afternoon breaks, but not lunchtime. Older pupils should have a minimum of four hours.

The DES recommended that every pupil under 8 should have 21 hours' teaching, with 23.5 hours for 8–13 year olds and 25 hours for 14 and over. Under the 1988 Act the governors were given the job of fixing school hours and holidays so it's up to them to see that this is done in their school.

As well as the obvious job of teaching pupils, the law says that teachers must record and report on pupils' progress to parents, must attend staff meetings and must help with public exams.

They do not have to supervise the lunchtime break. LEAS must provide lunchtime supervisors for that, although teachers can take on this job for extra pay. There's no obligation for teachers to supervise out-of-school activities unless these are in directed time. Of course many teachers do this out of good will.

They must attend in-service training as directed by the head and staff meetings. They must be prepared to provide cover for absent colleagues, usually for not more than 3 days unless there is no-one else to do it.

In addition to their 1265 hours, they must put in any extra time that is needed for their professional duties, for instance marking work, writing reports, preparing lessons.

How many teachers?

Parents are often surprised to find out that there are no rules about how many teachers a school should have. The law says that there must be enough suitably qualified teachers to provide a satisfactory standard of education for the children in the school, and there must be a headteacher.

It has been the Local Education Authority (LEA) who has decided how many teachers the schools in their area should have. The LEA decides on a pupil-teacher ratio – the number of pupils per teacher, and allocates teachers according to the size of school. Some LEAs are much more generous than others with their pupil teacher ratios. Primary school ratios are usually higher (fewer teachers) than secondary.

As an example, a school with 150 pupils and a PTR of 25 : 1 would get six teachers, perhaps plus a head and a deputy head. They might get some extra part-timers to cope with special problems or provide music or other subjects. This wouldn't mean that there were 25 children in each class. The size of the classes in a school also depends on the amount of teaching time each teacher has – *contact time*. Every teacher, even in primary schools, has some free periods for marking, preparation and other activities. The more responsibility a teacher has in the school, the less contact time. Time has to be found for in-service training, meetings etc.

There is also the vexed question of cover for teachers who are away. It's more and more difficult for some LEAs to find supply teachers to fill these gaps. In any case, supply teachers are often not a very satisfactory solution as they don't know the children or the work. Schools have to try to organise the arrangements for cover themselves, especially for short absences. They may do this by being generous with non-contact time, on the understanding that teachers will fill in for absent staff.

Class size also depends on how the head decides to organise the timetable. There may be small classes for some subjects, or in the sixth form. This must mean larger classes elsewhere. Very popular schools may have larger classes than less popular ones, because every place will be taken up. Even if they get more teachers, there may not be a classroom to put them in.

When Local Management of Schools (LMS) comes in, (see the chapter on School Finances) it won't be the LEA who decides how many teachers a school should have, it will be the governing body. The governors could spend more on teachers and non-teaching staff, and less on other things. Or they could decide to cut back on teachers who already take up 70% of most school spending, though this is unlikely, as most parents and governors believe in small classes.

If you are worried about the size of your child's class, find out the reason for the size first. Then you will know whether the LEA, the head or the governors are responsible if you decide that something needs to be done about it.

How are teachers trained?

Teachers have to have qualifications for teaching that are approved by the Secretary of State for Education and Science. All newly qualified teachers have to have at least Grade C in GCSE maths and English. They must also have a degree in education (BEd) or a degree in another subject plus a teaching certificate (PGCE). They have to do a year's teaching on probation before becoming fully qualified. It's usual for primary school teachers to have a BEd, while most secondary teachers have a degree plus PGCE.

When there is a shortage of teachers the Secretary of State can relax these rules. Graduates in maths and science have been allowed to go straight into teaching without a PGCE. The teacher shortage has led to plans for a new kind of teacher, a *licensed teacher*. The typical licensed teacher would be a person from industry who decides after some years that they would like to teach. They must have maths and English O level, and some higher education. They can start teaching at once without any formal training, but will have training on the job. If they successfully complete a year in the classroom, they become qualified teachers.

Needless to say the teachers' unions are very opposed to this proposal as they feel it would dilute the professional standards of teaching. The argument goes on about what teacher training should consist of. There is no agreement about how practical teaching skills can be taught or about how much academic knowledge teachers need for primary and secondary teaching.

When Her Majesty's Inspectors of Schools

(HMI) did a survey of new teachers,[1] they found that about three-quarters of the lessons they gave were satisfactory or better, but a quarter were unsatisfactory. Poor lessons were usually due to poor planning, lack of discussion with pupils, and a failure to provide work of the right level for different pupils.

When new teachers were asked about their training, almost a third were dissatisfied. They criticised the lack of time on learning about how to control pupils and manage their classes. Primary teachers felt that they hadn't had enough preparation to teach all the subjects now required at primary schools. They all felt they weren't taught enough about computers, special needs, the administrative chores they had to do. They wanted more support from the school during their first year in teaching and more advice from experienced teachers and LEA advisers.

So next time your child's class has a probationer as teacher, be a little sympathetic and also try to find out what sort of help and support they are getting from the school and the LEA.

In-service training (INSET)

Teacher training doesn't stop when a teacher leaves college. Most teachers continue to take extra courses, in their own time and in school time. Because of the National Curriculum, teachers will need new skills for teaching and assessing children's progress.

Even when the training is provided by the LEA it costs money, for tutors and materials. LEAs get special grants from the DES for INSET but these don't cover all the costs. When it takes place in school time someone has to cover for the teacher on the course. So schools are constantly having to strike a balance between helping teachers teach better, and avoiding the disruption of classes because their teacher is away.

[1] The New Teacher in School, HMSO, 1989, £4.50

This is why Mr Baker, as Secretary of State, made it part of the teachers' contract that teachers should put in five extra days every year when the schools are closed, for in-service courses arranged by the school or their LEA. These were known as the Baker Days. It's becoming quite usual for parents and governors to be invited along to the Baker Days too.

Parents can get very irritated about schools being closed for odd days' in-service training. In fact the children are still getting the same number of days' teaching as they were before because the term is made longer to compensate. Schools ought to discuss this with parents and to try to minimise the inconvenience it can cause. If they don't, take it up with the governors.

Teacher appraisal

The Civil Service, the Armed Forces and most of industry regularly appraise the performance of their staff. The usual form is for each individual to have an interview once a year with their superior, to discuss a report on their year's work. The object is to help people do a better job in the future. Very often, a good appraisal results in extra pay.

The government have been trying to introduce a national system for appraising teachers since Sir Keith Joseph was Secretary of State. It has been difficult because the teachers' unions were strongly opposed at first, and also because no-one was quite sure how you could appraise teachers in the classroom.

Now the DES are encouraging all LEAs to set up appraisal schemes, based on principles that had to be worked out by ACAS before the teachers' unions would agree to take part.

The main principle is that teacher appraisal is a continuous process with the aim of developing the teacher's skills. It is not linked to pay or any disciplinary matters. Teachers will have a say in the way in which their work will be appraised. When the yearly appraisal interview takes place, it should end up with an agreed statement and a set of targets for the next appraisal.

The role of the governors in all this is not decided, but it is clear that if governors are to be the people who select and appoint teachers, they will want to have something to do with how they are appraised.

One head didn't wait for this. When Stan Bunnell was head of Queens School in Hertfordshire, he set up his own system. It included a regular appraisal of himself by members of his staff and the governors. He took to heart what they said. For instance, they were concerned about his being out of school so much because he was in demand for committees and courses. He tried to cut that down. But it gave him the opportunity to explain that his style of management was to give real responsibilities to the deputy heads. This is an example of how appraisal is a two-way process.

One of the parent governors who took part had considerable experience of appraisal in industry and said that the problem from his point of view was that there were so few targets that could be measured. It's important to be very clear about what is being appraised.

Stan Bunnell himself feels that the main advantage of appraisal is that it gives teachers a chance to stand back for a moment, and take an objective look at what they are doing.

Parents who may themselves be used to regular appraisal in their own jobs may wonder why teachers are making so much fuss about it.

Who chooses teachers?

Until quite recently in many places, teachers were selected and appointed to schools by the LEA, or by the headteacher. This was changed by the 1986 Act which gave all governors the right to a say in appointments.

The LEA decides what should be the complement of teaching and non-teaching staff in a school. The governors select staff for any complement post when it becomes vacant, except that the LEA can insist that the governors take someone already employed by them. This could be someone who is to be redeployed from another school because of a fall in numbers.

Heads have to be appointed by a joint panel of governors and members of the LEA. The LEA is not allowed to have a majority on the panel.

This will change again under Local Management of Schools. Once a school has its own budget under Local Management, the governing body will select all members of staff including the head. Although they will have to consult the LEA, they won't have to take someone just because the LEA wants them to and they will be able to dismiss teachers.

What can be done about unsatisfactory teachers?

Parents often wonder why some teachers keep their jobs. It is certainly not a simple matter to dismiss a teacher, especially a headteacher. It is often difficult to prove that they are not doing their job, and the teachers' unions are very active in protecting their members' interests.

Before Local Management only the LEA, who is the employer, could dismiss a teacher, though the governing body could recommend dismissal. In voluntary aided schools, although the governing body is the employer, it has to get the LEA's agreement to a dismissal.

There are some official reasons why a teacher can be dismissed, though they do not come up very often. The Department of Education and Science can insist that a teacher is dismissed for:

- sexual offences and violence involving children and young people;
- other serious kinds of violence;
- misappropriation of school funds;
- deceiving the LEA about their qualifications;
- repeated misconduct.

The Rehabilitation of Offenders Act does not apply to teachers, and there are arrangements for everyone selected for a teaching post to be checked with the police before the appointment is made.

If the LEA or the DES has reason to think that a teacher's health is not up to the job, they can insist on a medical examination. A teacher who fails to pass this can be dismissed.

But most complaints about teachers are for incompetence. Teachers can be dismissed for incompetence like any other employee. But it is difficult to get firm evidence that teachers are failing in their jobs, and at a time of teacher shortage, LEAs are not necessarily very keen to start proceedings.

The procedure itself is straightforward, but it must be carried out very systematically, with the correct verbal and written warnings. The teacher must be given the chance and the help to improve. Even more difficult, the head, senior teachers and LEA advisers have to be prepared to give evidence against their colleague. All this takes time. Many cases of dismissal have failed at an industrial tribunal because they were not handled properly.

So it's not surprising that heads and LEA advisers prefer to try and deal with this sort of case in private. They may offer in-service training, or some sort of advisory or consultancy job, or a post at a less demanding school, or early retirement. This can be very frustrating for parents who think that nothing is being done.

Although under LMS, the governors have the right to dismiss teachers, they will still have to be able to justify their actions to an industrial tribunal. If they lose, and have to pay compensation, they might have to pay the costs out of the school budget. (They might decide it was worth it).

Many LEAs have agreements with local unions about redundancy. Under LMS, the governing body will not have to honour these, though there is always the risk of running into difficulties with the teaching unions if they don't.

How are teachers paid?

The old system of deciding what teachers should be paid was swept away by the 1987 Teachers Pay and Conditions Act. This put a dramatic end to the long-running teachers' dispute by imposing a pay settlement and new conditions of work on teachers.

All teachers except heads and deputies are now paid on the standard national scale. This scale has 11 points, and teachers go up a point for each year of service, until they reach the top. A teacher at the bottom would receive £9,000, (1990) while at the top without an allowance they would get £15,723.

There are five incentive allowances, A, B, C, D, E, ranging from £925 to £5,500. These are paid for extra responsibilities, like being head of a department, or overall responsibility for maths in a primary school. They account for only about 4.5% of the total salary bill for teachers, so they don't make a lot of difference. The number of allowances in a school is related to the size of the school.

Heads and deputy heads are paid according to the size of the school. They start at £18,588 for a small primary school and go up to £37,900 for the largest secondary schools. Deputy heads get a range from £18,300 to £27,600.

Governors and the LEA can decide to make additional payments to teachers above the national scales.

It's a lot of responsibility for not very much money.

SCHOOLS, PARENTS, AND GOOD BEHAVIOUR

In 1988, the government was so worried about violence and disruptive behaviour in schools that it set up a special committee of enquiry. The Elton Report[1] looked at the whole question of the way pupils behave in school. Their conclusions were that violence was not the real problem, though it was essential to create an atmosphere where children would not even think of being aggressive towards teachers or each other. What did worry teachers was persistent minor disruption. This seemed to be a problem even in well-run schools.

The report makes 138 very practical recommendations for encouraging better behaviour in schools, offering everyone involved in education good advice about how to manage schools. One of these recommendations reinforces what has already been said about teacher training. New teachers are not given enough training in managing their class. They need more help and support from the head and senior staff. The report stresses the need to select teachers that have the ability to relate well to pupils.

The Elton report found that schools which encourage parents to take part in the life of the school often have high standards of behaviour. In schools like this, partnership with parents means something – working together towards the same aims. Parents feel welcome in the school. Parent-school activities are organised that appeal to the whole range of parents, not just a small active minority. Having more adults around in school isn't regarded as a nuisance. It's seen as helping the school to have a calmer, more positive atmosphere.

All this tells us something about what helps to encourage high standards of behaviour in a school. It has a lot to do with that elusive idea, the *ethos* of the school.

[1] Discipline in Schools A report of the Committee of Enquiry chaired by Lord Elton, 1989, HMSO, £10

What is an ethos?

What do we mean by the school's ethos? The law describes it as the way the school is conducted.[2] This is the joint responsibility of the head and the governing body. The head has to organise and manage the school and supervise the staff. The governors must let the head get on with the day-to-day running of the school, but it's their job to look after the ideals by which the school is guided.

It is not just a question of looking at rewards, rules and punishments. It's making sure that the system is focussed on rewarding good behaviour rather than emphasising punishment all the time. It's also about how people treat one another in the school. Governors should be taking an interest in very practical things like the general appearance of the school.

What do parents, pupils, staff and the local community think about the school? Do the parents support what the school is trying to do. Are parents consulted about rules and discipline, school uniform, behaviour? If not what can be done about it?

Good behaviour

Under the 1986 Act governors can make a written statement of the principles that should underlie a school's policy for good behaviour and discipline. The head, who has the duty to promote high standards of behaviour must take these into account. It is helpful to have a written statement because it makes it easier for everyone to know what the behaviour policy is.

In other words, every member of staff, including the support staff, every parent, every pupil and every governor knows what the rules are. They can encourage the children to follow them all the time. When everyone understands the policy, they are more likely to support it and carry it out fairly and consistently.

Be consistent

Consistency is important. All parents knows how deeply children resent it when rules are applied differently by different teachers at different times. It's not fair, they say, and they are right. How can children know what the standards of good behaviour are if people keep changing the rules?

Schools will tell you that one of the big problems they have is that parents don't support the standards they are trying to preserve. "We try to stop the children using swear words in the classroom, only to find that parents waiting for their children in the playground think it's a joke when their children say the words we have been trying to forbid" said one primary school teacher.

Television and video are another area of conflict. The Elton Report says that popular TV programmes are an important part of children's culture. It is wrong for adults to ridicule them. "All of us tend to feel hurt if our tastes and enthusiasms are ridiculed." Rather, says the report, teachers and parents should use TV both to encourage children to view in a critical, way, and to reinforce the positive messages presented by many programmes.

But it's no good schools preaching tolerance and respect for others if what children watch on their TV screen constantly contradicts this. Parents do have a responsibility to see that children do not watch an excessive amount of video and other network material transmitting violent and other antisocial messages.

[2] DES Circular 7/87 Education (no 2) Act, 1986, Further guidance

Good management

The Elton Report thought that the main reason for an unruly school was bad management. Bad management of the school as a whole and, even more important, bad management of the teaching in the classroom. The work being offered to the pupils was unsuitable and was not planned and organised as well as it should be.

In 1987 Her Majesty's Inspectors of Schools (HMI) also produced a report on *Good behaviour and discipline in schools*[3]. HMI reckon that they can identify what makes for good behaviour in schools, and most of what they said then has been repeated in the Elton report.

Most important, they say, is the leadership provided by the head. Headteachers must insist on high standards and follow them themselves. Then teachers must expect a lot from pupils in their work and in the way they behave. But it's no good expecting high standards if you don't give the pupils the chance to do well. This means providing good teaching and opportunities for everyone to succeed. So a lot depends on the teaching and the way the school is run by the head.

Listen to pupils

Another good sign is if pupils are involved in making decisions about their education and how the school is run. A good school usually has a School Council run by the pupils, with elected representatives from each year. The head and staff take what the Council says seriously, and explain why if what they ask for can't be done. Pupils are given real responsibilities for what goes in school. The governors and the PTA make an effort to talk to pupils and find out their views.

It's well known that the 14 and 15 year olds are the most difficult pupils to deal with, and the Elton report suggests that this may be because schools fail to recognise that these children are growing up, and should be given more responsibilities and more privileges.

Schools need to be aware of the effect they are having on pupils, both in groups and as individuals. That sounds obvious, but it often seems that decisions are taken in the school without any thought of how they will appear to the pupils and parents.

Set a good example

The need for good examples is important. The head's treatment of staff when, say, passing them in the corridor, the way staff act towards one another or talk about one another in front of pupils, the way teachers behave towards non-teaching staff, above all, how staff talk to the pupils, all these are giving messages to the pupils about standards of behaviour.

School rules OK

In the long run, such messages are much more effective (or damaging) than a proliferation of rules and prohibitions. HMI say that the best schools lay down a few clear principles that most people would agree with. These are concerned with encouraging good behaviour rather than punishment.

Of course rules must be reasonable. Sometimes it seems that schools make up rules just for the sake of having them. But if the reason, say, for having a rule about not running in the corridors is understood, there's more chance that it will be obeyed. Children may disobey the most sensible rule, but at least they are usually

---

[3] Published 1987, available free from DES Publications Despatch, Honeypot Lane, Stanmore, Middlesex HA7 1AZ

fair-minded enough not to hold a grudge if teachers punish them for breaking it. It's when children are constantly punished for breaking rules about things that seem trivial that you get a climate of resentment in a school. That does nothing for high standards of behaviour.

HMI quote with approval a community school whose single school rule reads "All pupils are expected to behave in a responsible manner both to themselves and to others, showing consideration, courtesy and respect for other people at all times". But a rule like this is no use unless it is consistently enforced.

Reasonable punishments

However good a school may be at encouraging good behaviour, there will have to be some punishments some time. Corporal punishment, which includes slapping, throwing missiles and rough handling is no longer allowed in any state schools or other schools which receive any public funds. For example, although the Act doesn't affect independent schools, children with Assisted Places (help with fees) at independent schools must not be given corporal punishment.

If a teacher has to handle a child roughly in self-defence this will not count as corporal punishment.

Any other punishment must be reasonable, but apart from that education law has little to say about them. Elton points out that punishment should fit the crime, making a distinction between minor and major misbehaviour.

Detention is the most common punishment for a minor breach of school rules. If parents have been informed beforehand that detention is used as a punishment at the school and have not written to the school to say that their child must not receive that kind of punishment, the school will assume that detentions can be given when necessary. But if a child was in detention

and the parent went to the school to ask for them, the school could not refuse to allow the child to leave. This could be false imprisonment.

Parents ought to be informed in advance that a detention has been given. It is obviously wrong, though not against the law, for a detention to be given without warning. Parents may be worried about a child's safety, especially if the child misses the school bus and cannot get home. Other people could be involved. The child might be prevented from attending a music lesson or some other appointment or be unable to meet a younger brother or sister as arranged. If this does happen to your child you should make a strong protest to the school.

A court has ruled (Terrington v Lancashire County Council) that a whole class can be detained as a blanket punishment, but only when the whole class could be held to blame for bad behaviour.

When things go badly wrong

Nobody's perfect, least of all schoolchildren, let alone teachers. Sometimes a school feels that it can do no more with a pupil who is always in trouble in school. That's why heads are given the power to exclude children from the school, either for safety reasons, or because the school has reached the end of its tether. After all, the other pupils in the school have rights too, to be educated in peace, without being upset by disturbed and unruly pupils.

One difficulty is that there are not enough resources in the system to provide proper help for disturbed pupils. Schools complain that it takes far too long to assess pupils with behaviour problems and to provide special help for them. Very often children with special needs behave badly because they are frustrated by learning difficulties. Parents can support the school by helping to put pressure on the LEA for more resources for these pupils.

Exclusion

The 1986 Act made new rules about exclusions from school in an attempt to tidy up the procedures so that they are fair to everyone, and so that children were not kept out of school for long periods without receiving any education.

The new rules make it clear that it is only the headteacher who can exclude a child from school. Exclusions can be *temporary*, a cooling-off period after which the pupil will be allowed back perhaps after promises of better behaviour, *indefinite* while the school, the LEA and the parents consult about what should be done, or *permanent* – what used to be called expulsion. In all cases the parents, governors and LEA must be kept informed.

The 1986 Act makes it clear that unless there is a sudden crisis, exclusion from school should only come at the end of a long process of trying to help a pupil with behaviour problems. Parents should have been called in at a very early stage, long before exclusion is considered.

However, parents often say that the first they hear about it is when the head rings up to tell them their child may not come back to school. Sometimes this is because they haven't understood the messages the school has been sending home or have ignored them. Sometimes schools have sent these messages by the child, who fails, quite naturally, to pass them on to the parents. Sometimes the school has tried to cope with the problem without involving the parents and have finally reached confrontation. Sometimes tempers have been lost over a minor incident which then gets blown up out of all proportion.

It is important to go and see the school the moment you hear that something may be wrong. At an early stage it may be possible to sort things out before they get beyond repair. You should be given the information about the school's 'pastoral care' system in the school prospectus. Usually the first person to talk to would be the class teacher or tutor, who might call in support from senior members of staff if necessary. The school can also bring in outside serives like the Education Welfare Service or Social Services for more help.

The right to appeal

If it does come to an exclusion, parents should immediately be told about their right to appeal to the governors. Parents often feel that governors are bound to support the head and staff, but this isn't always the case. Many governors want to hear both sides of the question, and take pains to see that parents and children get a fair hearing.

If there is to be a hearing it is very important to make sure that the rules of natural justice are seen to be observed. Unsubstantiated evidence or hearsay ought not to be admitted, and it ought not to appear that the head is both prosecutor and judge.

Governors can overrule the head and allow the child back in immediately or earlier than planned. If the governors support the head parents can appeal to the LEA, who can overrule the governors and direct the school to take the pupil back.

Expulsion

If the school decides to exclude the child permanently, and the governors and the LEA back this decision, parents can appeal to an independent tribunal which is not connected with the school. The governors can also appeal to the tribunal if the LEA wants them to re-admit a child against their wishes.

In voluntary aided schools there is no right of appeal to the local authority over a permanent exclusion. Parents can still appeal to the independent tribunal.

Even independent schools may not exclude pupils permanently without reasonable grounds. Lord Justice Cockburn said in 1865 that although headteachers must have the right to expel pupils whose conduct was damaging the school, this power must not be exercised 'wantonly or capriciously'.

Exclusions are usually a painful matter for all concerned. The governing body ought to be kept informed about all exclusions, even when there is no appeal, and should be worried if the numbers seem to be exceptionally high, out of line with other schools in the area. This may be an occasion for parents, school and governors to get together and discuss behaviour policy.

It's often difficult to understand why parents would want to get their child reinstated into a school who is trying to get rid of them. But it may be the nearest suitable school, or the child may have friends there. Parents don't want their child to suffer the stigma of having been 'expelled'. If a child is reinstated, the school will have to make very strenuous efforts not to take it out on the child. If parents suspect this is happening, they should immediately inform the head and if necessary the governors. There should be no question of victimization.

A good discipline policy in a school should reduce hard cases to a minimum, but you will never be able to eliminate them altogether. Sometimes a change of school and a fresh start may be the right answer.

The local authority must provide an alternative school place for any child permanently excluded from any school.

Bullying and racial harassment

Some recent tragedies have made it clear that these are serious matters and schools can no longer afford to turn a blind eye to them as they sometimes have in the past. Schools can and should take a firm line about any kind of bullying. They have a responsibility to ensure the safety of pupils in the school.

The Elton report say that teachers have a duty to set a good example, especially in respecting racial and cultural differences. The curriculum should be used to promote tolerance and understanding of other people and other cultures.

Another of their recommendations is that senior staff should be 'visible and strategically placed' when children are moving from one room to another between lessons, and that there must be enough lunchtime supervisors who are properly trained. These are some of the times when bullying can cause real distress if it is not immediately checked.

Any parent worried about bullying should take it up with the head, and the governors. They can do something in the short term if they are prepared to give supervision a high priority. In the long term, they may need to be persuaded to make changes in the ethos of the school.

Police and schools

The government is very keen that there should be good relations between schools and their local police. Many police forces now have schools liaison officers. HMI have commented on[4] the good work these officers can do in schools in four areas:

informing schools and pupils about the role of the police in society;
informing them about the law and the rights and duties of citizens;
making young people aware of dangers;
helping to foster crime prevention.

[4] Our Policeman a report on police-school liaison by HMI 1989, published by HMSO

The school has to give the local police chief a chance to comment on the curriculum. Schools are asked to bear in mind the role police can play in personal and social education (PSE) lessons. For instance in some schools police officers teach the law and citizenship sections of the PSE course. In another project police officers, a teacher and a group of fourth years organised a clean up and repair of damage done by vandals in a local park as part of the PSE programme.

School watch schemes, like Neighbourhood Watch, have a good effect in reducing vandalism in and around schools.

A good community police officer can help to promote better relations between the police, the school and the local community and reduce local juvenile crime. But this does need to be carefully handled by the school and the police, especially if relations are already strained. HMI recognise that it can't work without mutual trust, and attitudes have to change on both sides.

SCHOOL FINANCES

Who pays for education

Taxpayers, the local community and parents pay for state education. Taxpayers pay through the grants that central government make to local councils. The community pays through the money raised by the community charge which is spent on education. Parents pay through the many demands from schools for help – whether it's the annual fete or a weekly sub to the school fund.

About 40% of local government spending on education comes from the government in the form of Support Grant. The rest is raised locally through the community charge and the small amounts Local Education Authorities (LEAs) earn from school lettings and fees for adult education etc.

A big shake-up of government and local authority funding for education is going on at the moment, as a result of the changeover from local rates to the community charge and the national business rate. This will tend to limit the amount a local authority can spend on its services, including education. What the government thinks an LEA needs to spend may be quite different from what the LEA wants to spend.

How is it spent

The local council decides how much of the resources at its disposal should go on education. This varies quite a lot from one area to another. Then the Education Committee decide how that money should be spent on schools, colleges, sports and youth facilities etc.

Some of the schools' share of the budget goes on services provided centrally, like administration at the Town Hall, school transport, inspectors and advisers, education welfare, educational psychologists and so on.

The rest is shared out between the schools. Both county and voluntary schools get all their running costs from the LEA. Teachers' pay is the biggest expense – around 65% of the whole budget. Support (non-teaching) staff use up another 10%, and maintenance, heat and light about 15%. The 'capitation' allowance for books, materials etc gets what's left, about 10%.

Local Management of Schools

Local Management of Schools (LMS) began when, under the 1986 Act, governors were given the right to an annual financial statement from the LEA. This sets out how much their school had cost the authority in the last year – for staff, support services, maintenance of buildings, capitation and any capital spending on the school.

This information has to be included in the annual report to parents. So parents as well as governors can see exactly what resources their school is getting. Governors were also given the power to decide how the capitation money is spent, though they can delegate this to the head.

The 1988 Act goes much further than this. The governors will be entitled to a much more detailed statement under specific headings, of the money spent on the school and its share of the cost of services provided centrally. This is in preparation for schemes of Local Management of Schools (LMS). All LEAs must have an LMS scheme in place by April 1990. The scheme sets out how schools will be brought into LMS. The procedure will be fully operational by April 1993 but most LEAs have already set up trial schemes in a number of their schools.

LMS means a big change in the way schools are run. Every school with more than 200 pupils will have a 'delegated budget'. This will include as much as 90% of the amount the LEA spends on each school. The budget will be managed by

the school itself. Many decisions that were taken by LEA officers at the Town Hall will now be taken by the head and governors in the school. The aim is to make better use of the resources available for education, and to help schools provide the kind of education the local community wants.

The governors and the head will have the power to decide how many teachers and support staff to employ. They will select and appoint them and decide what allowances they should get. The head will be appointed by the governors. They will have to consult the LEA about staff appointments but do not have to follow its advice. Governors will have the power to fire staff too, though they will be subject to the same employment laws as other employers. They could have to pay the costs of unfair dismissal if they acted against advice in dismissing someone.

The school will have to do its own purchasing of books, materials and some services. It will be able to decide which of these services it wants to buy in from the LEA or from other sources.

It will have to look after the general maintenance and repair of the school buildings, except for major building works that come out of capital spending. (More about buildings later.)

The LEA still has some important functions. It will be responsible for the standard of education in the area and will have a team of inspectors and advisers to supervise this. It will be responsible for in-service training of teachers and will support governing bodies in the new work they have to do.

One of its major tasks is to decide the all-important formula by which money is allocated to each school. This is where the arguments begin, because schools are very anxious to get their fair share of the money that is going. The government has said that most of the formula must be based on the number and ages of the pupils in the school. That seems fair enough, until you begin to look at the other factors in the cost of running a school.

45

One school may have an old building solidly built, but whose rooms have high ceilings that are difficult to heat. Another may have a building built in the 1960s with one of those fashionable flat roofs that constantly let in the rain. Some schools are on a number of different sites, which is bound to mean extra costs. Then you have to consider the area where the school is situated. Should a school in a prosperous suburb get the same for each pupil as one in a deprived inner city area?

There is a worry about what will happen to children with special needs in ordinary schools under the new arrangements. The LEA can either include the costs of providing for them in the school's general budget, (there would be no guarantee then that the school would decide to spend resources on them) or LEAs can earmark special funds to support them, so that schools get extra money for each child with special needs. This will depend on the local LMS scheme.

Another concern is about the cost of teachers. The government says that the actual cost of employing each teacher must be charged to the school. If a school has a settled staff who have been teaching a long time, they will be near the top of the pay scale. This will cost more than when a school has mainly newly qualified teachers. In a small school, this difference might be a large proportion of the budget.

Some teachers are worried that schools might want to get rid of long-serving staff because of their cost. This is unlikely because most governing bodies, like parents, want their schools to have good, experienced teachers.

There will be some provision for tiding schools over the changeover period so that no schools are big winners or heavy losers.

A new role for governors

Even in places where schools already controlled some of their own resources, the governors weren't very involved in what was decided. Often, they just approved a shopping list prepared by the head and staff. Now the governors have a lot more responsibility. Because they are legally responsible, they have to take much more interest in how the school is managed. They must let the head and staff get on with the professional job of teaching the children, but they must do their best to see that the way the school's money is spent helps to make their school as good as it can be.

Heads and staff work very hard. It is easy to be so bound up in the business of daily survival that there is never a chance to sit back and work out how the school could be managed more effectively, how to ensure that all the pupils are making all the progress they can.

This is where the governing body comes in. They can work with the head and staff to identify what the school's aims and objectives are. Then the school budget can be planned to support them.

Grant-maintained schools

The 1988 Act gives some schools the chance to opt out of local authority control altogether. Instead of being maintained by the LEA, the school receives a grant from the Department of Education and Science (DES) equal to what it would have got from the LEA if it has remained in the LEA system. Grant-maintained schools are run by the governing body, almost like an independent school, except that the DES is paying. They still have to keep to the same national education laws and regulations as schools which stay with their local authorities and they must teach the National Curriculum.

The governing body of any school with more than 300 pupils can apply to the DES for grant-maintained status. First, though, they must hold a ballot of parents to see if the parents are in favour. The vote will be decided by a simple majority of those voting, but if fewer than half

the parents take part in the ballot, it has to be re-run. There is no restriction about the numbers voting in the second ballot.

Parents can tell the governors to hold a ballot if they can get enough signatures to the request. The supporters of the ballot need the number of signatures equal to one fifth of the pupils. So in a school of 1000 pupils, 200 parents' signatures would be needed to hold a ballot.

Even if the ballot is successful, there's no guarantee that the Secretary of State will approve the application to opt out. He has to look at the governing body's proposals, and judge whether they met his requirements for the secure future of the school.

Schools which opt out would take with them all the existing staff. Any staff who did not wish to go would have to resign unless the LEA could offer them another job.

The reasons why a school might want to opt out of local authority control are that schools would get more independence and less interference from the LEA. A number of the schools which have already voted to opt out were threatened with being closed or amalgamated because of falling numbers of pupils in the area. Others were worried about LEA policy, perhaps for ending selection.

Some thought that they would have a better life for the school under DES control.

The financial arrangements are intended to ensure that the school would be no worse and no better off than before. Nor will the local community, because the money that would have gone to the school will be deducted from the grant paid by the government to the LEA. The DES can make special grants to a school on opting out, especially for extra staff costs during the changeover.

The arguments against opting out are that the school might suffer through being cut off from the local education system and local services.

It's also been suggested that the DES may be a harder master than the LEA, especially when LEA schools under LMS have the right to manage their own budgets.

An opted-out school may not change its character for a period of five years unless there are special circumstances. Changes can only be made with the Secretary of State's approval. There is the possibility, however, that a school might at some stage change its admission arrangements, perhaps to become more selective, or to draw pupils from a wider area. Local parents might then not be able to send their children there.

Objections have been made to the way in which the majority of the governors will be appointed. Although the DES can appoint its own nominees if it is worried about the school's management, most of the governors will be appointed by the governing group who first applied for the new status. There do have to be some elected parents and at least one elected teacher.

Grant-maintained schools are a controversial

issue. Those in favour say that schools will have more scope to develop their own excellences. Those against say that it will be divisive, and create a two tier system of schools. LEAs, they say, will not be able to plan sensibly and economically for pupil numbers. It remains to be seen just how many schools will take the plunge.

School buildings

Many surveys have shown that schools around the country are getting more and more dilapidated. It causes a lot of frustration to parents and governors when they find it so difficult to get urgent repairs, building work and maintenance done. Whether it is building an urgently needed new school, or making a small improvement to an existing one, it's nearly always a long struggle.

Local authorities can borrow money for capital projects, such as building a new school or major alterations to an existing one, but the government restricts the amount according to national financial policy. Even when LEAs sell off buildings and land the proportion of the proceeds they can spend is controlled by the government.

Voluntary aided schools

Because of their status, voluntary aided schools have to find their own money for capital projects and external maintenance, instead of getting it from the LEA. They get 85% of what they spend back direct from the DES if it is sanctioned. They are subject to the same restrictions on capital spending as the LEA and have to compete for funds from a limited budget. Internal painting etc is paid for by the LEA.

Redecoration, repairs and improvements

Until Local Management comes in, most LEAs have a rolling programme of regular painting and decorating for all the schools for which they are responsible. If there is a special case for earlier redecoration, perhaps because of some unusual damage, governors can put pressure on the LEA to move them up the queue. Unfortunately, the regular maintenance programme often suffers if budget cuts are made so even when a school is first in line, it may have to wait a long time.

Of course, every school wants to be redecorated in holiday time rather than when the children are there, but since there are only 12 weeks of holiday a year, some schools are bound to suffer.

The caretaker will usually be able to carry out or arrange for small repairs, up to a cost limit.

More serious matters may have to be approved by the LEA. This is where delays creep in, and it may be necessary to keep nagging the Education Office to get urgent repairs completed.

The difference between a repair and an improvement is often a very technical one, and can make quite a difference in the case of voluntary aided schools, where an improvement inside the building becomes the responsibility of the governors, whereas a repair would be paid for by the LEA.

In both county and voluntary schools, there are always many improvements which could be done, and not enough cash to do them. Both major and minor improvements come out of the LEA's capital budget, which is strictly controlled by the government.

When very simple repairs and alterations go untouched for months and sometimes years on end, parents sometimes ask why they can't do it themselves. There are various reasons why this is not as easy as it looks. Building and safety regulations are rightly strict about children's safety. There may be problems with local unions. The LEA may not want to accept a new piece of equipment or work area because it will then have the extra costs of insuring and maintaining it.

But even so, if the parents use tact, patience and professional expertise it is possible to get these jobs done to everyone's satisfaction.

Under LMS a school should have more control over all such matters, in exchange for the hassle of dealing with painters and builders themselves.

Charging for school activities

State education may be free, but there are some things parents have to pay for. It has always been difficult to draw the line between things which are part of the school curriculum, and so ought to be free, and optional extras which have to be paid for. The 1988 Act tried to settle this once for all, but with doubtful success. The law is explained in the DES circular on Charging[1] but it still leaves room for confusion.

When no charge may be made

The basic principle is that any activities that take place wholly or mainly during school hours (not counting the lunch break) must be free. The timing of the school day must be published in the school prospectus, so that parents know whether or not an activity is in school hours.

Any activity that takes place outside school hours which is part of the National Curriculum must be free. When an activity which is part of the preparation for a public exam like GCSE takes place outside school hours that too must be free.

This includes the free use of books, materials and equipment, though a charge can be made if pupils want to take home the finished product of home economics or craft lessons. Parents are expected to provide suitable clothing for craft, PE etc, though the local authority can choose to provide sports clothing and must provide safety equipment. (LEAs can also make grants for school uniform and other clothes for children of poor families.)

When charges can be made

A charge can be made for individual music tuition, even during school hours, unless it is for an exam syllabus or the National Curriculum.

[1] DES Circular /89 Charges for school activities

in the same way as for family holidays during term-time. (A maximum of two weeks in any one year is permissible.)

In these cases, the LEA and governing body would in theory be bypassed and the parents directly approached for payment. Consequently these activities would be fully chargeable even if they took place in school time. The school would have to make the position clear to parents, emphasising that it would not be responsible for the safety of pupils.

Voluntary charges

There is nothing to stop a school from asking parents to pay a voluntary charge towards the cost of a school visit or other activity that takes place in school time. The difficulty is that children must not be excluded from the activity if their parents don't pay. The school might not be able to afford to make the visit unless everyone pays. They can ask parents to volunteer to pay extra to cover the non-payers, though this seems a bit unfair. Or they could put the pressure on by making it clear that unless everyone pays, the trip won't take place.

(The national graded music tests don't count as a 'public exam').

A charge can be made for an activity that takes place wholly or mainly outside school hours as long as it is optional.

Third-party trips

To complicate the issue, a charge can be made for an activity such as a ski trip or theatre performance put on by an outside body during school hours, as long as it is optional and pupils have leave from the head and governors to miss school.

The headteacher and governors can approve requests from parents for the release of pupils

Residential visits

An activity that is part of an exam course or takes place mainly in school time must be free except that a charge can be made for board and lodging (not more than the actual cost).

Otherwise the full cost, including the cost of paying teachers to act as escorts, can be charged.

How can you tell whether a residential visit takes place mainly in school time? By calculating how many half day sessions it takes up. So a trip that began at Thursday lunchtime and ended on Sunday evening would take up seven half days, four of them not in school time. This would be chargeable. One that began on Thursday morning and finished on Saturday evening, making 6 half days, four of them in schooltime, would not be chargeable.

Help for parents who can't afford to pay

Parents who receive income support have a right to help with payment of the charges for board and lodging on residential trips that are part of the curriculum.

Otherwise, there are no national rules about remission of charges. Each LEA, has to draw up its own policy. Many LEAs will offer help to other poor families, so that their children can take part in optional activities provided by the school. The governing body can change these rules. If they charge more than the LEA recommends the LEA will deduct it from their

budget, so they won't gain anything. If they are more generous than the LEA provides for, they have to find the money from somewhere. The rules, stating clearly what will be charged for and what will be free, must be published in the prospectus.

Optional activities may not be part of the National Curriculum or essential to prepare for a public examination. But they may still have a good deal of educational value. It seems hard that children should be excluded from them because their parents can't or won't pay. This might be one use for PTA funds, to subsidise school outings so that everyone can take part.

Exam fees

The cost of entering pupils for exams is very high. The school must pay entry fees for all public exams entered through the school unless

the pupil is prepared for the exam privately. Fees may be recovered from parents if the pupil fails to take the exam without good reason.

School meals

Local authorities may provide school milk if they choose to do so, and must charge every pupil the same price for it. They no longer have to provide school meals except to children of parents on income support who must be given some kind of free midday meal.

School meals can be provided to other pupils but they must all be charged the same price. LEAs are not permitted to give free or cheap meals to pupils whose families are not on income support.

There are no other regulations about the prices charged for school meals or their food value.

School transport

Going right back to 1944 LEAs have had to provide travel to the nearest school for children who lived more than walking distance away. At that time walking distance for children under eight years old was considered to be two miles, and for children over eight, three miles. These distance are very carefully measured along the nearest available route.

There's been a lot of legal argument about what 'available' means. One judge held in 1985 that if a route was unsafe for a child, to walk alone, the LEA had to provide transport. A case in 1988 ruled that if the child's parent was able to take the child to school, it didn't matter that the route was unsafe.

The argument still goes on, and causes a lot of ill feeling especially because of the rigid dividing line. Some children get free travel, others using the same stop don't because their home is a few yards nearer the school. Efforts to reform the system have so far failed because of the expense and complexity.

The LEA, not the school, has to provide supervision and take reasonable care of children using school transport.

Boarding school fees

LEAs can make charges for board and lodging at state boarding schools. They can provide help for parents if this would cause hardship. The DES may provide help for parents of children at grant-maintained boarding schools.

If the child is at boarding school because the LEA think that this is necessary to make sure the child gets the right education, the LEA must pay the whole cost.

Damage to the school

Although it is not in the Act, Circular 2/89 points out that there is nothing to prevent schools from asking parents to pay for a broken window or a lost textbook if their child was at fault.

If governors decide to charge parents in this way, it should be mentioned in the school rules, so that parents and pupils know where they stand.

School lettings

Schools are the obvious place to hold local community events and activities, and most LEAs

offered this kind of event a special cheap rate to hire the school, or even free use if it was for something educational. Now that many schools are running their own budgets, they are allowed to keep net income from lettings. If they hope to make money from letting out the school they will have to balance costs, including wear and tear, overtime and energy costs, against any income. The temptation may be to price the rent so high that community groups, such as Scouts or Brownies, can't afford it.

A school is a community resource built and paid for out of everyone's taxes. The whole community ought to be able to use it, as long as this does not interfere with the education of the children. It may be difficult but the governors have to strike a fair balance between the school's responsibility to its local community and making a profit.

HEALTH AND SAFETY

Parents expect their children to be safe while they are at school but some recent very sad accidents have shown how easy it is for things to go wrong. Parents and teachers have to take reasonable care of children; no-one expects that it will always be possible to prevent accidents. The question is what standard of care is reasonable? Generally speaking, the courts are becoming much more sympathetic to parents who claim that schools have not taken enough care of their children. The new legislation continues to lay a very heavy responsibility on teachers and on the school authorities to make sure that schools and school activities do not put children at avoidable risk.

Who is responsible?

Health and safety regulations in school are enforceable by law and are there to make sure that the school is a healthy and safe place for pupils, staff or anyone else using the school. The LEA is responsible for health and safety in county schools. Even when the school has control over its own budget, governors must obey any directions from the LEA about health and safety. In voluntary aided schools, the governors are responsible for health and safety, though they can ask for the LEA's advice when necessary.

Responsibility for day-to-day health and safety in the school is usually handed over to the head. There may be a health and safety committee on which staff are represented. The head has to take the decision as to whether any area, plant, or equipment should continue to be used after a hazard has been reported.

Parents and governors should report any hazard as soon as they notice it. Governors must put it right at once if it is their responsibility or notify the LEA immediately if it is their's.

Vandalism

Protecting the school against vandalism is often a problem. It is important for everyone to realise that it's *their* problem, it's no good hoping that the police or the LEA can solve it on their own. Schools need to look carefully at the security both of buildings and grounds, calling in police help and advice if necessary. 'School watch' schemes that involve parents and the community keeping an eye on the school and reporting anything suspicious can prevent damage and thefts. There may be simple measures that can cut down the opportunities for vandalism. Involving the pupils in anti-vandalism schemes can help.

Parents have a responsibility to see that their children are not involved in vandalism out of school hours. As explained in the chapter on School Finances, parents can be asked to pay for damage done to the school by their children.

Insurance

There is quite a lot of confusion about how schools are insured and what the insurance will pay for.

Every school has to have *employers' liability* insurance, which covers the LEA and the governors against negligence towards any employee. So if an employee is injured because of some fault in the equipment or building, the insurers will pay compensation. This policy will also cover negligence by the staff. *Public liability* extends employers' liability insurance to cover death or injury to third parties, e.g. pupils.

When schools are responsible for their own budgets, most local authorities still provide public liability insurance to cover the staff and governors for accidents and damage caused by negligence to anyone, pupils, staff or visitors, while they are in the school. If the LEA does not provide this cover, the governors must arrange their own insurance.

Insurance cover for public liability means if the school is to blame for an accident, all the legal costs including compensation will be paid by the insurers. So if a child is injured through tripping over a hole in the playground that should have been repaired the insurers will pay up. But many parents don't realise that if the school has not been negligent, no recompense is payable. In a recent case, a boy paralysed by an injury received playing rugby claimed compensation from the school's insurers. The court held that it was a genuine accident in the normal course of play and no-one had been negligent. So the boy was not entitled to any compensation.

This kind of injury would only be covered by personal accident insurance, for which you don't need to prove negligence. Some schools offer this at a small cost to parents through a group scheme for all their pupils. One such scheme is run by the National Confederation of Parent Teacher Associations (NCPTA). The Central Council for Physical Recreation sponsor a low-cost scheme especially to cover sports injuries. It's worth looking into personal accident insurance whether or not your child is keen on sport. 3000 children a year are hurt in accidents at school.

Health and safety education

School is the ideal place to reinforce good habits of working, playing and living in a safe and healthy way. Health and safety education is not among the foundation subjects of the National Curriculum, but the 1989 Education Act requires schools to promote the physical as well as the mental development of pupils, and to prepare them for the experiences of adult life.

The National Curriculum Council has made proposals about how this can be achieved. It suggests that health education should be taught in two ways. It will naturally form part of various compulsory subjects, (for example, science and PE). But there should also be a time-

tabled health and safety education course, because this enables teachers to go into attitudes about health and safety in depth. What children think and believe about health is more important than factual knowledge when it comes to encouraging sensible healthy behaviour.

The Council gives an example of how young children might be introduced to safety education. They could look at their own classroom and see how safe different parts of it are. They could work in a group looking at safety in the playground or the gym. They could invite someone whose job involves keeping children safe in to talk to them.

Any health education programme has to include some discussion about smoking, alcohol, drugs and solvent abuse. This has to be handled carefully if it is not to have the unintentional effect of glamourising the problem. Experience has shown that it is no good laying down the law as that just puts young people off. The aim is to promote a life style that helps young people handle social pressures and make sensible well-informed decisions about their own health.

Every school should have a senior member of staff who is responsible for co-ordinating the school's drug education policy, and for dealing with issues about drug misuse. Schools are expected to involve parents, and to make sure that parents and school are working together with the same aims and attitudes.

Child abuse

Teachers are often the first to suspect that a child may be being abused, or children may confide in them. In 1988 the DES and the DHSS issued a joint circular (no 4/88) about tackling child abuse, including physical injury, neglect and ill-treatment as well as sexual abuse. If a member of the school staff has good reason to suspect that a child is being abused they must report this to the senior member of staff with responsibility for the school's response to child abuse. It's not the teacher's nor the school's job to investigate child abuse or to question parents. That's for the police, the NSPCC or the local Social Services.

The local authority must have a document clearly explaining the procedure for handling suspected cases. There must a named officer in the education department and the Social Services Dept to whom all cases should be reported. Any parent who has cause for concern about a child, perhaps one of their children's friends, can approach the school, who should be able to advise on what to do next.

School supervision

When a child is at school or on a school visit the teachers must take the same care of them as a careful parent would take of their own children. And like parents, that responsibility goes on for 24 hours a day if the child is away from home in the school's charge.

Under the Teachers' Pay and Conditions Act of 1987, heads are responsible for maintaining good order and discipline in their schools. There must therefore be a reasonable system of supervision during school time, and the head must see that this is carried out. The system is expected to take into account the ages and numbers of pupils, any physical or mental handicaps they may have, the school buildings and their environment, any particular dangers, what the pupils are doing, and the experience of the supervisors.

It is reasonable to expect children to be supervised before the morning session and after the afternoon session. This is usually only for the ten minutes before school begins or after it ends. The school should write to parents stating the school hours and explaining the supervision arrangements. If local transport arrangements mean that children are bound to arrive earlier or leave later than this, parents should press for supervision to be organised or for the school times to be changed. Schools cannot be expected to be responsible for children who arrive at school long before it opens, or leave long after it ends, unless special arrangements have been made.

A memorandum issued by the National Association of Headteachers in July 1988 says that no primary school child should be allowed to leave the school during school hours without clear evidence of a request from the parent or guardian, preferably a written request. No pupil should be sent out of any school, whether primary, secondary or special, on a personal errand for a member of staff, as there may be no insurance cover for this.

Schools have to make sure that children are adequately supervised during breaks and lunchtime. Teachers can be on duty during breaks as part of their directed time, or as volunteers. The Teachers' Pay and Conditions

Act says that teachers must have a reasonable break at midday and cannot be directed to do lunchtime supervision, though they may volunteer. In most schools extra staff, known as School Meals Supervisors, are employed at lunchtime. (Some of these are teachers doing the job for extra money.)

It may be very difficult to supervise pupils in wet weather. Schools must see that proper supervision of all children is carried out when they are allowed indoors, perhaps to stay in their classrooms, during breaks.

School journeys and visits

The rules about charges for school activities (see page 50) have made schools think again about the kind of school journey or visit they plan for pupils. One result may be that they make more use of local places of interest during term-time and do less travelling. Visits tend to be more closely tied in to the school curriculum.

Parents may not always realise that teachers taking school parties usually do so as volunteers. It would take up far too much of their contracted hours if, for example, the week's school camp was counted against their annual total. They don't get extra money (danger money?) for the privilege of taking 30 excited children to France for the day. Yet the safety of the children is their responsibility day and night.

Parents should always be asked for their consent if a child is to go out of school. They should be told about the purpose of the visit and the arrangements for supervision. If parents are to help with the trip, the insurance should be checked to make sure they are covered. Everyone should have clear written instructions about what to do in an emergency.

As a result of the fatal accidents to schoolchildren in Austria and at Land's End, the DES issued a new handbook[1] for teachers which gives very practical guidance about all the factors schools and teachers should take into account when leading school parties on outdoor events. It gives nine recommendations for ensuring the safety of the party:

- leaders must be experienced and have sound judgement;
- schools should appoint a co-ordinator to make sure all trips are planned safely and training is given;
- leaders must be fit, must have the right skills and must know about any likely danger;
- equipment should meet national standards;
- the way any expedition is to be run should be explained to parents and all those taking part;
- leaders should know the latest local weather forecast;

- the leaders should have with them a list of members of the group and frequent counts should be made; it is better to have small groups under one leader than a big party with several leaders;
- leaders should ensure that the party behaves responsibly at all times;
- leaders must know how to take precautions against risks, and how to cope in a dangerous situation.

Most of these rules make very good sense for any kind of school outing.

Out-of-school activities

School clubs and other 'extra-curricular' activities can add a lot to the quality of the education provided in the school. Again teachers are giving up their own time on a voluntary basis. This is not part of their 'directed time'. But if the activity is sponsored by the school, there must be the same standard of supervision as in school hours.

The school may also be used for play centres and youth clubs run by the local Youth Service. These are not usually anything to do with the school, although some school staff may work in them. The local authority is responsible for staffing and supervision and will provide insurance cover. Other clubs provided at the school by outside bodies have to follow proper safety standards, but are not superintended by the school or the LEA.

[1] *Safety in outdoor education* published by HMSO, 1989, £3.95

GETTING INVOLVED

It may be a long time since anyone saw that famous notice in the school playground 'No parents beyond this point'. Most schools nowadays recognise how important it is to encourage parents to take part in the life and work of the school. But some of the attitudes that lay behind that notice, that parents were a nuisance, in the way, might interfere with the professional work of teachers, are not too far below the surface.

Parents' new rights

One change the new legislation (see Introduction) has made is that because parents have many more rights to know what is going on in school, it is much more difficult for a head who would prefer to exclude them, perhaps because of bad experiences in the past. The governing body and the LEA can make it clear that schools are expected to do all they can to build up good relations with their parents.

This move isn't helped by the small minority of parents, often holding extreme views, who use their new rights as a way of harassing and intimidating teachers. The best defence against any kind of extremism is a good working partnership between the head, staff, governors, pupils and parents. It has to be based on mutual trust, and that takes time. Parents and governors must be able to trust the head and staff to do a good professional job in the classroom. The professionals must respect and trust the parents. Then they can work together with the same aims. Parents need to understand what the school is trying to do, and act as a candid friend, not afraid of telling a few home truths when necessary, but always ready to defend the school against unfair attacks.

You can't build up trust without effort on both sides. Schools must genuinely welcome parents in, so that they can see for themselves what is going on. Parents must respond when the school invites them and asks for their help.

A good school will make parents welcome from the start. The school prospectus, (as suggested by the Tomlinson Committee on Freedom of Information[1]) will tell them all the different ways parents are involved in the school – clubs, groups, school association, parent helpers, courses and meetings. It will explain how parents can arrange to visit the school, and what to do if they have a problem. This will all be done in a way that makes it clear that parents are valued partners in the education of their children.

Very often the professionals don't realise just how off-putting their jargon and language is. Parent governors are in a good position to point this out tactfully to the school. It may take a bit longer to write in a way that appeals to parents. This is a job an interested parent might be able to do with the guidance of the head and staff.

Many schools have a parents' room or corner where parents can have a cup of tea while waiting to see staff. They can chat with other parents, and use as a base when they are helping the school.

School news

A school newsletter will keep parents in touch with what is going on. This is often a joint venture between the head, governors and parents. The head will certainly want the right to see anything that is going out to all parents. Whoever is producing it, it is essential to have the head's support as it is very difficult to produce and circulate one without the use of school facilities. The governors may be able to do some persuading if the head is doubtful about its value.

Newsletters, like other letters home need to be presented in an interesting way if parents are to read them. A document that consists of two tightly packed poorly duplicated A4 pages is not likely to attract a high readership. If your school is still sending out papers like this, see if you can find someone with access to desk-top publishing facilities who can liven up the appearance. Illustrations done by the pupils and contributions from them can add some light relief.

Parent-teacher associations (PTAs)

The new legislation gives parents many rights to information about what is going on in schools. But it stops short of guaranteeing them a right to a formal home-school association, something that many parent campaigners wanted. The main reason given was that you cannot compel the head and staff to take part in an association if they don't want to. There are heads who are very active in promoting parent-school co-operation who set their face against a formal PTA because they feel it can be too exclusive. They claim that it can fall into the hands of a small clique or can interfere with the head's direct contact with all parents. One way of avoiding this is to make every parent of a child in the school a member automatically, without having to join or pay a subscription.

Most schools do now have some kind of school association, often called 'Friends of the school' so that past parents, old pupils, grandparents and others interested in the school can join as well as parents and teachers. This is all to the good in the new environment, because it will be very helpful for schools to be closely linked to their local community. Schools will be much more open to critical comment from outside, and will need all the support they can get from their neighbours.

[1] Informing Education A report on the freedom of information committee chaired by John Tomlinson, ILEA, 1987

This does not just mean financial support, though that will be even more in demand when schools are running their own budgets. It's inevitable that schools will want to use their parents to raise extra cash, but a relationship that depends entirely on fund-raising is not going to get very far. It can exclude parents who are worried that they can't afford to meet the school's demands. In any case the people who pay the piper will want to call the tune, eventually. Fund-raising may be a good way into the school's confidence, but it is only a beginning.

A good school association will also be doing its bit to educate parents about the changes taking place in education, for instance by holding workshops on topics like the National Curriculum. Note the word 'workshops'. What parents don't want is to be lectured. For some reason, teachers talking to parents tend to forget all they know about how children learn and go back to chalk and talk methods that they wouldn't dream of using in school. And if you ask an officer from the LEA to come and explain something like Local Management, they can sometimes be even worse.

Coral Pepper, chair of the National Association of Governors and Managers, describes one of the best day's training she ever had, on the curriculum in primary schools. 'We were pupils for the day; we could choose subjects, and we went into the classroom and had a typical lesson. If everyone could have that experience they would see their school in a different light. It was superb'. You learn a lot more from an experience like that than from any amount of lectures.

The school association is a natural breeding ground for parent governors, but the two jobs shouldn't be confused. You don't have to be active in the association in order to be elected as a parent governor. And once you become a parent governor, you have to take on a wider perspective than that of the school association. It is useful for parent governors to keep in touch with the school association, but they must keep in touch with other parents too, who may not choose to come to its meetings.

The annual report and parents' meeting

The 1986 Act made it compulsory for the governing body of every school to produce an annual report for parents and to hold an annual meeting at which the report could be discussed. If more than 20% of parents are present they can pass resolutions which have to be considered by the school, the governors and the local authority.

This had a very mixed response from the schools. Many schools complain that holding the meeting is a waste of time as so few parents turn up. This is a pity, as it provides a good opportunity for parents to find out about what the school and the governors have been doing and to discuss it with them. Unfortunately people tend to think of it as an opportunity to let off steam about problems and grievances. It should rather be the occasion for a celebration of the school's successes during the year, and a chance for parents to thank the school for what they have done well.

The annual report should be written by the governors, though all too often the head has to do it. Like the school newsletter it ought to be well produced, interesting and lively, something the school could be proud to show outsiders. Complain to your governors if it fails to meet this standard.

There are certain items that have to be included:

- names of all the governors, and who appointed them;
- address for contacting the chair and the clerk;
- information about the next parent-governor election;
- breakdown of school finances;
- exam results for secondary schools;
- links with the community and the police;
- the school curriculum policy statements;
- what the governors have done during the year to carry out their duties;

- details of complaints and appeals procedures.

Most schools will also incude other activities such as sport, music, drama, community work, industry partnerships, what happened to school-leavers.

The report must be sent out to all parents. At the same time, parents must be given at least two weeks' notice of the annual meeting. This doesn't have to be an evening meeting. Some schools have found that a Saturday is better, especially if it is combined with the school fete, or other social event. Parents are more likely to want to come if there is some entertainment such as a school concert or a video of the school journey. If it is to be held in the evening, it helps if a creche and something for the older children can be provided.

The purpose of the meeting is to allow parents to comment on the work of the school over the past year and on the way the school, the head, and the governors have played their part. If it is kept very informal, with a circle of chairs rather than rows, parents are more likely to speak up. Remember that the person taking the chair may be just as nervous as the parents. The chair must discourage personal attacks on individuals. It's not the place to air complaints about an individual child or teacher. Anyone with that kind of worry should see the head privately. The idea is to discuss the general life and work of the school.

Parents as helpers

Modern ways of teaching put a lot of emphasis on topic work, projects, use of tape recorder and videos. The pupils are expected to be active rather than passive learners. This makes many demands on teachers. Parent help at home and in school can make a real difference to the quality of education. But parents need to know what they are doing if they are to help rather than hinder. It's no good confusing the children by trying to teach them in a different way from the school. That's where the School Association can give support by keeping parents informed about educational ideas. It can also keep teachers aware of what the parents think about the way children are taught. Many LEAs now have schemes like the London PACT scheme (Parents And Children and Teachers) which is a planned way of helping parents help their child with reading.

It's particularly important for parents and teachers of children with special educational needs to work together. That's why many special schools have home liaison teachers who can visit parents in their own homes and discuss the child's needs together. This idea has proved so successful that some ordinary schools are now appointing a member of staff with the special job of building up good relations between parents and the school.

If you can spare the time to come into school and help regularly, this is an ideal way of getting to know the staff and the pupils. Most teachers will welcome an extra pair of hands to help with all the chores. An extra pair of ears to hear children reading is always useful and not only in the primary school. Secondary schools need help just as much with pupils who have problems with reading, especially if their first language is not English.

Dave Miller is a parent who is able to help in school because he is a fire officer who works shifts. He explains some of the advantages:

> 'I felt a bit doubtful at first but it's a very open school. Teachers welcome it when they see someone's interested and you are not just there to pick faults. Also the children get to know you and you can talk to them, see whether they are enjoying it, and what they are learning.'

Parent governors

The new legislation has strengthened the powers of governing bodies to have some say in what happens in a school. (More about that in the next chapter). There has certainly been a shift of power away from the professionals – the local government officers and teachers – towards governors and parents.

Although the idea of having elected parents on the governing body was around when the 1944 Education Act was going through Parliament, it was not until the 1980 Education Act that it became compulsory for every school to have at least two elected parent representatives.

Church schools had to follow suit, with at least one elected and one appointed parent governor. The 1980 Act did not come into force until September 1985, so parent governors have had quite a short history in many schools.

Although from 1985 there were elected parents and elected teachers, in most areas the political representatives still had a majority. The 1986 Act changed that. It laid down very strict rules for the composition of governing bodies, which now depends on the size of the school. Parents have a least one quarter of the places, the same number as the political representatives. This does not apply to voluntary (usually church schools). Their governors are still appointed mainly by the church or charity that founded the school.

Another change made in 1986 was that all governors serve for four years, unless they choose to resign. Previously, parents had to resign if their child left the school. Now they can stay on if they wish until the end of the four year term.

What do parent governors do?

Parent governors have the same status, duties and responsibilities as other governors. They are there to bring the voice of parents to the governing body, drawing on their own experience as parents and on the experiences of other parents. Parents have a very direct personal interest in the school and see it from a different perspective from other governors. They can bring insights into how the school works which are very valuable for the governing body. They also have a sense of urgency, that can cut through bureaucratic inertia. But parent governors are not delegates. Other parents cannot instruct them about what to say at governors' meetings. It would be impossible for them to represent all the different opinions of all the people with children

at the school. Naturally, when an issue is of great concern to parents they would want to bring it before the governors.

The elected parents may not be the only governors with children at the school, but because they have been elected by other parents, this gives them a certain status and authority.

Parent governors are sometimes worried that being a governor could have a bad effect on their own children, especially if they have to raise matters that appear to be critical of the head. It would be very unprofessional for staff to take it out on a pupil or to make snide remarks in class. It is not unknown to find pupils who aren't above saying to teachers, 'My mother's a governor, so you'd better watch out!' You depend on good relations between governors and the school to avoid these hazards.

Heads do sometimes complain about parent governors who are constantly talking about their own child's problems in governors' meetings. This is to be avoided at all costs. It is very irritating both for the staff and for other governors, and does nothing to improve the status of parents.

Being a parent governor can be a difficult role. It makes their life simpler if they keep it in mind that they are individuals who have to put the good of the school before any personal interests and loyalties.

Keeping in contact with parents

All governors, not just the elected parents, have a responsibility to keep in touch with parents. They can do this through the School Association, by coming into school whenever parents are invited for open days and report meetings, by doing their bit in jumble sales and other events. It helps if the governors are

clearly identified with a large badge or sign so that parents can get to know them.

It is natural for parents with a problem to approach the parent governor first. They will probably say that they don't want to bother the school. The parent governor may be able to act as a go-between, but must be careful not to usurp the role of the head. Parents with a problem must discuss it with the head or staff. The parent governor can offer to go with them

as moral support if they are reluctant to do so. Only when this has been tried and the parent is still not satisfied should the parent governor consider taking it up with the governing body.

It is very important not to take sides on any issue, especially before you have heard both sides of the question. 'Parent governors cannot themselves right wrongs. It can be the job of the parent governor to bring matters to the notice of the head or governing body. It is the job of the head or the governing body to examine the issues and put things right if necessary.'[2]

Keeping parents informed

Parent governors are often asked to report back to the parents about the governors' meeting. There is no difficulty about this as long as they avoid passing on confidential information. Items which are confidential, especially those involving individual members of staff or pupils, must not be discussed, however informally, with other parents. The papers for governors' meetings, without the confidential items, must be displayed in the school. Draft minutes of meetings can be put up before they have been formally approved, if the chair of governors has checked them.

Elections

The local authority, or the governors in a voluntary school, decide how the elections for parent governors should be carried out. It must be done by secret ballot, with an opportunity for a postal vote. The turn-out for parent governor elections varies a lot from school to school. Some schools and LEAs give the elections a lot of publicity, with leaflets in libraries etc, and news items in the local press and radio. Others don't bother much. The Department of Education and Science publishes two helpful leaflets, explaining what being a governor means: *Shouldn't you become a school governor?* and *School Governors: a new role* (available free from DES Publications). If an election is coming up details of the arrangements must be included in the annual report to parents.

If there are not enough candidates to stand for election as parent governor, the other governors can appoint people to fill the places. They must if possible be parents of children at the school, or if not must have a child of school age.

Who is a parent?

The governors must keep a register with the name and address of every parent. Only the parents on the register are entitled to vote in school ballots. Keeping this register is not as easy as it sounds. Nowadays children may have a number of parents and step-parents. The Department of Education Circular 7/87 says that a parent 'includes a guardian and every person who has actual custody of the child or young person'. Schools don't have to track down every conceivable person who might qualify as a parent, but they can't exclude anyone who comes within the definition.

How many votes?

One parent one vote for each vacant place is the usual arrangement, though some LEAs allow one vote per family or one vote per child in the school. Circular 7/87 says that LEAs can arrange for proportional representation if they wish, as long as it is clearly explained.

Who can stand for election?

Anyone who is a registered parent can stand for election. The rules about putting your name forward should be explained in the annual report or school prospectus. No-one who is not a registered parent can make a nomination. Otherwise the DES Circular suggests that there should be as few restrictions as possible and

[2] NAGM Paper 8 Parent governors obtainable from NAGM price 50p

that people should be allowed to nominate themselves.

Election meetings

Most schools hold an election meeting where parents can find out more about being a governor, and perhaps decide to stand for election themselves. There is usually a chance to meet the people willing to stand, who may be asked to say a few words about themselves. Sometimes they can do this in small groups instead of having to stand up before a big audience.

Voting

Voting papers with the names of all the candidates must be sent to all parents. This is usually done by pupil post because of the expense of postage, so you need to keep a sharp look-out for this in your children's pockets when you are sorting the washing. It's usual to include a brief statement from each candidate. The election papers should be translated into local minority languages if necessary.

Each school will have a Returning Officer who will be responsible for running the ballot. There has to be some control over the issue and return of ballot papers because of allegations of fraud in the past. These should not be so complicated that they discourage people from voting, and must preserve the secrecy of the ballot. Ballot papers may be returned by post, or by pupil post, or in person.

By-elections

If any parent governor resigns before their term of office is up a new election must be held as soon as possible. All the parent governors must be in place before any governors' meeting is held to decide co-options or the election of the chair or vice chair of the governors.

After the election

The school should write to parents with the names of those who have been elected, explaining how to contact them. Everything that can be done to keep parents informed about the parent governors and what they are doing helps. Then next time there is an election, more people will understand what is involved. They will have seen that parent governors can do a useful and important job for the school.

WHERE TO GO IF YOU HAVE A PROBLEM

Whatever the new legislation may say about rights, parents often feel at a disadvantage when they have a problem about their child's school. The most eminent parents may remember their own schooldays and be in awe of the head.

After all, it's bad enough complaining about something you've bought in a shop or ordered in a restaurant. When you have a complaint about a school, a whole assortment of human relationships and feelings are involved. You may feel that you are putting your child in the front line. It may be especially difficult if you are on good terms with your child's teachers and feel that you are being disloyal to them.

Parents' right to know

However, what the new legislation has done is to change the climate. It may take a while for the effects to come through, but the balance has swung in favour of the consumers – the parents and children – away from the providers – the teachers and local government officers. Parents and their children now have the right to be consulted about what is going on in schools and about how the system works.

This is nothing new in many schools, where heads have always understood the need to take parents with them if they are to get the best out of the children. But there was no guarantee that a head would accept the need for partnership with parents. There was no obligation to keep them informed. Now parents can claim that inside knowledge as a right and not as a privilege or favour.

You may say that the right to know doesn't give you any real power. But that misunderstands where power lies. If you don't know what the system is, you can't make use of it to help your child. To that extent knowledge is power.

It is even more important that schools have to spell things out to parents and governors. They

71

have to be able to explain how the school is organised, what the children are learning, how tests are carried out and what the results are. Once all this has to be made public, it has to be defensible. It's not so easy to gloss over failings and muddles and to forget about black spots. The National Curriculum is a good example of this process. It has already revealed the fact that staff shortages prevent schools from teaching all the compulsory subjects. This highlights the way in which many children were not getting a broad and balanced education under the old system.

Education is having to come to terms with these and many other changes. They affect the job of everyone who has a say in how schools are run.

The role of the head

There is no doubt that the legislation has changed the traditional power of the headteacher. Heads are now much more answerable to the governors about how they run their schools.

The National Curriculum gives them less freedom of action over what is taught and to whom it is taught than they had before. (Perhaps this will end some of the disputes with parents about the subjects children are to take in the last two years of secondary school.)

With the governors, heads will have responsibility for much administrative work on finance and buildings that was previously done by the LEA. They will be able to make more decisions for themselves about how money is spent in the school. On the other hand, the LEA will probably put more effort, through their inspectors and advisers, into making sure that all schools and teachers reach high standards.

Nevertheless, the head is still responsible for what goes on from day to day inside the school. It is the head who decides how the teaching and non-teaching staff should be used in the school and how the teaching should be organised. In

matters of discipline, it's not easy to over-rule the head's decisions. Ultimately it's up to the head to see that standards of learning and discipline in the school are as high as possible.

Governors and the LEA may seek to influence their heads and may be able to direct them on some issues. But heads have the ultimate weapon. They cannot be forced to carry out decisions they don't agree with. They can resign and it is not so easy to replace them these days.

The role of the governors

The governing body represents all the groups interested in the school. About a quarter are political nominees, made by the local education authority, often in proportion to party strengths on the local council. A quarter are elected parents, and there will be one or two elected teachers, depending on the size of the school. The head can choose whether to be a full member of the governing body, with a vote. Heads that decide against this have the right to attend all meetings of the governors. The three groups, parents, staff and LEA representatives get together to choose a fourth group, the community representatives who also have about a quarter of the places. Although they are co-opted they become full members of the governing body. There has to be at least one governor representing local business.

The rules are different for church schools, whose governors are appointed mainly by the church. The chair of governors in these schools is often the local parish priest, though this is not required by law.

The conduct of a school is under the direction of the governing body, except for functions which are specifically given to the head or to the LEA. This gives them a concern with every aspect of the life of the school, in particular how it appears to the outside world. But they should not interfere with the professional job done by the head and teachers.

With the head, they decide on the aims and objectives of the school. As explained in earlier chapters, they can issue policy statements on the curriculum and discipline. They can decide whether the school should offer sex education. Under Local Management of Schools, they will be responsible for the school budget. One very important job is the appointment of the head and the staff employed in the school.

It is now accepted that schools have to be accountable to their local community for the way in which they are providing education to that community. Yet this does not mean that a governing body can lay down the law to the head and staff and expect to get its own way. The professionals cannot be forced to work in ways that they don't support. It's often said that governors have to earn the right to be listened to. They can only do this by taking time and effort to get to know their school.

The relationship has to be one of partnership with the head and staff, working together to improve the quality of the education provided in the school. The professionals do have to explain and justify what they are doing to the governors and through them to the parents. Certainly one of the most important jobs governors do is to ask the right questions. After all, if the head and staff can't explain to the governors what they are about in an convincing way, there must be some doubt as to whether they can put it over to the pupils. That's one of the reasons why it is important to have a wide range of people on the governing body, with different experiences of life and work. Schools have to cater for all sections of the population, and try to meet all their needs, not just those of one group who may be particularly good at putting their views across.

So parents should see the governors as the guardians of the public interest in their school. They should not hesitate to contact the governors if they feel that something is wrong and cannot get it put right.

The role of the LEA

Local Education Authorities are part of local government. Some of the councillors elected to the county or metropolitan borough council form an Education Committee which looks after the Local Education Authority and its education officers.

LEAs have to make sure that every child in their area has a place in a suitable school. They must provide other educational services to the local community including leisure and youth activities. Within government restrictions they decide how much should be spent on education in their area.

The 1986 and 1988 Education Acts have had the effect of reducing many of their powers. They have much less say in the appointment of staff. The delegation of most of the education budget to individual schools means that they have less financial control. They can no longer

dominate governing bodies by appointing a majority of the membership.

However, they are still responsible for planning and organising the education system in their area. They are also responsible for its overall quality. Heads and governing bodies have to answer to them about how they carry out their own responsibilities. The politicians who run the Education Authority still have a good deal of political control over the system, and are subject to the discipline of the ballot box. They can be voted out if local electors aren't satisfied with what they do. So it is worth contacting your local councillor if you can't get satisfaction from the school or the Education Office.

In the case of voluntary schools, you may need to contact the diocesan board for education instead. They do not directly control church schools, except through the governors they appoint to their governing bodies, but they can exert moral pressure.

LEAs have no influence over what happens in grant-maintained schools. If you can't get satisfaction from the school, the next stop is the Secretary of State for Education and Science.

The role of the government

The government's part in education is carried out by the Department of Education and Science, under the Secretary of State for Education and Science who is a member of the Cabinet.

It used to be said that we had a national system of education, administered locally. That was not altogether true, because although the central government in theory had to supervise the whole system, in practice they had very few powers with which to exercise any control over it. The 1988 Act changed that, because through the National Curriculum and the national system of testing, the Department of Education and Science can have a very direct effect in what is happening in every school in the country. For the first time it also directly controls some schools – the grant maintained schools.

The government has also taken the sole power to control teachers' pay, so that the local authorities, who are technically the employers, no longer have a say. It has put limits on local government spending, first through rate-capping, then with the poll tax and the unified business rate. It can exert very strong controls over how much money local government spends in all its services, including education.

It's also taken on a new role as information provider. Now that the law has given many powers to governors, the DES realises that it has a responsibility to see that they can do the job. As well as encouraging LEAs to support their governors, the DES sends out free information leaflets and guides about the work of governors and about the national curriculum to every governor in the country. (It is usually

the LEAs who have to do the actual distribution). It also publishes information for parents. This was unheard of a few years ago. Most of the material is well-produced, easy to read and very helpful. You can get copies free from DES publications if they don't come through from the LEA.

Even before the new legislation, you could always appeal to the Secretary of State if you felt that an LEA or a governing body was acting unreasonably. Section 68 of the 1944 Act still gives this right of appeal. Even if the LEA has followed the letter of the law, the Secretary of State can overrule its decisions in favour of an individual. This doesn't happen very often and there are some limitations on what the Secretary of State can consider unreasonable.

Another section of the same Act, Section 99, can be used to compel a governing body or an LEA to carry out their duties if they are failing to do so. Again, this has not proved very effective in the past. LEAs have used the excuse that they are trying to fulfil the law, but have a good reason for being unable to do so.

However the fact that these two sections exist is in itself a protection for parents, a safeguard against unreasonable behaviour on the part of those responsible for the system. Just the threat of using them will sometimes be enough to persuade an authority to change its mind.

The DES is also the base for Her Majesty's Inspectors of Schools (HMI). HMI have a long and independent history of inspecting schools and collecting information about education all over the country. They publish this information in a series of very useful, practical pamphlets, for example the *Curriculum Matters* series, which describe the good work (and some of the mistakes) that are going on in schools in different parts of the curriculum. They also carry out inspections of schools. The reports on these full inspections have to be made public and must be included in the stock of material about a school which is available to parents.

Recently they have also been inspecting whole LEAs, and publishing reports on them too. They have a powerful role in overseeing the way the National Curriculum is brought into schools.

Where to go for help

Although some specific rights to appeal or complain to the governors or the LEA are given under Section 23 (1) of the 1988 Act, you are usually expected to go through an informal procedure first, in the hope of sorting out the problem before it need come to an official complaint.

When you have a problem, it is often quite difficult to find out whom to ask, and where to find them. It's a waste of time to tackle the wrong person. You need to know what level to begin at. Many people make the mistake of starting at too high a level. They ask to see the governors about a simple problem that the class teacher could have sorted out. On the other hand, it's no good blaming the class teacher if there aren't enough computers in the classroom.

Very briefly:

- The head is responsible for everything to do with the day to day running of the school.
- The governors are responsible for deciding school policies, which the head carries out.
- The Local Education Authority (LEA) is responsible for providing schools and organising the local education service. Church schools are supervised by the diocesan boards of education.
- The government is responsible for education law and for training teachers and deciding their pay.

Which means that:

- If you have a problem about something that goes on inside school, including discipline, you go to the head.
- If you aren't happy about the outcome, or

you think that school policy is wrong or not being carried out, you go to the governors.

- If you are still not satisfied, or your problem is to do with finding a school, or other matter of local policy, you go to the LEA. The diocesan board may be able to help in a church school.
- If you are still not satisfied, or your problem has to do with national policy laid down by the government, you go to the Department of Education and Science.

to parents. If they don't you could ask a question about this at the annual parents' meeting.

The governors may be reluctant to intervene in a dispute with the school unless the matter involves a school policy for which they are responsible. It helps if you can show that other parents besides yourself are concerned about the issue.

Contacting the head

In a big school some of the work of running the school will be delegated to heads of year and heads of subject departments. Class or subject teachers may be able to help with straightforward problems about classwork. But some heads prefer all queries to go to them first. You can check with the school what the policy is.

Some schools have special regular times when someone is always available to see parents. If not, try to make an appointment to come in, as then you can be sure that someone will be free to see you. You can usually do this by telephoning or sending a note to the school office. It's not a good idea just to turn up. It can be very unhelpful to try to corner the class teacher when you bring the children to school, just as 30 children are arriving in the classroom.

Contacting the LEA

The Education Office address should be in the post office or library. It is often quickest to talk to the local government education officer in charge of the appropriate section first, because they may be able to help straight away. In a big authority it helps to know what room or telephone extension you need. The school, or a friendly councillor may help you to find out which officer to contact, and at which office. If your library has an information section they may be able to find out for you. Otherwise you can spend a long time trying to find the right person or section.

If the officer is not helpful, you can go to your councillor. Most councillors have a regular surgery to which you can take any problems, but if all else fails, write to them at the Town Hall, addressing your letter c/o the Members' Lobby.

Contacting the governors

The school brochure or annual report should explain how you can contact the chair of governors or the clerk to the governing body. Or you can write to them care of the school, though these letters don't always get through. You may know the parent governors and prefer to approach them first.

Governors ought to make themselves available

Contacting the DES

The Department of Education and Science in London is known for having a very helpful switchboard but if you have a complex problem it is probably better to write in. They are good at deciphering fine points of the law, but they can't help with individual problems over schools unless you have gone through the procedures at a local level first.

How to make a case

You may have rights but you must take care how you use them. Most problems with a school can be sorted out if there is good will on both sides. If parents feel nervous when they approach the school or the Education Office, they can come over as very aggressive and unreasonable. If you are angry, try not to let your anger get the better of you.

The first way to approach anyone about a problem is to take the line, 'I'm in this predicament and I'm hoping you will be able to help me.' People respond better to a request for help than to a strident complaint.

So you don't go to see the head saying 'That maths teacher is a hopeless idiot and shouldn't be allowed near children'. You say 'I'm afraid that my Jo doesn't seem to be making much progress with maths. Is there anything I can do to help?'

It is also essential to get your facts straight. Everyone tends to exaggerate to make a good story, but you must be careful not to say anything you can't substantiate. The slightest inaccuracy, totally irrelevant to your main concern, could be seized on as a defence against taking you seriously. On the other hand if you do get your facts right and can show a reasoned argument, the chances are that you will be astonished at your success. Schools and officers want to do the right thing; they don't set out to do you down.

If it seems to be taking a long time to get a reply, it may be worth contacting your MP. MPs have surgeries too, or you can write to them explaining what the problem is. They may have some territorial political clout, especially if you are a member of their party. Otherwise there's not usually much point in contacting them about local problems until you have tried all the local processes.

If you are seriously concerned about a school, you could try writing to HMI about it. You may not get a direct answer, but your letter will be noted and may prompt a visit on their part to the school.

It is always better to muster the support of other parents if you can, as that will help to convince the powers that be that you are not just interested in getting an unfair advantage for your own child. The difficulty is in finding other parents who agree with you and are not afraid to stand up and be counted. Many a governor or parent who has tried to raise an issue against the wishes of the head or chair of governors will find that they get no support in the meeting only to be told afterwards in the pub that they were quite in the right. The way to get around this is to canvass support before you make your point. People need to be prepared beforehand to support you, they like to have a chance to think it over.

Formal complaints procedures

If you have made an informal approach and are not satisfied, you can use the official complaints procedures. Under Section 23 of the 1989 Act an LEA must set up a clear procedure for hearing complaints about the following:

- the provision of a broad-based curriculum including religious education;
- the National Curriculum not being properly provided;
- the school offering a qualification that has not been approved by the Secretary of State;
- the provision of religious education and worship (there may be special arrangements for voluntary aided schools);
- the need to act reasonably about exemptions from the National Curriculum;
- charging for school activities;
- providing information as required by the Act.

Anyone whose complaint under Section 23 is rejected can still appeal to the Secretary of State under Sections 68 and 99 of the 1944 Act if they are not satisfied.

It is up to the LEA to decide on the procedure but it has to be approved by the Secretary of State. It must be well-publicised and make it clear whom to contact about a formal complaint. There must be a way of sorting out which complaints can be heard and which complaints need to be heard urgently. All complaints should be dealt with 'speedily, efficiently, fully and fairly'.[1] There must be a series of distinct stages to pass through, and parents must know how each of these is handled. At each stage the complainer must be

told what the result is and what is to happen next.

The governing body must be involved at the first stage of the complaint and must make sure that it has been properly investigated in the school before it goes to the LEA.

Regular reports must go to the governors and the LEA about the number of complaints and what was decided about them with an annual summary to the DES. So woe betide any school that has an unusually high number of complaints against it.

Last resorts

The local ombudsman

You can complain to the Local Ombudsman (Local Commissioner for Administration) if you have reason to think that the LEA has not carried out its own procedures correctly. If an LEA has acted with bias, neglect, delay or inefficiency the Ombudsman can rule that there has been maladministration and suggest what could be done to make up for this. The LEA is not obliged to put things right, but usually does. You can't complain about the internal running of the school but a number of parents have successfully complained about not getting their choice of school or about free school transport.

The Ombudsman cannot deal with complaints about voluntary schools.

The law

If you have an exceptionally strong case and can get support from a solicitor or local Law Centre you can go to the courts for Judicial Review of a decision. You have to be able to show that the DES or LEA or governors did not keep to the strict requirements of the law. It's not something to be undertaken lightly.

---

[1] DES Circular 1/89 *Local arrangements for the consideration of complaints*

Where to find out more

Useful addresses

Government

Department of Education and Science
Elizabeth House
York Road
London
SE1 7PH
071 934 9000

DES Publications Despatch Centre
Honeypot Lane
Canons Park
Stanmore
HA7 1AZ
081 952 2366

Her Majesty's Stationery Office
Mail Order
PO Box 276
London
SW8 5DT
071 622 3316

Local Ombudsman
Commissioner for Local Administration in England
21 Queen Anne's Gate
London SW1H 9BU
071 722 5622

Commissioner for Local Administration in Wales
Derwen House
Court Road
Bridgend
Mid-Glamorgan
CF31 1BN
0656 61325

National Curriculum Council
15–17 New Street
York
YO1 2RA
0904 622533

School Examinations and Assessment Council
Newcombe House
45 Notting Hill Gate
London
W11 3JB
071 229 1234

Governors

National Association of Governors and Managers (NAGM)
Christopher Hatton Centre
26 Laystall Street
London EC1K 4PQ
071 833 0399

Parents

Advisory Centre for Education (ACE)
18 Victoria Park Square
London E2 9PB
081 980 4597

National Confederation of
Parent Teacher Associations (NCPTA)
2 Ebbsfleet Industrial Estate
Stonebridge Road
Gravesend Kent
DA11 9DZ
0474 560618

Prospect Trust
Newpoint House
St James' Lane
London
N10 3DF
081 444 5816

Campaigns

Campaign for the Advancement of State Education
National Secretary
4 Hill Road
Carshalton Beeches
Surrey
081 669 5929

Useful publications

Education (weekly magazine)
Longmans
The Pinnacles
Fourth Avenue
Harlow
0279 29655

Times Educational Supplement weekly paper available from newsagents

These should be in your local reference library.

St Andrews
BOOK SALE

Victory Memorial Hall

New Books at a Fraction of the Original Price

Saturday 20th September

10am-4pm

ADMISSION FREE

In memoriam
T.J.H. 1924–1999

Sheep in the Cotswolds
The Medieval Wool Trade

Derek Hurst

TEMPUS

First published 2005

Tempus Publishing Limited
The Mill, Brimscombe Port,
Stroud, Gloucestershire, GL5 2QG
www.tempus-publishing.com

British Library Cataloguing in Publication Data.
A catalogue record for this book is available from the British Library.

ISBN 0 7524 2898 5

Typesetting and origination by Tempus Publishing Limited
Printed in Great Britain

Contents

No browne, nor sullyed black the face and legs doth streak,
Like those of Morland, Cank, or of the Cambrian hills
That lightly laden are: but Cotswold wisely fills
Her with the whitest kind: whose browes so woolly be,
As men in her faire sheep no emptiness should see.
The staple deepe and thick, through, to the very graine,
Most strongly keepeth out the violentest raine:
A body long and large, the buttocks equall broad;
As fit to under-goe the full and weightie load.
And of the fleecie face, the flanke doth nothing lack,
But every-where is stor'd; the belly, as the back.
The faire and goodly flock, the shepheards onely pride,
As white as winters snowe, when from the rivers side
He drives his new-washt sheepe; ...

Extract from *Poly-olbion* (Song XIV)
by Michael Drayton (1563-1631)

Notes for the reader

Prices are stated as in the original source, and conversion rates to modern decimalised currency are as follows: 1 shilling (s) = 5p; c.2½ old pence (d) = 1p. A common unit of medieval currency was the *mark* of 13s 4d (in pre-decimal currency, or about 67p). Old units of weight and measurement are as follows: 1lb = 0.454kg, 1 yard (equivalent to the medieval *ell*) = 0.914m. Other terms in general medieval use may be found in the Glossary.

Quotations from original sources have generally been transcribed as written, except that in the passages from the Cely letters, which are all from the Early English Text Society edition (Hanham 1975), 'y' has been substituted for the Middle English letter 'yogh'.

Medieval monetary values are difficult to gauge without knowing the average contemporary income at different levels of society, and the values of some basic commodities. The following prices may help to provide a very rough guide to the value of medieval currency in terms of its purchasing power, and so enable the scale of the sums stated in this book, for instance in wool deals, to be better appreciated (daily incomes mainly after Dyer 1989, and 2002a, and prices after Rogers 1866 and 1882):

Century	Daily income		Wheat	Ale/beer /cider	Salt
	Labourer	Craftsman	(per quarter) ★	(per gallon (4.5l))	(per bushel)★
13th	1d	2½d	5s–6s	½d (cider)	4d
Early 14th	2d	4d	4s	1d (ale)	5d–6d
Later 14th	3d	4d	5s	½d (cider)	6d–8d
Early 15th	3d	5d	5s	2d (beer)	6d
Later 15th	3d/4d	6d	6s	1½d (ale)	6d
Early 16th	4d	6d	8s–12s	2d (ale)	9d

★A quarter weighed about 450lb (204kg), and a bushel 56lb (c.25kg).

References to counties are to the pre-1974 historic counties, unless otherwise stated, and the English places referred to are generally now in Gloucestershire, unless otherwise stated.

ABBREVIATIONS

AgHEW	*The Agrarian History of England and Wales*, vols I–IV (Cambridge, 1967-1991)
BL	British Library
Cal LPFD	*Calendar of Letters and Papers Foreign and Domestic* (published vols)
CPR	*Calendar of Patent Rolls* (published vols)
DoE	Department of the Environment (buildings listing, now under Department of Culture, Media and Sport)
EPNS	English Place-Name Society
NA	The National Archives (Kew)
SA	Southampton Archives
VCH	*Victoria County History* (Gloucestershire vols II (1907), VI (1965), VII (1981), IX (1976), XI (1965); Oxfordshire vol II (1907))

Acknowledgements

The impetus to address the subject of this book owes much to the enthusiasm and interest of the large group of volunteers who took part in the 'Sheepwashes in the Cotswolds Area of Outstanding Natural Beauty' Local Heritage Initiative project, which was funded in 2001-3 by the Heritage Lottery Fund and sponsored by the Cotswolds Area of Outstanding Natural Beauty (AONB) Partnership.

In the course of researching the book I have benefited from discussions with many; in particular with Sebastian Payne and Ian Baxter about early sheep from the archaeological viewpoint, and with Lyn Gibbings, John King and Joe Henson (both the latter being of Cotswold Farm Park) about the Cotswold sheep breed. Duncan Brown (Southampton City Museums) guided my appreciation of the fine imported ceramics found during archaeological excavation in Southampton and which constitute a tangible link between this medieval English port and the Italian wool merchants, who came in pursuit of Cotswold wool. I would also especially like to offer my thanks to David and Linda Viner, who first encouraged me to start collecting material; to David Guyatt, who fathomed medieval texts with his customary generosity; and to Carolyn Hunt, who supported my efforts at computer-aided illustration and generously provided artwork. Other colleagues in the Worcestershire Historic Environment and Archaeology Service also provided much-needed encouragement on occasion.

The generosity of many has assisted in the provision of contemporary material to illustrate the book. Accordingly I am grateful to the following: The Council of the Early English Text Society for permission to quote extracts from *The Cely letters 1472-1488*, as edited by Alison Hanham (1975); Cambridge University Museum of Archaeology and Anthropology (*11*); Joe Stevens (*23*); the Society for Medieval Archaeology (*28*); the Koninklijk Museum voor Schone Kunsten in Antwerp (*31*); Oxford University Press (*33*); the British Library (*34*); Iona Antiques, London (*58*); Lyn and Shaun Gibbings (*59*); and the Cotswold Sheep Society (*66*), who all generously gave permission for reproduction of their material. The Mercers' Company of London kindly provided a grant in support of arranging for some of this material to be included in the book.

Peter Kemmis Betty, Lyn Gibbings, Bob Tatam and Simon Woodiwiss, amongst others, generously read parts of earlier drafts, with beneficial results for the contents. Of course, any mistakes or omissions that remain are my own.

Preface

The term 'Cotswolds' today describes an area of limestone uplands in western England. It takes in a large part of Gloucestershire, as well as parts of Oxfordshire, Somerset, Warwickshire, Wiltshire and Worcestershire. This area is still largely rural, and the countryside is now renowned for being especially tranquil and attractive, which is reflected in its official designation as a nationally acclaimed 'Area of Outstanding Natural Beauty', the largest such area in England. As well as its natural beauty, the Cotswolds can also claim to be well endowed with some of the most attractive of old buildings in its towns, villages and farmsteads. Taken together, these qualities are the principal ingredients of one of the most quintessentially 'English' places, today deservedly popular and enjoyed by many thousands of visitors every year.

History has contributed much to the appearance of the modern Cotswold landscape. Activities commonly acknowledged to have been of great significance in the Cotswolds in the past are the farming of sheep for the production of wool and the manufacture of cloth. These made a substantial impact on that landscape and, equally importantly, were the source of considerable wealth. Though the medieval and early post-medieval sheep farmers, wool merchants and clothiers are long gone, some of their works are still evident in that landscape, particularly the fine stone buildings where they invested their profits. But there are also other clues to their activities, not the least being the existence of a distinctive Cotswold sheep breed.

Sheep grazing has been instrumental historically in creating and maintaining the open character of the Cotswold scenery, though the few surviving sheep-walks of today (e.g. Cleeve Hill near Cheltenham and Minchinhampton Common) may now have been turned into amenity areas where alternative users, such as golfers, have taken the place of sheep. In an earlier age these large open spaces of grassland would have been repeated many times over across the length of the Cotswolds as upland pastures. The visual impression of openness would have been even more striking in the past, as any substantial land boundaries may have been entirely absent over large areas of arable in the common fields cultivated communally in medieval times. Today, however, the sheep runs of the past are rarities, and generally they have now been ploughed up for arable farming.

Other local traces of the formidable medieval industry of wool production and woollen cloth manufacture are much more subtle, such as the frequency of the street name Sheep Street in the Cotswold townscape (e.g. Chipping Campden, and Burford), or village (e.g. Charlbury); or of public houses with names such as The Ram or The Golden Fleece. Then there are the occasional funerary brasses commemorating wool merchants (e.g. at Northleach church), or some other arhictectural detail at a local parish church. But, taken together, these mementos from the past still represent a good body of surviving physical evidence for wool production in the Cotswolds, and the eventual emergence of a cloth industry, that initially will have relied on the local wool.

Fortunately the documentary sources are much more eloquent, and these provide both a national and international perspective on the Cotswold wool trade from the medieval period onwards. Archaeology also provides some additional information, but very much performs just a supporting role for the moment. In future, however, as more account is taken of wool production due to its economic and social importance, it is likely that archaeology will play a greater part in revealing its local significance, as more local features are discovered that may be recognised as relating to this major trade.

This book, therefore, brings together diverse sources of information about the Cotswold wool trade, and touches as well on the Cotswold cloth industry, and provides an archaeological viewpoint by linking the historical record with surviving archaeological remains. This viewpoint is intended to relate the documentary evidence back to the people and settings in the Cotswolds where the original wool production took place, as it is often the local sites that get forgotten, even while the trade is being extensively celebrated as an important aspect of our national history through the good services of historians. The early Cotswold cloth industry is also touched on as it benefited from the availability of good-quality local wool in its early days, though later it sourced the wool for its fine woollens from other regions.

A visit to a derelict sheepwash site at Sutton-under-Brailes in south Warwickshire in 2001 was a first introduction to the medieval Cotswold wool trade. This sheepwash was a tangible link with a famous agricultural heritage, which had not only impacted on the enduring appearance of the Cotswolds today, but had also contributed enormously to the national economy in its time, and so been a major force for the betterment of society both in this country and abroad. By carrying out a survey of numerous similar sites across the Cotswolds, under the auspices of the Cotswolds AONB Partnership, it has been possible to gain a real sense also of the local scale and importance of the wool trade at first-hand through this one type of site, the sheepwash. Hopefully this book will also help others to appreciate this aspect of Cotswold history, and provide further impetus towards the conservation of sites associated with this impressive achievement by the sheep farmers and wool merchants of medieval and later Gloucestershire and its adjacent counties.

I

Introduction

It is important to start with the landscape itself as this was one of the principal factors in the success of the medieval wool trade. The Cotswolds are a range of limestone hills in the west of England defining a major watershed between the Severn and Thames river valleys, and covering some 800 sq miles (over 2,000km²) (*1*). They have a distinctive character in various ways. A sharply steep slope marks the western edge of the hills, while, in contrast, to the east there is an almost imperceptible dip slope. They have several notable high points, such as Cleeve Hill at 1,040ft (317m) above sea level, but the general impression is of gently rolling hills, which give settlements in the folds of the hills a high degree of seclusion and protection from the worst of the elements. On the steep scarp slope to the west there are a series of steeply cut valleys associated with rapid streams, which were once important as a source of water power. There are also economically useful outcrops of fuller's earth and stone building materials, giving rise to other local industries, and providing a diverse economic base. But the chief wealth was in the extensive pasture and, the high ground being very dry, it was primarily suited to sheep rather than cattle. This was the key to the maintenance of large flocks of sheep, and, in addition to their wool, they provided manure to increase the fertility of the thin soils and hence boosted arable cultivation on lower ground.

The name *Cotswold*, which has been used since at least the twelfth century (Hooke 1998), has sometimes been taken to mean a place associated with *cotes* or sheepfolds, but the derivation favoured by modern commentators derives the *cot* element from the personal name *Cod. Cod's wold* was a place name originally for a piece of land around *Cod's dene* (Cutsdean) and this usage seems to have gradually spread out to include the rest of the region as well (Smith 1976). The term *wold* would imply that this expanse of higher ground was once characterised by woodland during the Anglo-Saxon period. But *wold* has also been considered to be country with scattered stands of trees rather than being densely wooded at the time of the English settlement, as *ley* names are usually common in the latter case (Fox 1989), and place names ending in *ley* are generally rare in the

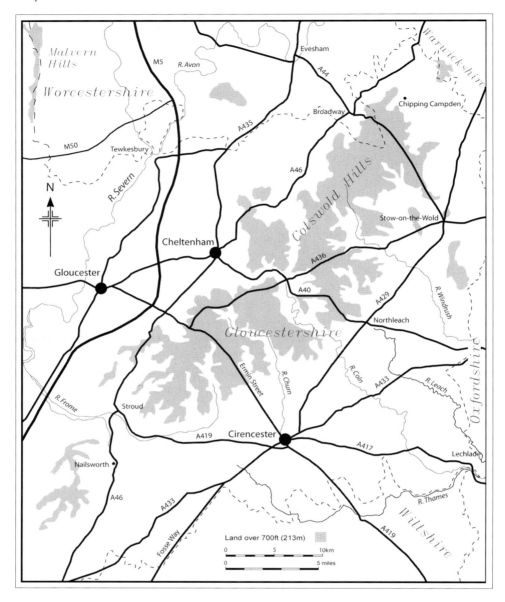

1 Map of the Cotswolds showing principal routes and places

Cotswolds. Some corroboration of this latter interpretation comes from *ley* names being much less rare on the western scarp slope (Dyer 2002a), which often remains heavily wooded even in the present day.

The region was notable in Roman times for its degree of Romanisation both at the main town *Corinium*, now Cirencester, and in the surrounding countryside with its numerous large estate houses (usually referred to as villas). This was eventually reflected in its standing towards the end of the Roman period when Cirencester became the capital of one of the British provinces. The end of central Roman control left individual towns as regional centres and Cirencester remained a force to be reckoned with until AD 577, when it was overcome by the west Saxons at the Battle of Dyrham. Even in the subsequent period Cirencester (where seven hundreds met) remained the main administrative and market centre in the south Cotswolds, though a new administrative and market centre developed at Winchcombe in the north Cotswolds by the ninth century. Around 1016 the county of Gloucestershire itself was created from these units (Finberg 1975).

Wool came to the fore in the Middle Ages to be recognised as a major economic asset and a particularly potent symbol of English power by the fourteenth century. Wool was used for outer garments, in combination with linen (from flax), which was relatively coarse, for underwear, and cotton was not yet imported on a sufficiently large scale to compete. In both the cases of linen and cotton, some specialised centres on the Continent did achieve a high standard in both these alternative textiles, but the importance of wool as an established commodity, on which national economies had been founded, meant that these alternatives to wool made little real headway in the medieval period.

Wool was, therefore, the first choice in the Middle Ages for textiles which were affordable, comfortable and attractive to wear. Apart from the obvious economic value which wool acquired as a result of its popularity, the subject clearly affected some Englishmen in a peculiar way, as they sometimes waxed lyrical in public about the superior quality and value of this English asset. For instance, John Gower (d. 1408) called wool 'that noble lady, goddess of the merchants … so nice, so white, so soft' (van Uytven 1983, 177), while John Lydgate (d. *c*.1450) referred to wool as 'cheeff tresour in this land growyng'. These sentiments, however, do reflect the situation where large numbers of people were making plenty of money out of the wool trade.

This brings us to the other main factor that brought about the success of the Cotswold wool trade, which was, of course, the sheep itself, which managed to outshine most other sheep in the country in the quality of its wool. This is all the more mysterious as the origins and character of the local sheep are less easy to fathom. The pedigree of the Cotswold sheep, and even its appearance in the Middle Ages, remain controversial. It is uncertain whether it was bred primarily for wool, or whether it had been employed initially for other purposes such as maintaining soil fertility in arable fields by being moved around in pens (folding), and for milk for cheeses, and only later came to be prized for its wool as well. Further archaeological investigation, using the latest techniques such as DNA analysis, eventually will hopefully shed some light on this darkest corner of Cotswold history.

When the interest in English wool brought foreign merchants to our shores, the Cotswold sheep were immediately held in high regard and their wool quality was never in question. But surprisingly the exact attribute of the wool that signified this quality and made the wool so sought-after, remains today somewhat of a mystery. Another principal region for best quality wool was the Welsh Marches around Leominster (north Herefordshire), and here the wool was definitely being celebrated for its fineness, as it was being compared to the 'silkworm's thread' (in Drayton's *Poly-olbion*). It is likely, therefore, that it was also the fineness of the Cotswold wool that was its main attraction to the Flemish and Italian, and then later, the English weavers.

Cotswold wool, together with other English wool, shares a less reputable place in English history. It was in the medieval wool trade that the English government first developed an interest (subsequently undiminished) in raising money from trade by taxation, and thereby discovered a whole new way in which to interfere in, and exploit, to its own advantage, the conduct of business, whether conducted by its own subjects or by foreigners. This may be symbolised by the Lord Chancellor still sitting on the woolsack in the House of Lords today. In 1938 the stuffing was found, contrary to tradition, to be horse hair and so it was restuffed with wool from the United Kingdom and all the Commonwealth countries.

The Cotswold wool industry, therefore, sheds light on both the workings of local communities and of national governments, whilst, for about 300 years, being the source of some of the greatest wealth, which both bolstered the aspiring middle classes and helped make practical realities of the aggrandising schemes of English kings.

2

The Cotswold sheep

... but Cotswold wisely fills
Her with the whitest kind: whose browes so woolly be
(Extract from the poem *Poly-Olbion* by Michael Drayton dated 1612)

The origin of the Cotswold breed is difficult to establish with any certainty. Some have claimed that these sheep were simply Spanish stock brought over by Eleanor of Castile, the wife of Edward I, or, alternatively, Flemish stock brought over by Philippa of Hainault, the wife of Edward III (Brill 1973). But these seem to be just romantic ideas which have no firm historical basis.

The earliest sheep in England are generally regarded as being akin to Soay sheep (*2*), an ancient breed that survived into the twentieth century on the remote island of St Kilda off the north-west coast of Scotland. These are small, predominantly dark-woolled sheep which look more goat-like than

2 Soay sheep. Ram to left, ewe to right, the latter showing the tendency to shed wool naturally by late spring

conventional modern sheep. They are also more like goats in their behaviour for they are capable of jumping over high obstacles. Their wool is black, brown, or blonde and both sexes are horned. They are now kept in order to demonstrate the appearance of earlier sheep, for instance at the Cotswold Farm Park in Gloucestershire. The fleece of the Soay is relatively short at 2in (50mm), and is moulted annually (Ryder 1964, 3) so that it can be plucked rather than requiring shearing. It averages annually some 2lb (0.9kg) of wool. Some of the best evidence for the early wool type has come from Bronze Age burials where waterlogging has preserved traces of textiles. Here the wool has included the coarse, bristly fibres typical of the outer coat of the fleece of wild sheep and was mainly brown in colour just like the Soay (Ryder 1964, 4). The ancestry of the Cotswold sheep, therefore, certainly begins in this way, but the intervening progression to the medieval Cotswold sheep, and through to the Cotswold breed of today, is much more problematical.

Sheep tend to be hairy rather than woolly, so that the fleece naturally remains undeveloped (Ryder 1984a). The development of woolly sheep appears be part of a long trend beginning in the Middle East after c.1000 BC, with the eventual emergence of fine fleeces in the Mediterranean area from the Classical period onwards. Selective breeding had other effects resulting in the continual growth of the outer coat rather than moulting, a whiter appearance, loss of horns, and a longer tail, while some have seen the proportionally shorter neck as another such indication. These are all signs of improvement through selective breeding.

There is some archaeological evidence that the Soay-type sheep underwent development before the Roman period with a greater tendency towards woolliness and towards white wool, presumably through selective breeding. Ryder (1981a, 18) has demonstrated from the archaeological evidence of contemporary wool remains that white, shorter and longer woolled sheep were present in Britain by the end of the Roman period and some commentators (e.g. Trow-Smith 1957 and Whitlock 1965, 133) have placed the origins of the Cotswold breed with sheep introduced to the region in the Roman period, particularly in the area of Cirencester. Indeed some excavated sheep bone from archaeological sites in eastern England does support the idea of a larger and polled sheep being introduced by the Romans (Armitage 1983), and there is also now some evidence for this in the Cotswolds (Maltby 1998).

In the medieval period there is much more evidence, though this does not necessarily add up to a clearer picture. One early medieval source (twelfth century) makes reference to curly woolled sheep being more valuable than coarse woolled sheep and there is plenty of evidence of sheep being deliberately traded for breeding purposes. All of this suggests that at least two different breeds of sheep had been brought into existence by about the beginning of the medieval period at the latest. The presence of hornless rams, as demonstrated from archaeological evidence, has also been taken to show that there were definitely differing types of sheep in medieval England (Ryder 1981a, 23).

It is not yet possible to equate archaeological evidence with particular regional types of sheep, though this may eventually come about with the closer study of the skeletal remains of breeds in existence today and the concomitant use of DNA analysis of excavated bones where there is good preservation (Sebastian Payne pers comm). In the meantime, archaeological observations remain broad-brush, though none the less useful for that. This current evidence may be best interpreted as indicating variability in sheep, and the local development of different types aided by the relative difficulty of transporting large numbers of animals over long distances. For instance, there is evidence from sheep bones from archaeological sites for an improved (larger) breed of sheep in parts of the Midlands from at least the Saxon period (Albarella and Davis 1994). However, direct evidence from the Cotswolds suggests that the medieval sheep here were not much bigger than later prehistoric examples (for instance based on a sample of 452 sheep bones from the deserted medieval village of Upton; Yealland and Higgs 1966), and there is even some evidence from Bishop's Cleeve that the medieval sheep were slightly smaller than their Romano-British predecessors (Maltby 2002). These sheep were usually at least three or four years old when culled, and so had clearly been kept for their wool. Given their location, these sheep are likely to have been the source of some of the 'Cotswold wool', in which the bishop of Worcester is documented as being a major trader.

The character of medieval wool is obviously of great interest given that this determined the varying levels of success in economic terms of sheep from different parts of the country. However, there have been no archaeological finds of wool from the Cotswold region, as there have from elsewhere. Generally no wool finds have yet been recognisable as coming from long-woolled sheep as defined today (i.e. longer than about 6in (160mm), which suggests that medieval fine wool was of the largely shorter stapled type (Bowden 1956-7) by modern standards. As far as the fifteenth-century merchant was concerned Cotswold wool came in four grades: 'good', 'middle', 'good young', and 'middle young'. 'Young cottys' was shorter in the staple than wool from fully-grown sheep, and of less value for cloth making. There was £3 difference in price per sack between this and 'good' (i.e. finest) Cotswold wool (Hanham 1985, 268), with the 'middle' wool being of intermediate quality and price.

Even parchments have been pressed into service in pursuit of an understanding of the evolution of sheep. Their study, based on microscopic recording of surviving wool fibres, does suggest that the medium diameter wools, likely to have been longwools judging by today's longwools, first appeared in the fourteenth century. The actual size of some parchment has also indicated that some medieval sheep were definitely bigger than Soay sheep. This is the first tentative proof of a larger and longer-woolled medieval sheep. Longer wool has been claimed by some historians (notably Eileen Power, e.g. 1941) to explain the popularity and high value of Cotswold wool, and to suggest that it was used to make worsted rather than the more common woollens. But this interest in size and length ignores the, albeit sparse, documentary evidence that it was simply fineness of woollen fibres that attracted the buyers to the highly prized wools such as from the Cotswolds. For instance, in 1480 Richard Cely the elder passed comment that some Cotswold wool he had just had packed was 'much finer than the year before' (Hanham 1985, 77).

Where the written historical record is found so wanting, images become of great significance. Though these are useful for the general study of medieval sheep, few are specific to the Cotswolds. Most are English and Flemish illuminated illustrations in manuscripts, and are of sheep in religious or general scenes, showing the prevalent type of sheep to be a white-faced animal, with the ewes being polled, or hornless (34). Other images of sheep also occur occasionally in funerary monuments, and these are potentially much more significant sources of information about the Cotswold breed, as there are examples from the Cotswolds. Some are flat images in the form of the important series of monumental brasses in Cotswold parish churches, in particular at Northleach (3), and others are sculptured, such as on top of a corner buttress of the fifteenth-century tower of Compton Abdale church (4). It may be particularly significant that in some respects the brasses, in particular, show a different type of sheep from those in the painted illustrations.

There has been much debate about the sheep depicted on the Northleach memorial brasses of the eminent late medieval wool merchants. These brasses have been taken to have been made in a style not imitating an earlier conventional design, and, therefore, potentially much more likely to reflect real sheep (Armitage and Goodall 1977). However, the brasses have been attributed to London workshops and, therefore, it is considered unlikely that the designer would be familiar with Cotswold sheep. Certainly the long-necked and fine-limbed character of the medieval sheep on these brasses is reminiscent of the primitive Soay sheep, and so deviates markedly from the style of sheep representation usual in illuminated manuscripts of the period (34). The longer tail (e.g. on the brass of John Taylour who died in 1490) at the same time betrays a definite move away from the ancient breed (3). Limited archaeological evidence also supports this appearance of the medieval sheep as the general type (Armitage and Goodall 1977). That there is on the Northleach memorial brasses a conscious depiction of the medieval sheep is encouraged by other details in the design, such as the closely observed woolpack, while it may be assumed that the wool merchants themselves are also accurately reproduced to some degree. Such details suggest that the pattern-maker may have been faithfully reproducing contemporary medieval sheep, though whether this reflected the sheep of the Cotswolds is uncertain.

It is tempting to think that the pattern-maker had some knowledge of Cotswold sheep, as the mid-fifteenth-century sheep on the John Fortey brass (5) resembles a more slender version of the modern breed. Here the sheep is hornless and the fleece hangs loose under the belly suggesting that it was approaching a longwool.

3 Detail of the John Taylour brass in Northleach church showing a sheep and a woolpack. Dated about 1490

4 Figure of a sheep with horns surmounting the south-east buttress of the fifteenth-century tower of Compton Abdale church

5 Detail of the John Fortey brass dated 1458 in Northleach church, showing a sheep

6 Detail of the Thomas Bushe brass dated 1525 in Northleach church, showing sheep

7 Sheep's head corbel of about 1200 in the nave of Windrush church

This may, therefore, be the most authentic medieval depiction of a Cotswold sheep to survive. The sheep shown on the William Midwinter brass of the very beginning of the sixteenth century also look similar (67). This is in contrast with the sheep shown on the Bushe brass of 1525 (6), where both sexes are horned, the more curled example being the ram. Here the sheep look more like the more ancient breed seen in the Soay sheep, though their long tails and shorter necks do mark them out as more developed. Horned sheep, probably rams, are also depicted in the fifteenth-century sculptured representations at Compton Abdale (4) and Fairford churches, again suggesting that horned sheep were also to be found in the medieval Cotswolds. The earliest surviving sheep carving in the Cotswolds also shows a horned head and this dates to c.1200 (Windrush church; 7). The basic character of the medieval Cotswold sheep, whether they were usually horned or not, should be capable of being determined by archaeological means.

Another argument against the medieval development of the long-woolled sheep, in the modern sense, is the weight of fleeces, as a medieval Cotswold fleece normally only weighed about 1.85lb, as when 48 fleeces of coarser grade 'middle' Cotswold wool in the later fifteenth century weighed in at c.89lb (40.4kg; Hanham 1985, 112). Though the average weight on this occasion should not, however, be taken to be necessarily entirely typical of a Cotswold medieval fleece, as it has been demonstrated that fleece weights varied over time and were dropping, for instance, in the mid-fifteenth century, while bad winters could cause temporary declines to under half normal fleece weight (Stephenson 1988). Moreover, heavier fleeces of around 4lb (2kg) were associated with some enclosed pastures by the early 1600s, and in some areas 6–7lb fleeces were already being obtained (*AgHEW* IV, 666), though there is no detailed information on this from the Cotswolds. However, this suggests that sheep responded positively to their change to richer pastures. The modern Cotswold fleece is far heavier, weighing about 22lb (10kg) and 13lb (6kg) for the ram and ewe respectively (National Sheep Association 1998) indicating a gross increase in size. Such figures are also quite in keeping with contemporary commentators who also observed the increasing size of the fleece in the eighteenth century. Although part of this increase may be from better nutrition, it must mainly be accounted for as the extreme outcome of selective breeding.

There does, therefore, seem to be ample evidence that the Cotswold sheep was a distinct medieval type. The demands of farming in this region are the most likely way in which a local type evolved. The soils were very thin and the pasture sparse, which was known from distant antiquity to favour the development of a particularly fine woolled fleece. There was also a distinctive Gloucestershire custom of farming (known as hitching) which shortened the fallow, either by sowing part of it, or by not having any fallow at all (Tate 1943, 19). This intensive arable production would have required some method for rapidly replenishing soil fertility at the end of each growing season and folding with sheep would have supplied this need. This sheep-corn husbandry was very much a feature of the Oxfordshire Cotswolds in the medieval period (*AgHEW* IV, 249). Demanding local conditions will, therefore, have favoured the development of a local sheep type. Specialist flock management, most obviously by the monastic houses, as elsewhere in medieval England, realised the potential for high-quality wool production offered by the local sheep, as the monks sought to make profits from their large estates with a minimum of labour. Their contacts with the Continent and, in particular, with papal agents will have also been an incentive to widening markets and winning greater opportunities for trade. In the Cotswolds there is some evidence of selective breeding being actively pursued, as Kingswood Abbey, for instance, imported Lindsey rams all the way from Lincolnshire in the mid-thirteenth century. This district was at the heart of longwool territory in later periods, and close study of medieval fleece weights has demonstrated that heavier fleeces were also reared here in that period, at over 2lb (Bischoff 1983, 156) suggesting that the genetic disposition to long wool growth in some sheep was already recognised.

The earliest surviving written accounts of Cotswold sheep date from the sixteenth century. William Camden in the later sixteenth century described the Cotswold sheep as having 'the whitest wool, having long necks and square bodies'. Michael Drayton, who was born in Warwickshire and certainly had some first-hand knowledge of the Cotswolds, in his popular poem *Poly-olbion* of 1612 also similarly described the Cotswold sheep as being the whitest sheep, 'with no black or brown on the legs or face', with woolly brows, and the staple deep and thick on a large body. The sheer size of the Cotswold sheep and its fleece seems to be expressed by Drayton by reference to 'the buttocks equall broad; as fit to under-goe the full and weightie load'. This description equates well with the larger size of the Cotswold breed today, as does the reference to a woolly brow, which suggests the forelock, a characteristic of the breed today.

Michael Drayton in his *Poly-olbion* (Song VII) also made reference to Herefordshire wool ('Lemster ore'), and drew special attention to its fineness since 'with the silke-wormes thread for smalness' it 'doth compare'. So fineness was presumably also the outstanding feature of the best medieval Cotswold wool, though it fell short of the Leominster wool in this respect, 'yet quite he puts her downe for his abundant store' suggesting that the sheer abundance of Cotswold wool was in its favour. Throughout the later medieval period these two wool producing regions had vied for the top position in the wool stakes, Leominster usually winning out with the highest prices, though its short supply meant a ready market for Cotswold wool as well.

These descriptions of the Cotswold sheep give a definite impression that it was a large animal which had a thick heavy fleece, and this is in keeping with its nickname of the 'Cotswold lion', as well as with the appearance of the modern-day Cotswold. The allusion to a lion presumably came about because of the shaggy headed appearance of the Cotswold sheep and the earliest such reference was in the mid-sixteenth century (L. Gibbings pers comm), when it was common parlance, as in 'she is as fierce as a Lion of Cotsolde' (John Heywood (?1497-1580), *Proverbs*, part 1, chapter XI). This is a particularly telling confirmation of the comparative size and woolly appearance of the Cotswold sheep, presumably reflecting its characteristics in the later medieval period as well.

By modern standards the medieval Cotswold wool may have been of medium length and fineness, which would be in keeping with the needs of the Flanders and Italian weavers, who, it is generally assumed, were working with shortish stapled wool and would have been manufacturing woollens. The key to its success may have been inherent in the wool (e.g. its fineness, its whiteness, or its ability to take up dye), but it may also have had something to do with the organisation on the ground that made its purchase easier for the export market. Here its bulk export via Southampton on private licences granted as favours by the Crown, and its availability in large quantities from bulk suppliers may have been additional advantages. The financial ties and political allegiances of the English Crown, where the main markets were concerned, may, therefore, have also been powerful incentives in favour of Cotswold wool, as it established its worth in the medieval period. This wool must have had inherently desirable qualities and today this is characterised by the lustre and the clarity with which it accepts dye, but it is uncertain whether these would be some of the same qualities recognised in the Middle Ages.

Movements gathering pace in English agriculture were to affect the character of the Cotswold wool and it seems likely that the true long-woolled Cotswold sheep was only developed in earnest from the sixteenth century onwards, when enclosure and breeding favoured the growth of a much heavier fleece. The effect of better pasture on the wool was well understood in the sixteenth century when Welsh sheep were being brought into the Midlands to produce useful wool so that 'ther corse wolle chaungith to staple wolle' (Tawney and Power 1924a, 101). Adam Speed, writing in the early seventeenth century, regarded both the Herefordshire and the Cotswold as being fine wools, suggesting that this desirable quality was maintained into that century (Armitage 1983).

In the early eighteenth century, the Cotswold was described as still unimproved, and 'a small light carcassed polled animal, bearing ... a fleece of fine wool of about 3lb weight, but lighter and finer before that period'. The same commentator recalled that they were previously cotted but that this practice had since ceased (Turner 1794). Defoe (1725), when he reached the Cotswold Hills, proclaimed that they were 'eminent for the best of sheep, and finest wool in England', but that now fine wool had to be imported from Spain. In the course of the eighteenth century, therefore, the Cotswold sheep must have been transformed into a much heavier animal. Where once about ten sheep had to be shorn to produce a *tod* (28lb or 12.7kg) of wool, now only four were needed (Bowden 1956-7, 47). The size of the sheep and of its fleece had increased enormously, with the latter being useful for the new textiles which required longer and tougher fibres. In this case, the change in the character of the Cotswold wool was entirely in keeping with the demands of the contemporary textile industry and served to keep the breed in demand at home, suggesting that breeding was being directed according to the market.

In 1749 William Ellis said that the good wools still came from the Leominster area of Herefordshire and from the Cotswolds and that it was still the fineness that attracted comment 'for from it a thread may be drawn as fine as silk'. The Herefordshire sheep also increased their wool yield after the sixteenth century from about 1lb to 2lb (0.9kg) in the nineteenth century. Changing methods of farming had clearly increased their wool yield as well, but they are not thought to have changed their character significantly as a breed. If so, it shows that the local environment and sheep management regime do have an impact on the quality of the wool, but only to a lesser degree than if selective breeding is undertaken.

With an animal that begins breeding at one- to two-years old its characteristics could change very quickly through selective breeding, and it seems likely that the Cotswold was transformed so that its wool was more suitable for the new English cloth industry, and its meat could be sent to the rapidly growing towns. Generally this pattern of sheep development is confirmed by the archaeological evidence as there is little skeletal change in sheep from the later prehistoric period until the seventeenth/eighteenth century (Ryder 1981a). In this most recent period, therefore, both historical and archaeological evidence converge to tell the same story.

In around 1780 Rudder also commented on the coarseness of Cotswold wool by saying that 'the Cotswold wool ... never fine within the memory of any man I have converswed with ... is now become still coarser'. But a local farmer from Dowdeswell in the late eighteenth century reckoned that the Cotswold sheep had improved greatly in carcase weight and quantity of wool with the use of enclosures in the last 200 years (Tate 1943, 33). Clearly such comment suggests that the fine quality of the wool was no longer paramount and that quantity was preferred instead. In the eighteenth century when it is first possible to reconstruct well-defined zones of types of sheep based on good breed descriptions, longwools stretch along the Jurassic ridge from the Cotswolds in the south across the Midlands and into Lincolnshire. Complete uniformity of flocks, however, should not be taken for granted for earlier periods (Ryder 1984b, 17), and there was great variation in grades of wool produced within each flock.

This was now the era of the pasture sheep (e.g. the Leicester) with their long wool replacing the folding sheep, and some of the former had huge fleeces of long semi-lustrous wool of reasonable quality. These produced wool on the English grasslands, especially in the Midlands, which was ideal for the new cloth-making practice (worsteds), and by c.1700, worsted production exceeded the broadcloths in value and importance. It is generally considered that the new Cotswold sheep came about crossed with these pasture sheep, and that, fed on the new feed of turnips and clover, they ended up giving the very large fleeces of long wool suitable for combing wool, and worsted textile production.

In the early nineteenth century the size of the Cotswold sheep and its fleece at 9-10lb (4.5kg) were favourably commented on (*Gloucestershire VCH* II, 256). A later description (Bravender 1850) also reflects the breed as it is now (cf *8*, *58* and *66*). But the Cotswold Hills had mostly by then become the domain of the Oxford Downs, which originated as a cross between a Cotswold ram and the Hampshire Down ewe in around 1835. These seem to have inherited some of the qualities of the old Cotswold (i.e. the ability to fold well and to fatten quickly on less food than the improved Cotswold; *Gloucestershire VCH* II, 256), though intended mainly as meat.

The Cotswold sheep was already becoming rare as early as c.1800. Fed on turnips, its meat was poor and its wool coarsened. The Cotswold Sheep Society started in 1891 (-1922 and re-established in 1966), but decline in breed numbers continued and there were only 476 Cotswold sheep left in 1902. One of these flocks could be traced to the early 1600s and another to the early 1700s. The Garnes played a leading role in saving the breed for posterity and it is interesting to note that a Margaret Garne had sold Richard Cely woolfells at Chipping Norton in the late fifteenth century (Hanham 1985, 151), giving a direct link between this family and the medieval heyday of Cotswold wool sales.

8 Cotswold ewes with lambs on a hot spring day at the Cotswold Farm Park near Guiting Power

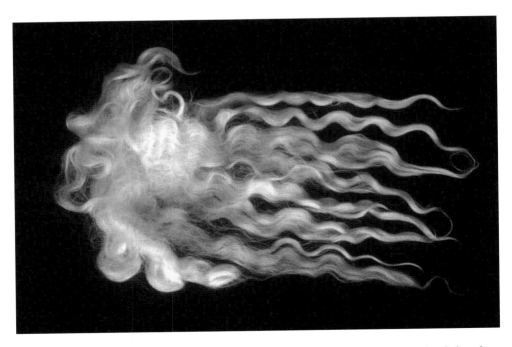

9 Wool shorn from a Cotswold ram (first shearing) showing the characteristic crimp (staple length 200mm)

Detailed descriptions of breeds did not generally occur until late on. Such a description of the Cotswold breed was first produced in 1892, and is still used today as the show standard of the Cotswold Sheep Society, with one of the distinguishing marks being the fine tuft of wool on the forehead (Harmer 1892). Cotswold sheep can still be seen today at the Cotswold Farm Park at Guiting Power near Stow-on-the-Wold in Gloucestershire (8). These sheep are longwools and have a lustrous fleece of generally up to about 16lb (7kg) from the ewes (L. Gibbings pers comm) with a staple length of up to 10in (250mm) (9 and 66).

3

Early sheep farming in the Cotswolds

Sheep had been domesticated in the Middle East by at least the beginning of the sixth millennium BC, and in Britain by the fourth millennium BC. It is uncertain when sheep started to be a common sight in the Cotswolds, but they were ideally suited to the limestone uplands and it was probably in the Iron Age or Roman period when they appeared in numbers. They would have benefited from the early eradication of the wolf in most of England, though it was only finally eradicated from the wilder areas in the later medieval period.

BRONZE AGE

Archaeology provides a crude picture of the development of domesticated sheep in Britain *c.*3500 BC, and then charts their rise in agricultural significance during the Bronze Age (*c.*2000–800 BC), as the prominence of pigs declined. This may reflect changes in the landscape, as the pig would have been more useful in a woodland environment, whereas the sheep is more suited to grazing on open grassland (Clark 1947), signifying that by the Bronze Age, large areas had been cleared of trees and shrubs. Sheep may, therefore, have quickly become part of a more cleared landscape, which they would have helped to maintain, and where, by providing manure, arable production could also have been more quickly intensified as a result of their presence. This is also the period that woollen textiles first appeared in this country whereas earlier textiles were based on plant materials (Clark 1947, 134), and the development of textiles continues today with wool still playing a major role. Sheep have, therefore, been the source of an essential commodity for the last 4,000 years.

Archaeological evidence for the earlier prehistoric Cotswolds is sparse and suggests that it was an area of small Bronze Age settlements and some larger enclosed settlements. Most significantly there is little indication of land division using ditches and pit alignments, so there is no reason to suggest larger-scale clearance and settlement before around 800 BC. Unfortunately there has, as yet, been little investigation of the prehistoric landscape through environmental techniques such as pollen analysis, which would provide a guide to broader trends.

IRON AGE

Few sites in the Cotswolds offer many clues to animal husbandry in this period. A large assemblage of late Bronze Age/early Iron Age animal bones from Potterne in Wiltshire, though just outside the Cotswolds, does seem to imply that male sheep were being kept for meat whereas the ewes were probably already being managed for wool, and in increasing numbers into the Iron Age (Locker 2000). There are few archaeological observations about the nature of the sheep of this period, other than the general comment that they were small in stature compared to modern sheep, as at the major defended enclosure at Bagendon (Jackson 1961), and, therefore, very similar to Soay sheep.

ROMAN

Sheep remained important for their wool throughout the Roman period, though, by the later Roman period, cotton cloth was also becoming increasingly popular (Mazzaoui 1981). Fine quality cloth was a feature of life in the Roman Empire, as it had to be a lightweight material in the warmer climate of the Mediterranean. This cloth was mainly produced in Italy itself and Tarentum (modern Taranto) in southern Italy was famous for its fine wool from a breed of sheep with fat tails (Toynbee 1973), and here there were dye works using the hugely expensive purple dye derived from shellfish. Guilds of wool workers were known and many of the fullers in particular became wealthy, suggesting that they organised much of the industry. Imported wool was required to keep up with production and this was documented as coming from Spain (Carus-Wilson 1952), while in the first century AD, Gaul also had a reputation for some of the more valuable sheep (Columella *De Agricultura* VII, 3).

Wool workers were situated all over the Empire, and, for instance, north Gaul (France) has many funerary monuments to workers in the woollen industry and there were official state workshops in this region. Great funeral monuments near Trier (Germany) point to this also being one of the areas engaged in large-scale cloth production (Drinkwater 1982), and this may have been organised by the local estate owners (Wild 2002, 28). At Arlon (southern Belgium) sculptures depict dyers at work stirring deep vats of dye. Traditionally, working wool into cloth was regarded by the good estate manager as a way of keeping slaves occupied during the quieter work periods such as in the winter (Carus-Wilson 1952, 623). Though 700 years earlier than the well-documented Flanders cloth industry from which the Cotswold wool growers benefited so greatly, there seems to be here some hint of what was to follow in the Middle Ages.

There is evidence for careful breeding of sheep under the Roman Empire, as it is recorded that a large sum was paid for a sheep of the *Coraxi* (in the Black Sea area) because its fleece was so special. A first-century BC description of the best type of sheep was that they should be:

> ... large, with plenty of soft wool of long fibre and thick all over the body, especially around the neck and shoulders. The legs short and the tail long.
> (Varro *Rerum Rusticarum* II, 3-4).

Several other references are suggestive of later practices. For instance, Varro describes keeping the sheep indoors if wet, using salt to encourage appetite and wanted his sheep ideally to have thick, white, long wool, while Columella (*c*.AD 60) recommended the washing of fine-woolled sheep 'three times a year as long as the weather was fine', which is the earliest reference to the careful washing of sheep (*De Agricultura* VII, 4). Columella also described the best winter shelter as 'long and thin', which closely echoes the design of medieval sheep-cotes over 1,000 years later.

The situation in Roman Britain is, however, far from clear. Documentary and iconographic evidence (Toynbee 1964) is not very helpful, while archaeology has also not yet provided any definitive evidence about the development of sheep and wool in this period. Generally sheep were probably kept primarily for their wool, as mutton was not highly regarded as a meat and evidence from army camps bears this out, though there are some exceptions such as Bar Hill on the Antonine Wall and at Corbridge near Hadrian's Wall, where the animal evidence from excavation suggests that mutton was commonly consumed. In the first case this was the base of a Syrian unit of archers which may account for this dietary variation (Applebaum 1958). At the Roman fort of Vindolanda near Hadrian's Wall, a variety of different wool types from the older native sheep to fine wools (both short and longwool types) has been discovered (Ryder 1981b, and 1993, 207). The fine wools are assumed to have been Roman imports.

There is some literary evidence for the burgeoning reputation of Romano-British sheep after 200 years of farming under the influence of Rome. In AD 300 Dionysius Periegetes commented that British wool was so fine that it was comparable to a spider's web, and in the time of the Emperor Constantine (307-37) Eumenius praised Britain for 'its innumerable flocks of sheep ... weighed down with fleeces' (Incert., *Pan. Constantino Aug.*, 7.9; Wild 2002, 5). This sounds remarkably similar to the situation that prevailed in medieval times. Wool-combs, such as examples from Roman Suffolk (Manning 1972), also seem to point to the availability in this country of longer fibred wool, as this equipment was used in later times to straighten long fibres and to help the removal of short fibres, prior to spinning.

Certainly by the fourth century, Roman Britain was famous on the Continent for its production of an overcoat known as the *birrus Britannicus* (a hooded cape; Wild 2002, 27), as well as for two varieties of *tapete Britannicum* (a thick cloth for a saddle or couch; Richmond 1955). A British *birrus* cost a maximum of 6,000 denarii, the equivalent today of perhaps £18,000, though any such calculation is fraught with problems. But, regardless of this, the relative value against other textile goods in the Roman Empire shows that the Romano-British textiles were some of the most luxurious and expensive available. They were the only items in Diocletian's Edict of Prices that hailed from the British Isles and together they hint at some startling developments in the quality of wool and textile production being achieved in Roman Britain.

However, it remains uncertain how widespread the Romano-British textile industry was and archaeological evidence has remained scanty. Across the Roman Empire the production of clothing for the army was organised by the fourth century on the basis of state factories and, where these are known on the Continent, they were placed in proximity to areas supplying good-quality wool (Jones 1960). In Roman Britain an imperial works supplying the army garrison with clothing is documented at *Venta* (probably the Roman town underlying modern Winchester; Wild 2002), and it is possible that this was the source of all the British garments in the Diocletianic list.

Roman villas are very much a feature of the Cotswolds and about 50 such sites are known in the area, of which the best known is at Chedworth. Most were founded in this particular style in the later third-fourth century. These buildings boasted some standards that many houses still fall short of today. Their artistic magnificence and quality of construction declared the prosperous background of their owners. One major question is whether these buildings relied on money brought into the Cotswolds, possibly from abroad, or whether the wealth was sourced in the Cotswolds itself. It has sometimes been suggested that this late Roman prosperity was based on wool (Finberg 1964; Reece 1976). However, a recent major archaeological survey along Ermin Street, which cuts right across the Cotswolds via Cirencester, considered that there was no indication of any Roman specialisation in sheep farming. But, thereagain, the same survey found no evidence to substantiate any such specialism for the medieval period either (Mudd *et al* 1999), and so the conclusion for the Roman period should perhaps be viewed with some doubt (see below).

Though the evidence is limited, there are several Romano-British archaeological sites which provide evidence for some specialisation in sheep farming in the Cotswolds. At Frocester, situated just below the scarp of the Cotswolds, a villa eventually succeeded a native Romano-British farmstead. Though sheep then became less a feature of the archaeological record, there was, however, a parallel trend towards more elderly animals, together with a greater size than a Soay, and this certainly suggests that wool had now become the primary concern here (King 1988; Noddle 2000, 228). High proportions of mature sheep, suggestive of wool production, were also found at the Barnsley Park villa (Noddle 1979). Significantly, an increase in size was also noted at this site. At Shakenoak Farm villa at Wilcote, south of Charlbury (Cram 1973), mature sheep were being retained most likely for their wool, and a similar pattern occurred at a villa at Marshfield (Morgan 1985), where, from the third century until the decline in Roman occupation, mature sheep of at least four years old were normally culled for meat. On other sites across the Cotswolds, a larger hornless sheep is also indicated by the archaeological evidence (Maltby 1998). Skeletal evidence, therefore, suggests the introduction of new genetic material. Sheep bones have also been recovered in quantity from the Roman temple at Uley, which was dedicated to Mercury (*10*), a god that was associated with sheep, as well as goats and cockerels. The site was notable for the large number of sheep and goat bones, which showed that, while goats increased in size in the Roman period, sheep, in contrast, underwent no consistent anatomical changes (Levitan 1993).

10 Conjectural reconstruction of the cult statue of Mercury with an accompanying sheep from Uley Roman temple site. © *English Heritage*

Archaeological field survey, involving large-scale prospection and excavation along Ermin Street, both to the north and south of Cirencester, has provided a transect through the whole central Cotswold landscape. This saw a number of occupation sites being investigated (Mudd *et al* 1999). At Birdlip (second to fourth centuries AD) mixed farming was taken to be the basis of the economy, but there is little consideration as to how soil fertility could be sufficiently maintained and the sheep are taken to have been kept largely for wool with few very young being eaten and most being eaten at two to four years old (Ayres and Clark 1999). The picture from the Roman town of Cirencester is similar to that from the countryside, with sheep were being culled at three years old in the early Roman period, while in the late fourth-century town they were culled either at around 15 months or at two- to four-years old (Levitan and King 1986). The presence of older sheep again suggests the growing of wool.

Other indicators of wool production are iron shears, which have been found in Roman contexts at Chedworth villa, and these would have been most useful for a more improved sheep where the wool was no longer plucked. Chedworth is, however, regarded by some as a shrine rather than an estate centre of the type usually presumed to have gone with a villa (McWhirr 1981). And, in contrast with East Anglia and southern England, there have been no finds of wool-combs (Manning 1972) in the Cotswolds.

Archaeological assemblages, therefore, present endless problems of interpretation, mainly stemming from not knowing how much has survived and how representative this might be. Clearly many more animals must have been consumed than the number indicated by the surviving bone evidence. Much of the bone has not survived and was probably ground up by dogs or burnt as fertiliser. The bones of smaller animals may have been most vulnerable to this type of treatment. Archaeological assemblages may well, therefore, only convey a small and potentially biased picture of animal demographics. Even large assemblages of bone fragments end up with many bones not being identifiable and only small numbers of individuals being counted. The structure of the sheep population would be one way of indicating the predominance of wool over meat, but so far these studies have not been done on a large enough scale as individual sites do not have enough material evidence. There is, therefore, a good case for combining the results of many sites together in an expanding database in future, which would be helped if specialists were more consistent in their recording of data to estimate the size of the sheep.

The evidence from animal bones will remain especially ambiguous if lamb and mutton did not really figure very much in the native diet in the Roman period, as then the least desirable meat of the older animals may not have been consumed, and the meat bones discarded as rubbish on domestic consumer sites. This would bias the overall pattern in the archaeological record for these sites so that there was no clue to the real scale of wool production. This would also apply if the bones were burnt and ground down as fertiliser, or otherwise processed or disposed of, so that they fell outside the archaeologist's net.

Unfortunately, therefore, animal bone assemblages from archaeological sites are often too small for much useful interpretation and, besides, bear no resemblance to the amount of meat consumed or otherwise husbanded on a site. Another aid to reconstructing the past landscape which could hold implications about the prevalence of sheep pasture is general environmental study, especially pollen analysis. But this is usually impossible in limestone areas, though a recent investigation has successfully extracted this sort of evidence in the Cotswolds, and has indicated an at least partially pastoral medieval environment (Scaife 1999). Where archaeological evidence is available, therefore, only some very general trends can be discerned. At the outset of the Roman period the sheep remained small (as at Cirencester; Thawley 1982) suggesting that a sheep breed close to the Soay was still predominant, but soon there is some evidence for a larger hornless sheep in the region as well (Maltby 1998). In Gaul a more developed animal (Ryder 1993, 206-7) was around by the second century, as shown by toy figurines of a ram (a horned short-woolled animal with a long tail) found in a child's burial at Arrington in Cambridgeshire (*11*), and probably made in the Cologne and Bonn areas (Taylor and Green 1992; Taylor 1993). These figurines are taken as evidence of a curly woolled sheep. The Arrington burial was accompanied by some fine wool textiles, though the strong foreign element in this burial left open the possibility that the cloth was imported. A similar enlargement of the sheep has been suggested from several Cotswold sites (see above), and in southern Britain generally, by the latest Roman period, sheep had grown in stature and seem to have been kept largely for their wool. Though there is presently little clue as to the breed of sheep that was responsible for this change.

The wealth of the Roman Cotswolds, as expressed by the number of substantial Romanised houses (the villas), seems reminiscent of what happened much later on, in the fourteenth to sixteenth centuries, when the Cotswolds was definitely renowned for its agricultural wealth based on wool, which resulted in equally impressive building works in stone, most evident for later generations in the scale and quality of the churches, and of some of the surviving medieval houses. However, this may be deceptive as stone is the local vernacular building material given its widespread availability, and this inherently tends to produce a more substantial and longer-lasting building. More significantly, it is perhaps the wealth that underpinned both the affluence of Roman Cirencester and Bath, as well as that of the surrounding country houses, that suggests a booming economic situation locally. That this area stands out in the west as much more heavily Romanised than the norm for this part of Roman Britain could indicate that its natural assets were exceptionally in demand in this period. However, some have interpreted this later Roman affluence of the Cotswolds, as indicative of incomers fleeing the uncertainties of the Continent and bringing their wealth with them to settle in one of the most desirable parts of Roman Britain. But there are few indications that the villa owners were necessarily foreigners and there is also no

11 Roman pipeclay figurine of a sheep from a burial at Arrington in Cambridgeshire. The figurine has probably been made in Germany in the mid- to late second century AD. © *Cambridge University Museum of Archaeology and Anthropology*

reason to assume that the Cotswolds in this period was as obviously the place to settle for any wealthy immigrants. On balance it seems more likely that the wealth of the area was derived from local resources, which, in the absence of any particularly productive industry, must have been tied to agriculture.

It may be possible in future through the in-depth archaeological study of the landscape to establish whether Roman sheep pasture was a major feature of the region, though it is inherently difficult to find evidence for an industry such as wool production, which generated no obvious waste product, nor was associated with any particularly obvious type of building. Environmental analyses of pollen and other related data, used to reconstruct landscape history, could contribute most to this debate, especially now that suitable deposits have been found to exist in the Cotswolds.

POST-ROMAN TO LATE SAXON

Sheep grazing may well have remained a major feature of the Cotswolds until the emergence of the English kingdoms, as place-name evidence indicates little woodland existed, especially in the north Cotswolds, at the time when place names were created across the Cotswolds (Hooke 1978). In addition, there is some archaeological evidence in support of the prevalence of raising sheep in this region. Anglo-Saxon sites in the Thames and Evenlode confluence suggest stock rearing, and sheep usually predominate (Blair 1994, 20), and at the decaying site of the Shakenoak Roman villa sheep bones were well represented in a seventh-century enclosure ditch. This fits well with the general archaeological evidence that shows that fine wools continued to be a feature of English textiles compared with, for instance, coarse Viking wool (Ryder 1983a). However, the archaeological evidence is again not very informative about the type of sheep, except to say that they are still quite slight, standing 20-28in (0.5m to 0.7m) high at the shoulder, and so similar to their Roman predecessors.

A much-quoted letter from Charlemagne to Offa, the King of Mercia, suggests that Britain had long had a reputation for high-grade textile goods and that it survived the demise of Roman control in the early fifth century and continued at least into the later eighth century. In this letter of AD 796 Charlemagne states that his subjects would like cloaks of the same pattern 'as used to come to us in the old times'. It is tempting to equate this garment with the renowned *birrus Britannicus* of the fourth century. The choice of words also hints at some recent disruption in this trade. This is the first potential hint in the written sources that wool from the Mercian part of England (which included Gloucestershire) had some special quality to recommend it for personal garments.

Fortunately there is now much more certainty about the extent and importance of wool production in the Cotswolds, as a result of the surviving documentary evidence, and place names are particularly useful. The minster church at Withington, founded in the eighth century, was clearly actively engaged in the sheep and wool trade. Nearly 800 acres had been acquired on the east bank of the River Coln, the land sloping from hilltop all the way down to the river and with part of the estate being called *Shipton* (literally 'a sheep farm'). Clearly the hilltop sheep walks were being actively extended showing that the economic value of the Cotswold hill pasture was appreciated. Wool, as a consequence, has been identified as a major source of revenue for Mercian churchmen generally (Finberg 1957a).

Shipton was a fairly commonplace name element in the region, such as Shipton Moyne and Shipston-on-Stour (from 764-75), and at Shipton-under-Wychwood and at Shipton-on-Cherwell (from 1005). Shipston-on-Stour (now Warwickshire, but formerly Worcestershire) was originally *Scepwaeisctune* (literally 'farm by the sheepwash'), a place name from at least the later eighth century (Mawer and Stenton 1927). This was the part of the Tredington estate where the sheep were assembled for washing (C. Dyer pers comm). The place name is particularly of interest as it is an early documentary reference to the washing of sheep before shearing. Other place-name evidence also helps to show the extent that sheep were an integral part of this landscape. For instance, there was *Sheepscombe* in Painswick (Baddeley 1907), and *Yanworth* (literally the 'lamb enclosure', and so a farm for breeding ewes; Finberg 1977, 75) in the central Cotswolds. Several instances of streams in the region being named *Washbrook* from an early date (Finberg 1977, 74-5) are also indicative of the long-lived practice of washing the sheep before shearing.

The continuity of estate boundaries in Withington has also been suggested, where the Anglo-Saxon estate could be the same estate as centred on the local Roman villa, and where this has later been fossilised in the medieval parish boundary (Finberg 1955a). If such continuities took place, then it is also very likely that the economic basis of the estate was also constant. Since this was evidently wool in the Anglo-Saxon period then this may be more evidence, albeit from an unexpected quarter, that the Roman estate also specialised in the same way.

The church of St Peter at Gloucester was also endowed with a considerable landed estate in the eighth century, which included an upland estate in the Cotswolds at Chedworth. This interest in the uplands was further developed by the third abbess of St Peter's, Eafe (734-767), who added a large estate at *Pinswell* (in the vicinity of Upper Coberley, near Withington), which was specified as being for running sheep. This is the first firm documentary reference to the importance of sheep in the local agricultural economy, and the scale of the operation is impressive. Despite being 10 miles from Gloucester, Coberley represented an increase in the summer pastures available for the abbey's flock from the eighth century. Gloucester Abbey also had land at Colesbourne for gathering its monastic flocks and paid for a lease at Evenlode with 100 sheep (Smith 1976, 66).

Other churches were keen to share in the income that could be earned from wool. By the mid-eighth century, the church of Worcester was also acquiring land in the Cotswolds and this was located at Bibury, Withington, Batsford and Woodchester (Dyer 1980, 11). It also came to include Cutsdean, formerly part of the royal endowment of Bredon in the eighth century (Dyer 1980), as this eventually came under the authority of the church at Worcester (Grundy 1935-6). However, corn production would also have been the intention, though it was probably understood that this went with the keeping of increasing numbers of sheep which maintained the soil fertility through careful stock management.

Place names incorporating a 'sheep' reference continue to appear. A *sheep-edge* in Dowdeswell is given in a charter of 800, and a *scepe clef* or 'sheep slope' was mentioned in tenth-century (974) Cutsdean. *Ramescube* and *Ramsford* in Hawling and Roel are mentioned in an 816 charter. Tagmore farm in Bourton-on-the-Water and Tragmore Pool in Temple Guiting include the element *tagga*, a young sheep that had yet to be sheared for the first time. Some indication of the extensive nature of some sheep farming may also be reflected in territorial links between sometimes widely separated areas. These are indicative of transhumance agriculture involving the movement of stock between distant pastures (e.g. links between the Thames and Cherwell valleys, and the Cotswolds). Parts of south and west Warwickshire also exhibit similar links (Blair 1994, 51). The first English regulations relating to wool also occur in this period when a tenth-century code states that 'a wey of wool shall cost 10s' (Lloyd 1977), a *wey* later being recorded as 182lb (83kg). Such a weight was exactly the equivalent of half a medieval sack-weight of wool.

The abbot of Eynsham (Oxfordshire) in the first half of the eleventh century wrote a monastic schoolbook that described the shepherd's work (Jones 1994). One of the jobs was to milk the ewes twice a day and to make cheeses and butter. Each day the shepherd drove the sheep out to pasture very early in the morning, and, during the day, guarded them from wolves, returning them safely to the folds in the evening. The latter were probably wicker hurdle enclosures, which, after the harvest, were set up in the arable fields. To achieve coverage of the whole field the fold had to be regularly and systematically moved.

Downland pasture was not explicitly recorded for William the Conqueror in the Domesday Book in 1086. This omission is usually attributed to villagers not having to pay rent for access to the grazing. There are, therefore, few indications here of the extent to which sheep were kept in the Cotswolds, except that Cirencester wool was reserved for the queen. It is perhaps significant that, where documentary evidence is more informative for other parts of the country, which were also later destined to be prominent in wool production such as East Anglia, this indicates large numbers of sheep already belonging to the lord of the manor in the mid-eleventh century (Snooks 1995, 39). And for other well-known areas of medieval sheep production, such as the Lincolnshire wolds, the Domesday Book is also silent, as for the Cotswolds (Hallam 1988, 124).

By around 1000 Flanders was advancing to its premier position in wool production and cloth manufacture, the latter being poised to develop as a major industry of the European Middle Ages. At the heart of this was the rapid growth of Flemish towns and the expansive marketing of the new cloth. Almost every town had its street of fullers and another of dyers, each on a watercourse (Carus-Wilson 1952, 627). Though England was not advancing so quickly, much was already in place. Even further away the shoots of one of the highest quality textile industries in medieval Europe were appearing in the ninth century at Florence where convents sometimes had a specialised interest in weaving high-quality garments for the clergy (Thompson 1931, 258), and eventually the Florentine weavers would be insisting on high-quality wools such as from the Cotswolds, much to the advantage of English wool producers.

Hardly any relevant mid- to late Saxon archaeological evidence is available for the Cotswolds, and so, but for the historical evidence, the Cotswolds would have been declared as having no special character or potential for future growth. The best that archaeology can do is to provide some indication of the normal quality of wools in the period, based on evidence from outside the Cotswold region. General archaeological evidence from textile finds, especially from London, reveals that fleeces of the ninth to eleventh centuries were chiefly of 'hairy medium' type wool suggesting that the sheep were still of a primitive type. These textiles were made of wool from mature animals not lambs and the preference was for white wool which would most readily take up a dye (Pritchard 1984, 50). It seems, therefore, that fleeces remained similar to their Romano-British precursors.

4

Cotswold wool in the Middle Ages

Records of sheep after 1100 become far more prolific. They occur regularly, for instance, in medieval manorial accounts, though sometimes, where sheep management was organised centrally across several estates, the manorial accounts will be silent and a master shepherd would have kept their own accounts (Harvey 1965). The keeping of sheep permeated rural society, and the sheep was integrated into country customs with many places in the Cotswold Hills having a documented association with wool production from the Middle Ages onwards (*12*).

The following parts of this chapter cover some of the broader themes of medieval sheep management, wool growing and trade in wool, including some reference to textile production, which would have consumed local wool at least some of the time, though this is difficult to corroborate. A chronological account of the Cotswold wool business resumes in the ensuing chapters.

SHEPHERDING

The reconstruction of sheep rearing practices in earlier periods is largely beyond the reach of archaeology, so must rely on historical evidence and take some account of modern practices. Fortunately, two treatises on medieval farm management have survived and both make reference to sheep rearing (Oschinsky 1971), and provide many details relating to medieval sheep farming. The most detailed of these has been attributed to Walter of Henley and is dated to the later thirteenth century, while it has also been suggested that he was writing about Gloucestershire, or possibly Herefordshire, as he makes much of the use of sheep-cotes, which were such a characteristic feature of these areas (Oschinsky 1971).

Though eclipsed by wool, it should not be forgotten that sheep were also producers of milk and cheese. Royal manors in Gloucestershire were notable

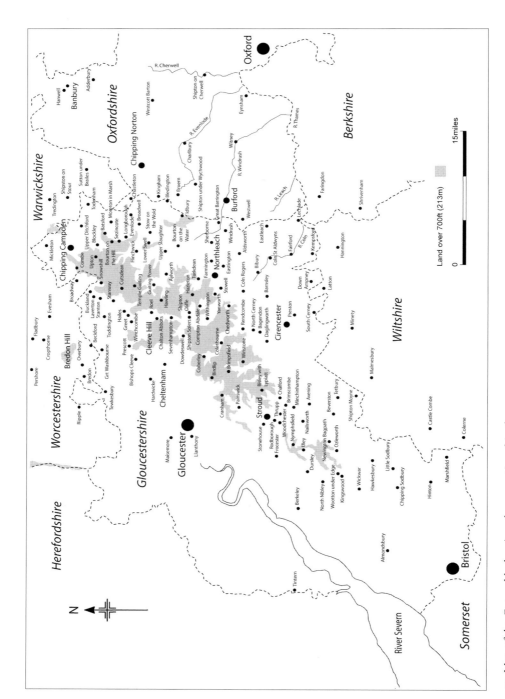

12 Map of the Cotswolds showing places mentioned in the text

for sheep products. For instance, Kempsford sent 120 weys of cheese from the sheep fold, and Adderbury (Oxfordshire) produced wool and cheese worth 40s (Hallam 1988, 126). By the sixteenth century the milk of five ewes was judged to be equivalent to that of a cow, with the lambs being weaned on 1 May and the ewes milked on until 1 August (Seebohm 1927, 200).

Sheep farming generally required little input of labour compared to arable and could produce ready cash through the activities of the travelling wool dealers (Power 1941). Sheep were also useful for raising the fertility of dry or just poor land, as they did not need water (Seebohm 1927). The importance of sheep farming lay as well in the possibility of a repeated valuable cash income from wool, and this meant that winter culling was undesirable and that the sheep had to be kept over the winter. The value of wool meant that as many wethers as possible were kept, while sufficient ewes were needed to replenish the flock. The male fleece was larger and was the best wool, as it was not so prone to stress breaks in the fibres, which inevitably affected wool from the ewes, after they had given birth. But rams could not be kept together in a flock without fighting which would be detrimental to the general condition of the wool. Instead the system of keeping wethers (castrated males) was evolved, which ensured a ready supply of good quality wool. The number of ewes kept also tended to be large, as few gave birth to more than one lamb and fatalities were frequent. Eventually specialised breeding flocks came about with the wethers and ewes being kept separately (Whitlock 1965, 31).

The keeping of sheep was not without expense and one of the largest items was the construction of special buildings, the purpose of which has been the source of some dispute. Both the surviving thirteenth-century treatises on keeping sheep mention these buildings, but there is scepticism that they could ever have housed all the sheep over a winter. Rather it is suggested they were used for ewes with lambs and so that the ewes could be milked for cheese production, and for the storage of winter fodder (Oschinsky 1971), as an extensive winter diet was necessary for the sheep.

The housing of sheep at night has been associated by some with the maintenance of a fine fleece, and by others with the need to protect the animals from cold as they were not otherwise robust enough to stand the winter (e.g. AgHEW IV, 190). Luccock (1809), however, disagreed and thought that danger from wolves was the main reason for cotting, and that it was potentially harmful to the sheep! However, Luccock notes that in his day (nineteenth century) the Herefordshire wool was still particularly fine, and that cotting was still practised here. Rather than a lack of cotting Luccock thought that the new diet of artificial grasses and turnips was the reason that the Cotswold fleeces of his day degenerated to give longer, thicker wool more suited to combing. He viewed his contemporary Cotswold sheep as very different from their medieval predecessors if the fame of the breed was to be believed (Luccock 1809, 233).

The sites of sheep-cotes have been identified across the Cotswold uplands (Dyer 1995), and some can still be seen as earthworks, for example at Stanton, near

Broadway (*29*). Their ground-plans show a long, narrow building representing a specialised purpose (see below and *28*).

According to Walter, sheep should be housed in a sheep-cote from 11 November till Easter depending on the weather, presumably meaning when the weather was cold and wet. He advised carefully on freshly marling the floor of the sheep-cote every 15 days and adding straw to this to produce better dung. This makes an important link with arable cultivation, as the dung would have been a valuable addition to the soil to boost fertility. The sheep were, therefore, integral to the fertility of land and some lords of manors claimed the right to have sheep folded on their land to manure it (Lockett 1974), which also demonstrates the close association of sheep with soil fertility. This process was referred to as 'folding', and the chance to fold animals on fallow and on stubble could have favoured the small producers in particular, as it was quite a cumbersome process (Hallam 1988, 125).

The shepherd's basic equipment was a hook, a knife, shears, a dog, and, for marking sheep, a mixture of tar and pitch (Seebohm 1927, 202-3). The dog could be fitted with a spiked collar as it was depended upon to ward off wolves (extinct in the Cotswolds by the twelfth century; C. Dyer pers comm), which invariably went for the throat. The salves that were used in around 1300 were mercury, copper, verdigris, or wine, but later in the century these were being replaced by the widespread practice of using grease and tar (Scott 1959). A tract on agricultural practice of the thirteenth century advised that a shepherd should have 300 sheep in his charge (Hallam 1988, 125). It is possible that much of the success in high-quality wool production was due to localised skills being developed following specialisation over a very long period which both benefited the breeds and their management. Even areas such as Norfolk, Suffolk, Devon, Sussex, Kent, Wiltshire and Dorset were regarded as producers of coarse wool in around 1400 (Power 1933, 367, fn 56), and only the Cotswolds and Herefordshire wool producers succeeded in achieving the very highest quality demanded by the foreign buyers.

Stocking densities seem to have varied, though in the post-medieval period over-stocking was extremely common. A sheep farm in the early seventeenth century might have a stocking density of six sheep per acre with fleece weights of 4lb, which was typical of good quality enclosures. The medieval stocking density is much less certain. Contrary to popular perception it couldn't have been normal to cull the majority of sheep before the winter, as wool was best from mature animals. Large flocks were, therefore, necessary. According to Walter any culling occurred between Easter and Whitsun, which is earlier in the year than most would expect, and was for sheep which were not going to recover condition after the winter. Another contemporary source suggests culling should have been planned before 1 August (Oschinsky 1971), and this would have involved some sheep being picked for fattening, as a result of being too old or weak to survive another winter.

It was standard practice in some areas, where the natural yolk or oil in the fleece was insufficient, to smear grease with tar on the fleece in an effort to keep the sheep warm and well, and to keep the fleece soft and rich (Luccock 1809). Thus the washing of wool was particularly essential to remove this grease, which attracted dirt, while washing also made the wool more pleasant for the shearer. Importantly washing also led to better storage quality (as long as the drying was done properly), and an easier product for the buyer to work with. It was an ancient practice and had been advocated in the Roman period for fine-woolled sheep.

Farmers waited until the wool was loose and raised from the skin before shearing, as this meant there was some undergrowth that left the sheep was some protection after the shearing. The timing of the shearing was considered with a view to the wool being dry, after washing, and with good weather following. Washing removed impurities that increased the weight of the wool, but the wool had to be well washed and dried for this arduous process to be worth doing. Medieval washing seems to have been carried out in convenient sections of local streams, and only from about the eighteenth century were purpose-made structures generally used. It was possible for a skilled washer to wash 100 sheep a day, when in 1641 a washer was paid 3d per 20 sheep. Purpose-built sheepwashes survive today (see chapter 12), and these are usually large enough to accommodate three or four sheep at a time. The sheep were thrown into the wash, and the shepherd and helper would rub the fleece with their crooks.

Shearing was not as quick as washing and, in the seventeenth century, a shearer with manual clippers was expected to deal with 70 sheep per day. Tar had to be on hand to dab any injuries and to mark the sheep afterwards. Winding the fleece seems to have been a specialised task sometimes done by women (see below), and the flesh side of the wool was wound outermost, as this was whitest. Two winders were needed to keep pace with five shearers (Ryder 1983b), and sometimes they were caught hiding the less good wool by winding it inside!

WOOL TRADING

Wool, in common with several other commodities such as salt, was capable of long-distance marketing (Campbell 1997, 243). There was a long chain of processes from wool to cloth, and in some cases individual stages were either very laborious or were definitely in need of some mechanisation to achieve the desired standards of workmanship. Therefore, investment was a requirement for a successful industry and lords, in most cases, were too conservative to take these risks on capital (Langdon 1997). Besides, industry had no enhanced social status attaching to it, and so was positively avoided by those with inherited positions. It was only in the later Middle Ages, from the fifteenth century onwards, that investments of this kind become more common as other entrepreneurs gained access to land leased out by the large landowners.

There was a regular seasonal rhythm to the wool trade. In the summer packhorse trains could be seen carrying away the wool and in autumn there was another consignment as whole sheepskins were sent away (the woolfells) after some of the sheep were culled before the winter. Having been transported great distances from the growing grounds the wool was again put into temporary storage: in London this was at Leadenhall, which was rented by the wool-staplers from the City of London (Bowden 1962, 92). Long-term storage was a feature of the wool trade, as dealers often awaited an upturn in prices before selling.

Wool sorting was important for quality production, and up to the sixteenth century was done by the quality of a fleece as a whole and only later was staple within the fleece sorted. As sheep breeds developed from the sixteenth century there was a greater diversity in a single fleece and so complex sorting of wool had to be developed (Bowden 1956-7, 51).

From the thirteenth century, when the sarplers (two or three sacks of wool bundled together) arrived in London, they were weighed at the Custom House in order to calculate duty. The sarplers were sealed after weighing and the merchant paid custom at this point (or rather gave security for payment at a later date), and was given a cocket of the weight or number of fells. It was illegal to ship without the cocket. A searcher checked the cargo against the paperwork before sailing and gave a bill of discharge to the purser. On arrival at Calais, port dues had to be paid of 4d per sack, or 2d per 100 fells (Salzman 1931). Charges were levied, therefore, at every stage of the passage of the wool from the wool grower to the foreign buyer.

English boats by the later medieval period could carry about 200 tons and certain ports, such as Southampton, saw the arrival of foreign ships eager to take away their precious cargo of wool. More often the wool was carried in fleets from English ports to the staple port on the Continent, which, throughout much of the Middle Ages, was at Calais. As a form of early insurance it was the custom for a merchant to split his wool between ships in order to minimise losses as much as possible. Such ships were also invariably armed as pirates or the French were a constant menace at sea, and it was also a safety measure that the wool was usually moved in organised fleets.

In the meantime, other specialist materials were being imported into England to support the home textile industry (47). Picardy woad import duty produced around £96 in 1194 but had soared to £600 20 years later. In the late medieval period the woad came from Toulouse (Carus-Wilson 1954). Alum and other dye stuffs were also regularly imported, especially as a result of the Italian trade (see chapter 7).

YARN PREPARATION AND TEXTILE MANUFACTURE

From the fleece the fibres would be aligned either using a comb or cards. There is no evidence for the latter before the medieval period, when they were used for shorter wool, the combs then being confined to longer wool. Iron wire was used to fashion the cards and the combs were also made from iron, as they needed to be heated for use. Spinning was carried out in the time-honoured way, using a lightly weighted spindle and a distaff, to produce the yarn, though the spinning wheel was introduced from the fourteenth century onwards. The yarn was turned into cloth on the loom, which from the early medieval period was a horizontal mechanism which had replaced the earlier vertical frame used previously in England for about 2,500 years. Most cloth was dyed using a colorant, which had to be fixed with a mordant such as alum, in order to give a more permanent colour.

Cloth finishing was a separate craft that involved raising the nap with teasels, and the use of long shears to give an even appearance to the surface of the cloth. Craft skills of a high order are evident at every stage in the cloth–making process, and it comes as no surprise that, given the care lavished on the textile working, the cloth makers wanted to use the very best raw materials. These guaranteed that some cloth makers could produce the finest cloth and so reap the reward of the highest prices.

5

The eleventh
and twelfth centuries

Cotswold wool was now set to become an important commodity in the Middle Ages and its trade was to have a beneficial economic impact on many places across the Cotswolds (*12*). Unfortunately, the Domesday Book does not say very much about stock holding in the Cotswolds, probably because grazing was a communal right that was not paid for. However, this is not the case for the whole of England and some detailed returns for sheep do survive for elsewhere, and on this basis a national figure of 7.5 million head of sheep has been estimated (Hoskins 1955), compared to a figure of 12 million in 1940 (Thomas 1955). The only definite Gloucestershire mention of wool in 1086 was that the queen was entitled to the wool of the Cirencester area, which implicitly indicates its special quality. Domesday Book also suggests that the north Cotswolds, especially between Cirencester and Winchcombe, i.e. the upper Thames valley, was the most populous area of the Cotswolds and this coincides with the greatest area of arable cultivation in the region (Smith and Ralph 1996, 28). Indeed the number of ploughs listed in the Domesday Book indicates that much of the Cotswolds was down to arable cultivation in this period (Dyer 1987). This fertility must have had much to do with sheep husbandry being integral with the arable cultivation and is another indication of the extent of sheep rearing in the region. The high valuation placed on some places such as Blockley in 1086 has also been attributed to extensive sheep rearing for wool (Hilton and Rahtz 1966, 77).

The development of the wool trade is entirely a native English achievement as there is no obvious link with the settlement of land on Flemish supporters by William the Conqueror, for these mainly took land to the east and south beyond the Cotswolds (George 1926). Instead the weaving of textiles and, therefore, demand for wool may have received a fillip from the introduction of the horizontal loom from about the mid-eleventh century (Munro 1994, 30), as this was capable of much faster working.

Trade contacts over long distances were an important element in the success of the wool trade. These were fostered by national and international fairs, which were an important element in the development of the wool trade as they were a ready-made system for specialised trade. They were characterised by merchants from much further afield than the usual weekly market in a provincial town, and usually merchants from the nearest ports would also attend. The presence of foreign merchants, in turn, had the effect of boosting other English industries.

The Norman Conquest had opened England up further to foreign trade, especially with France. Trade with Germany continued to be strong and Henry of Huntingdon, writing in 1155, described the English trade with lower Germany as 'extensive', with the English exports being tin, lead, fish, cattle, jet and above all wool (Thompson 1928, 508). Champagne, to the east and south-east of Paris hosted the famous fairs in medieval Europe at this time. Its location was suitable because it was at a pivotal junction of many rivers looking in all directions, and woollen cloth was a principal commodity for sale (Thompson 1928, 589).

The earliest literary reference to the export of English wool to Flanders occurs around 1100 and records the arrival of several Flemish merchants who travelled widely to gather wool before returning to the Low Countries via Dover (van Uytven 1983, 180). This contrasts with the situation in the eleventh century when Flanders seems to have been self-sufficient in wool. A commercial guild or *hanse* called 'the seventeen towns' had been set up in Flanders by the late twelfth century, and this was intended to regulate relations with the fairs of Champagne (Carus-Wilson 1952), presumably in such a way as to ensure a good supply of essential commodities such as wool.

During this early medieval period the first very large English flocks are encountered in the historical record, usually found to be in monastic hands. For instance, Caen Abbey had 1,700 sheep on Minchinhampton Common (*13*) in 1100-35 (Power 1941). It is also in the early twelfth century that the regular export of wool to Flanders commenced (Lloyd 1982, 98). By the mid-twelfth century, the Cistercian abbeys were already making long-term deals with foreign merchants based on future wool harvests, and, as in any futures market, this led in some cases to financial disaster (Farmer 1991, 397). This trend in dealing may mark the beginning of a more general increase in flock sizes to serve the foreign demand. There is also the first proof by the end of the twelfth century of some improvement in the fleece quality, as curly woolled sheep were being valued at nearly twice the price of a coarse woolled sheep in 1194 (10d as opposed to 6d; Rothwell 1975, 305), though there is no clue as to when, or where, this better quality wool was first developed.

Upland pastures were becoming increasingly sought-after and valuable economic assets and sometimes disputes arose, as in 1196 where a dispute involved the sheriffs of both Gloucestershire and Worcestershire (Finberg 1975). In the twelfth and thirteenth centuries, the demand for wool for export was increasing and this must have had an impact on the English countryside with

13 Minchinhampton Common as an example of the open Cotswold uplands of the Middle Ages; now partly a golf course

pasture being used more intensively. Paradoxically, this may have led to increased fertility and even expansion of arable through folding. The countryside was also seeing widespread population increase (Hallam 1988), which also applied simultaneous pressure for the expansion of arable. The latter was documented by the fresh clearance of new land for ploughing. Meanwhile, the growth of towns also boosted trade, and merchants were able to thrive by specialising in commodity products such as wool, which were now in good supply.

Secular estates had also developed landholdings where wool might be exploited. For instance, the family of the Beauchamps were conscious of the wealth that came with sheep. Though their estates were largely lowland manors elsewhere in Warwickshire and Worcestershire, they held some land in the Cotswolds at Sezincote and Sutton-under-Brailes (Mason 1980), and presumably participated in the wool trade.

For the first time cloth processing on a large scale is now documented in the form of fulling mills, which were used to clean and treat the cloth before sale. These were specialised machines and large investments. In the twelfth century there are only four fulling mills documented in England, including one on the Knights Templar estate of Barton in Temple Guiting on the upper River Windrush in the Cotswolds in 1185, as 'the brothers made a fulling mill at *Beretone* which was held by *Wireht* for a rent of 32s' (Lees 1935, 50). This high rent shows that it must have been well patronised by cloth makers, suggesting that the Templars may have been specialising in cloth production, as well as raising sheep in the region.

Water-power rapidly became more widely used for milling generally and it soon became necessary to replace the simple term fullery (*fullonia*) by 'fulling mill' to distinguish it from the ever-present corn mill (Carus-Wilson 1952). England had, however, long been a land of mills as evidenced in Domesday Book, and it is possible that the number of fulling mills has been underestimated for the twelfth century and earlier periods in the past.

The new mills gave more (and new) regions possibilities relating to a major national industry and the most suitable streams were often situated in the more hilly areas, which previously had had less chance to develop economically. The Cotswolds was ideally situated, especially on its steep western scarp, to take the fullest advantage of this new textile technology. By the end of the twelfth century Minchinhampton had four fulling mills (Smith and Ralph 1996). Other fulling mills soon followed, for instance at Bourton-on-the-Water in 1206 and at Stanway also in the thirteenth century (Smith and Ralph 1996). A general westwards movement of cloth makers has been suggested based on this documented appearance of fulling mills (Carus-Wilson 1954), which predominate in the west of England. This seems to have eventually replaced cloth production in the towns, especially in eastern England, where regulations did much to deter trade.

The Cotswold fullers had the additional advantage of easy access to local supplies of fuller's earth, as this was widely available over the south and middle Cotswold Hills (Dreghorn 1967, 125) and would have been an essential ingredient for the fulling process. The fuller's earth also had the beneficial effect of giving rise to rich pasture on the valley sides, while the Great Oolite limestone formation provided good pasture on the higher ground, an ideal mixture for guaranteeing well-nourished sheep and excellent quality wool. Any exposures of fuller's earth would have been evident locally, as this material is prone to ground movement. Natural geology in the Cotswolds seems, therefore, to have favoured both wool production and cloth making to a remarkable degree.

By the later twelfth century England was also no longer self-sufficient in woad, suggesting that cloth manufacture was now increasing markedly (Carus-Wilson 1952, 628). Another sign of its growth was the attention it attracted from national government, for in 1196 (Bridbury 1982, 106) the *Assize of Measures* decreed that the production of dyed cloth for the market should only be carried on in cities and boroughs, and that it should be 2 *ells* (2 yds) wide and of the same quality across the whole width (Carus-Wilson 1952, 628). A great many towns in 1202 paid to be exempt so that they could continue producing cloths of other sizes. Nothing was said about length specifically, so the traditional lengths are assumed to have remained which were variable between cloth types.

The main body of regulation was found in the towns, where the weavers and dyers in particular were rigorously governed, and these were clearly aimed at stopping the build-up of stock and, therefore, any challenge to the established merchants. This is shown in a consultation that the London municipal authority carried out with other towns at the end of the twelfth century (Ponting 1957, 18). It is clear from this that merchants in both wool and cloth were now established as important members of English commercial life and that new centres of cloth production were beginning to take shape. In the West Country these were Winchester and Marlborough, both recognised as cloth-making centres by 1200 (Ponting 1957, 15).

Wool rather than cloth was, however, the premier source of wealth and the profits from Cotswold wool were now beginning to be a serious matter. By the end of the twelfth century, Winchcombe Abbey was deriving one-third of its cash revenues from wool sales (Finberg 1955b, 69). Famously, when in 1192 Richard I (the Lionheart) was captured by the Duke of Austria returning from the Third Crusade and the Holy Roman Emperor demanded a ransom of 150,000 marks, Cistercian monks (and other small orders; Bridbury 1982) provided a year's wool clip in 1193 towards the ransom (Lockett 1974). Their part of the ransom was accordingly paid in 50,000 sacks of wool (Postan 1973, 342) because the Cistercians had no gold or silver as was said at the time (Bridbury 1982) and Richard I was finally released in 1194. Some of this wool may have come from the Cotswolds as the Cistercians had interests here, such as at Kingswood, Bruern, and Bordesley Abbeys.

By the end of the twelfth century the wool trade was already a potential instrument of foreign policy whereby the king of England could even hope to undermine the allegiance of Flanders to the king of France (Lloyd 1982, 99).

6

The thirteenth century

In Europe the best wool is English,
in England the best wool is Cotswold
(From a popular Flemish weavers' song)

During the thirteenth century the wool export trade grew to about 33,000 sacks (Power 1926, 22), representing the wool of about 7 million sheep, with exports then accounting for about 60 per cent of the total home wool production (Donkin 1973). Politicians were clearly taking care to safeguard such a valuable trade. In 1236 a new treaty was made with Flanders that probably brought about a further increase in trade (Lloyd 1982, 99), as the new treaty established safe conduct for both English and Flemish merchants by land and sea and in both territories. It was even laid down that conflict between rulers would not automatically involve their subjects in similar hostility! (Lloyd 1982, 99). This seems a novel (though rather impractical) way of trying to ensure that this vital commerce could continue to flow even at times of inter-state conflict.

Wool benefited by the taxes on trade being intermittent into the thirteenth century, as state taxes focused instead more on property, and, therefore, the wealth that wool had created (Bridbury 1982). Commerce was quickened by the presence of such a major commodity such as wool. Towns across the Cotswolds hosted fairs and some of these were later summer fairs where the fresh clippings could have been on sale, for instance at Northleach, Cirencester or Tetbury (Finberg 1957b). Much trade was also done through the important national fairs at Winchester (Hampshire) and Boston (Lincolnshire) in that much of the wool taken to these was already spoken for (Lloyd 1977). Credit was a necessary part of these transactions, purchases at one fair being paid for at a subsequent fair. In this way, large quantities of goods could be placed on order and safely delivered at the next major fair in the annual calendar with a guaranteed sale. This was a system that clearly relied heavily on trust and honesty, where the honour of the merchants was part of the currency invested in the trade.

The buoyant English wool industry relied ultimately on the excellent reputation of fine-quality woollen clothes that could be manufactured from this material. Surprisingly, this reputation was not merely the product of vanity, but also had a practical foundation. Medieval handbooks on how to maintain good health, while concentrating on the benefits of different foods, specifically endorsed the 'thin' Flemish woollen cloth as the best, especially if worn together with thin linen cloth as undergarments. These handbooks have mainly survived today in the form of fourteenth-century Italian manuscripts with lavishly illuminated pictures, but they were largely based on Arabic texts of the eleventh century (Arano 1976). Such documents, therefore, hint at the long established prominence of the Flemish cloth makers in medieval Europe and the unassailable reputation they had achieved working with the very best English wool, such as from the Cotswolds. Such textbooks on health reveal how fundamental fine woollen clothing had become in medieval culture, where the demand was based on a belief in its health-giving qualities, as well as the fine appearance that it bestowed on the wearers.

Foreign merchants were now playing a major role in stimulating the demand for English wool. Towns in Flanders (notably Bruges, Ghent, Antwerp and Ypres) were the principal cloth-making centres of the Low Countries. In the later twelfth and thirteenth centuries the Flemish cloth manufacturers were desperately seeking wool in England to take back home and initially they had found suitable supplies in Lincolnshire, especially from the Lindsey region. At the time the only other countries that were supplying wool were Spain and Germany. The Flemish merchants were also the main suppliers of cloth to the English royal household by the mid-thirteenth century, and their deals were sealed at the major annual fairs such as at Winchester. Hence some of the wool must have been taken on a return journey back to England, and found itself displayed at royal court and in other noble households as part of the livery which set the rich and powerful apart socially.

While cloth making boomed at some Continental centres it was also becoming more important in England, as it emerged from the towns and colonised the countryside. Some English towns, including some in the west such as Gloucester, Hereford and Worcester (Power 1926, 65) had already developed good reputations for their textiles, so that some English cloth was well known abroad for its high quality. For instance, cloths known as *Stamfords* were known in Genoa by 1200. However, the average English cloth worker was under the thumb of the local merchant and unable to sell his own products. Only in the royal towns were the cloth workers able to avoid this oppression by buying the right to set up their own guilds. However, the trend was towards rural production, sometimes with the involvement of the lord of the manor who set up a local fulling mill for his own profit, though the weavers sometimes constructed their own fulling facilities and so avoided the lord's mill, for instance at Hawkesbury, Gloucestershire (Miller 1965, 73). This was a period when the lords of the manor were still extending their rights and the building of a local fullery was a large investment, so the lord tried to insist that it was used by all his tenants.

New cloths were now being sold such as *Cotswolds* and *Ludlows* (Carus-Wilson 1941), their names betraying their more westerly origins. Presumably this new West Country industry used the local wool, in which case it is a chapter in the history of Cotswold wool that has not been widely noted, and has been eclipsed by the interests of the foreign cloth makers. Various places in Gloucestershire offer evidence of local cloth making in this period. For instance, the abbot of Winchcombe Abbey straightened a watercourse to give a more powerful flow of water to his fulling mill, and paid 8d in damages to another fulling miller, John Blundell, after water had been diverted away to the abbey mill (Perry 1945, 52).

Fulling mills seem to have especially proliferated across the Cotswolds in the later thirteenth century, perhaps as a result of a temporary lull in the foreign trade as a result of the new taxation, or during temporary bans on foreign exportation of wool. In 1285 a fulling mill was built at Cerney near Cirencester and another at Fairford in 1296 (worth 13s 4d), while the tenants of Chedworth had their own. In the Stroud district, fulling was established by 1272 at the latest when one 'Roger the fuller' was listed in the Rodborough court rolls, while another fuller in the same period was Thomas de Rodborough at Brimscombe and at Thrupp by the end of the thirteenth century (Perry 1945), apparently running two mills (Watson 1932, 265). The thirteenth-century Minchinhampton custumal mentions seven tenants as fullers and several tenants were also digging fuller's earth (Watson 1932, 265). Cloth production was being encouraged at local level long before it received any official encouragement in national policy. For instance, the custom of the manor of Minchinhampton allowed any weaver living by his craft, and in need of a home, to enclose part of the common.

The Gloucestershire wool growers and merchants were, of course, keen to benefit from this burgeoning market in wool. By *c.*1200, Winchcombe Abbey had already been deriving one-third of its income from wool from its extensive Cotswold estate. Winchcombe town merchants were also engaged with wool exports, as they were fined in 1276 for contravening a ban on exports (Royce 1892). Another Gloucestershire abbey that was heavily involved in the wool business was the Cistercian house at Kingswood. The monks here specialised in sheep rearing, selling lambs at 6d and sheep at usually over 1s each, and there was a sheep-house at *Aldrinctun* (Perkins 1899). The monks were also apparently breeding sheep, as they bought rams in *Lindesay* (Lindsey in Lincolnshire) for 25s 4d in 1241. In 1242 at least £167 was received by Kingswood monastery for wool, mostly of the 'better' sort, whereas expenses of a shepherd were £3 8s 8d. In 1256 the Kingswood monastery was employing 33 shepherds (plus five villagers) at £4 6s 6d. In 1263 the same monastery was paying £22 18s for hay for the sheep, which was a large expense, but the business was still profitable. The washing and shearing of 20 sheep cost 2d according to one late thirteenth-century source (Oschinsky 1971), but the annual wool crop from those sheep was probably worth annually about 12s, so clearly it was worthwhile to keep sheep in the Cotswolds.

The importation of *Lindesay* rams into the Cotswolds is particularly interesting, as a similar practice is recorded in 1208, when the bishop of Winchester ordered 16 rams for his large Wiltshire flock (Scott 1959). This suggests a routine practice that was aimed presumably at improving the wool. And since 16 rams might be expected in modern breeding to serve 50 ewes each, then they were sufficient for nearly 1,000 ewes, and so may signify a major effect on the character of the flock. Whether it merits being called selective breeding is uncertain in the absence of a detailed account of medieval sheep rearing, though it does seem to point in that direction. The Lindsey sheep were another regional type that were recognised at the time as being high value medieval wool producers, and the preference for breeding stock from this area, which was later to be known for the heaviest and longest fleeces in England, does suggest as well an interest in fleece weight and staple length by the medieval Cotswold sheep rearer.

One of the largest thirteenth-century flocks in southern England consisted of the 29,000 sheep on the bishop of Winchester's estates in 1259 (Ruddock 1951, 18; Stephenson 1988). But very large flocks were also being kept on the Cotswolds in Gloucestershire. By the end of the thirteenth century John de Gameges (abbot of Gloucester 1284-1306) had increased his Gloucester Abbey flock to 10,000 sheep, which produced 46 sacks of wool annually. It has been estimated that Winchcombe Abbey had a flock of 8,000 sheep since Pegolotti (late thirteenth/early fourteenth century) expected it to provide 40 sacks per annum, and this at 13 marks (£8 13s 4d) a sack would make the annual wool harvest worth over £300. Both these producers were in the top 55 of wool producers in England recorded by Pegolotti (see chapter 7). Winchcombe Abbey was already very well endowed with Cotswold manors at Domesday Book, but this Benedictine abbey was so intent on its farming interests that, in around 1200, it purchased three almost adjacent manors, Hawling, Hazleton and Yanworth, from a Flemish noble called William of Béthune. The price was £228 with a rent, thereafter, of £20 per year. This process of purchasing Cotswold manors continued with the manor of Roel in 1318, which was bought from the Abbey of St Évroul for £550. The success of sheep-corn husbandry was presumably the key to this increasing agriculture investment.

Other monastic estates also increased their sheep holdings in the later thirteenth century. The bishop of Worcester was a substantial farmer, who, in around 1290, had 5,650 sheep in flocks of between 120 to 800, with the largest on the Cotswold manors, together with other livestock such as 542 oxen and 67 horses (Dyer 1980). The bishop was clearly exploiting a lucrative market, and, as early as 1246, the flocks were organised centrally around his Blockley manor. In 1299 he was keeping 1,000 sheep on Cleeve Hill pastures in the summer and 200 in the winter. His records of his Cotswold manors in this year showed 500 wethers at Upton, 492 ewes at Blockley, 340 wethers at Northcombe, and 280 hoggasters at *Alvrichesdown*. This picture contrasts with that recorded by the auditors who valued the estate around 20 years earlier and then estimated that about half this number was to be expected (Hilton and Rahtz 1966, 77). In the following century this trend continued with the size of the flock increasing again to 872 wethers, 803 yearlings and 390 lambs at Michaelmas 1383.

The pattern of English rural life was affected by the ambitious profiteering in wool by the landlords, as some tenants on manors in the Cotswolds owed duties that reflected the local prominence of wool. For instance, Idbury in 1279 had villagers who owed customary duties of washing and shearing the lord's sheep (Jones 1994, 89). The Sherborne tenants of Winchcombe Abbey also had services of washing and shearing sheep, and these services were owed mainly by the cottagers. Hired labour would also have been needed, possibly with the customary tenants acting in a supervisory role (Hilton 1957). This meant an increase in paid work opportunities for the villagers, and was another local bonus of the wool industry. The tenants also usually had their own sheep, some having about 100, for instance at Abbots Barton in 1291 (Dyer 1988, 377), so that they could also participate in the lucrative market for Cotswold wool. A similar pattern of duties was attached to the inhabitants of Eastington manor, which lay adjacent to Northleach, and was in the hands of the abbot of Gloucester.

Far from the Cotswolds, there were important developments in this century in Italy, which were to have a bearing on the wool trade in England over the next two centuries. Florence was a city with a sophisticated cloth industry where there were seven guilds representing different stages of production, and it has been claimed that about half the population, about 30,000 Florentines, came eventually to be engaged in the wool trades (Thompson 1928, 466-7). There was also a great interest in Italy in producing wool. One monastic order called the *Humiliati*, which had been active since the mid-twelfth century, even specialised in sheep ranches and in helping through their charitable acts the poorer wool workers in both Lombard and Tuscan Italy. Eventually they moved mainly to the Tuscan area as they were being financially oppressed by the Lombards, and Florence invited them to settle in their area in 1239, where they established a school for training in the arts of wool.

Though few Italians were yet to be seen in the Cotswolds (Ruddock 1951, 18-19), as they were busy buying wool in eastern England and exporting it to Flanders, thence to be conveyed overland to Italy. Yet in March 1251 the king ratified the sale of Cotswold (*Coteswaud*) wool by Westminster Abbey for a period of six years to James Offreduc and Reyner Barboti and others of Siena (Italy), and their safety was also personally guaranteed by the king. He even agreed to underwrite the sale in the event that Westminster Abbey became financially embarrassed (*CPR* 1247-1258, 90). The shrewd Italians were clearly taking as few risks as possible in the course of their international trading and knew that the trade was so valuable and prestigious to the English king that they could expect special favours. Equally, this particular agreement seems to reflect the fragile 'futures' market, where deals could go badly wrong and even jeopardise powerful institutions. Italians would also pursue debts vigorously, such as in 1280, when the *Riccardi* sued five dealers in Banbury for five sacks of wool (Bridbury 1982).

Since the Italians had only a small percentage of the trade out of Southampton in the late thirteenth century, then other merchants must have been handling much of this trade. And trade there certainly was, as Southampton exported in 1286-7 1,938 sacks of wool, while in 1290-1 this increased to 2,299 sacks (about 374 tons of wool). Flemings and Frenchmen such as Robert de Sancto, Fussino de Amiens and Hugo de Corbie will have accounted for some of this trade, but most of it went out in the names of English merchants based in Winchester and elsewhere in the hinterland of Southampton. The interest of the Flemings no doubt indicates where most of this wool (including by this period Cotswold wool) was destined to be sent. This contrasts with the overall export trade in English wool in 1273, when about two-thirds had been accounted for by foreign merchants (Power 1933).

However, it was not all plain sailing. Intensification of wool production, not for the last time in English agriculture, probably contributed to an increase in disease. The serious disease of sheep scab became a widespread problem in the 1270s and major outbreaks continued into the fourteenth century (Farmer 1991, 400). However, this was not a total disaster as the fells could still be sold. The *Chronicles of St Albans Abbey* (Ryder 1983b) suggested that sheep scab in 1274 was introduced by imported Spanish sheep. Spanish sheep had also been blamed for the scab in Wiltshire in *c*.1272 (Scott 1959 and *Gloucestershire VCH* IV). Disease continued to be a problem into the 1280s, when the bishop of Worcester was complaining about losing his sheep.

Though not explicitly stated in the historical record, there is here a hint that Spanish sheep were also being brought in for breeding purposes, though none can yet be placed in the Cotswolds. Spanish sheep farmers were certainly intent on producing wool of a high standard for in 1273 all the Castile shepherds were organised together into a guild. This lasted until the early nineteenth century, maintaining the standards of the merino flocks for the purpose of wool rather than meat (Lipson 1953, 37). This move was probably instrumental in the later emergence of Spanish wool as a superior product.

However, the main driving force behind the growth of the wool trade was the foreign demand by the Flemish weavers for English wool, though the trade was sometimes threatened by political problems, such as a ban on wool export to Flanders after 1270. These temporary restrictions had the effect for future generations of revealing some of the normally hidden wool business, as merchants were caught trying to evade the ban. For instance the Shrewsbury merchant, Nicholas of Ludlow, was caught in south-east Gloucestershire taking his wool to Southampton for export (Hilton 1966). By the later thirteenth century, Flanders was also beset by its own problems, as tensions erupted between the urban and rural cloth makers. But places such as Ghent were able to benefit from this situation by gradually stiffening regulations that prohibited cloth processing and production in its surrounding countryside, and Bruges and Ypres did the same. This was to change in the fourteenth century when the country producers gained more concessions in their own favour (van Werveke 1971, 354-5), and then the whole country, both town and village, came to rely on cloth production.

The 1270s, therefore, saw a host of changes in the wool business, some of which were of temporary duration, while others were to have a more lasting impact. The 1270-4 political breakdown in Anglo-Flemish relations, when English wool exports to Flanders were banned by the English king Henry III, had been a temporary move in order to maintain the loyalty of Flanders by demonstrating forcibly its economic dependence on English wool. The more lasting effect was from the imposition of a customs levy on wool exports (see next chapter), which, once introduced, was eventually used increasingly to raise money for the Crown. These changes, however, had the beneficial effect that more records were created, and this includes the first of a series of surviving medieval price lists for wool. The Douai wool-price schedule of 1275 may have been drawn up to assist in settling various claims for compensation following the confiscations of merchants' goods that had taken place on either side of the Channel (Munro 1994). If so, then the only Cotswold monasteries involved seem to have been Kingswood Abbey, whose wool was not counted amongst the best, and Bruern Abbey (both Cistercian). Yorkshire and Lincolnshire abbeys were by far the most numerous in this list of 95 religious houses.

The *Maltote* (literally the 'evil toll') of 5 marks (£3 6s 8d) per sack of dressed wool was first levied in 1294. This probably had the effect of depressing prices paid to the wool producers as well as raising the selling price. Prices dropped to about 60 per cent of their level in the 1280s (Hallam 1988, 730), and in the later 1290s wool could even be difficult to sell.

In 1297 there was a great wool famine in Flanders for political reasons, which ended with the signing of a treaty of alliance with England. The English parliament declared that the wool of England amounted 'to some half the value of the whole land', meaning that most of the export earnings were from wool (Lloyd 1977). This was also a period in which the Jews lost their royal patronage based on their ability to lend large sums, which was forbidden under Christian law, and they were replaced by the Italians, whose interests focused especially on the wool industry, thereby perhaps overcoming the laws against usury, as they generally advanced money in return for wool trading privileges rather than being repaid in cash.

At its thirteenth-century peak the best Cotswold wool on the Flemish market had fetched 28 marks (£18 13s 8d) a sack, or about 1s per lb (Power 1941). Putting this into perspective, a 1lb (0.45kg) of wool was the equivalent of over a week's income of a waged labourer. Or, to compare it with another commodity, the market price of 1lb of best wool was the equivalent of 168lb (c.76kg) of salt. The price of wool was buoyant, as there was competition from merchants for the wool and both the Flemish and Italian industries were now competing for the same wool. The Italians tended to buy the most expensive wool and this has been put down to their preference for prepared (i.e. washed) rather than raw fleeces (Munro 1978, 129). With the increasing prosperity of medieval Europe and its insatiable demand for high-quality cloth in order to give expression to its hierarchical social frameworks, English wool was now set to take centre-stage in national trade.

WOOL MARKETS AND FAIRS

As well as sheep being driven between their summer and winter pastures, the wool itself was also moved over long distances and it must have been a feature of road transport at the time, as the wool was being either conveyed to secure warehouses or to ports. Occasionally routes were labelled 'wool-ways' betraying the extent of this trade, in much the same way as the contemporary saltways. Examples are the Woolpack Way at Westcott Barton, the Woolway at Chipping Norton, and Wool Slade Way at Hanwell just north of Banbury (Gelling 1953). These names are significant indicators of major routes plied by the wool merchants in the Middle Ages, and all occur, significantly, in Oxfordshire en route between the Cotswolds and London.

Many markets and fairs were established in this period and the Cotswold region was no exception. Unfortunately fairs are often poorly recorded historically, as they were occasional events without any permanent officials. They may have played a significant role in the wool trade, at least locally, as they would have attracted wool gatherers and merchants. The fresh wool clip would have been a feature of the mid- to late summer fairs, but wool seems to have been available all year around, indicating that a lot of it was stored for long periods.

The following are some thirteenth-century (or slightly later) fairs in the Cotswolds where the season of the fair is known (based mainly on Finberg 1957b):

Summer fairs: Chipping Campden, Chipping Sodbury, Cirencester, Fairford (fourteenth century), Lechlade, Marshfield, Northleach, Painswick, Stow-on-the-Wold (fourteenth century) and Tetbury (fourteenth century).
Autumn fairs: Blockley, Guiting Power (fourteenth century), Hailes, Moreton-in-the-Marsh.

The Italian merchants certainly held to the view that around St John's Day (24 June) was the best time to be looking for wool at fairs in the Cotswolds (Origo 1957), and so summer fairs from late June onwards may well have been visited for this purpose.

SOME MONASTIC ESTATES WITH INTERESTS IN COTSWOLD WOOL

Large estates of all types engaged in sheep farming, but the monasteries seem to have been particularly active in the pursuit of profit from wool, mainly because their records have survived to tell the tale and have attracted the interest of historians. The monasteries were major consumers of wool themselves, and so, in accordance with the rule of St Benedict, it was woollen not linen bed cloths (*lectisternia*) that had to be used (Pantin 1933, 224). The Cistercians are well known for their success in wool production, especially in northern England and they were equally successful in the Cotswolds, suggesting that this order had a particular method of raising sheep or preparing the wool, that appealed especially to the foreign merchants. Their interest in breeding is suggested by the acquisition of Lincolnshire sheep; however, it remains uncertain whether the Cistercians were responsible for any breed improvements. Their business skills do not always seem to have been a match for the foreign merchants, and in the thirteenth century in particular, they were often heavily in debt, probably as a result of wool deals that had not flourished. The following are some of the main religious houses, which produced wool in the Cotswolds (*14*), despite sometimes being situated well outside the Cotswold region.

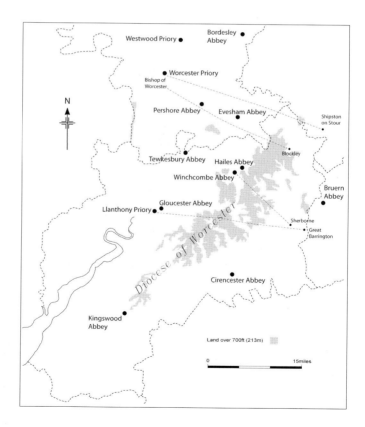

14 Some monasteries in the Middle Ages and their Cotswold pastoral estate centre

Bordesley Abbey, Worcestershire (Cistercian)
Though based in the Midlands this abbey had pastures in the Cotswolds including Combe grange near Chipping Campden. It seems to have fallen on hard times in the fourteenth century even before the Black Death (Rahtz and Hirst 1976). The monks sent Cotswold sheep to a house in Surrey (Donkin 1958), and this may have been a deliberate attempt to improve quality, as the wool of Surrey was generally poor.

Bruern Abbey, Oxfordshire (Cistercian)
This abbey was actively engaged in the wool trade and in 1233 the monks obtained from the king a grant that no one should interfere with their sheep in the event of debts, so long as they had other goods of value. This must have proved useful in 1284 when their debts reached 2,100 marks (£1,400), presumably having come unstuck in wool deals where they had effectively borrowed money on the promise of being able to deliver a set quantity and quality of wool in future years. The debt was down to 1,000 marks (£666 13s 4d) by 1340 (*Oxfordshire VCH* II).

Abbey of Holy Trinity, Caen, Normandy (Benedictine)
Some early surveys of around 1120 show that the manors of Minchinhampton and Avening were carrying up to 2,000 sheep belonging to Caen Abbey, together with a lot of arable in their possession as well (Chibnall 1982). The flock was composed at that time of 344 ewes, together with 223 wethers at Minchinhampton and 600 milking ewes, 496 lambs, 36 wethers, 36 maiden ewes and 24 older rams at Avening.

Cirencester Abbey, Gloucestershire (Augustinian canons)
This abbey was heavily involved in the wool trade. Sheep-houses are known on various outlying parts of the abbey estate, for instance at Aston in around 1250 and another at Shrivenham (Ross 1964). A *shephouse close* was known in the town in the later medieval period and this was the demesne sheep-house (Baddeley 1924). By the sixteenth century the abbey sheep-houses were farmed out with the flock of 300 with rights to pasture on the stubble and this provided half the profit from the manor (*Gloucestershire VCH* IX, 161). At the Dissolution this was the richest of the nearly 200 Augustinian abbeys in the country (Evans 1998).

Evesham Abbey, Worcestershire (Benedictine)
The monks had a fulling mill (*molendinum fullonum*) at Bourton-on-the-Water by 1206 (Carus-Wilson 1941). Pegolotti has Evesham low down in his list of productive abbeys, with wool production at only 10 sacks per annum valued at 12 marks (£8) each (Bond 1973).

Gloucester Abbey, Gloucester (Benedictine)

This abbey was an ancient foundation (*15*), and clearly it had well–established interests in sheep and wool production. Some parishes on its estate were evidently dedicated to wool production, such as at Eastleach, for instance, where some peasant tenures included the duty of washing the sheep of the lord of the manor for one day a year, and of shearing on another day (a service valued at 2d in 1266-7). In all there were eight tenants owing this duty, including 'Matilda the shepherdess'. Tenants at the nearby manor of Aldsworth owed similar services, and here the duties lasted two days each, and there was the additional duty of marking the sheep for a day with bitumen (Hart 1867, 182-5). This fitted in well in the farming calendar, as work on arable would have slack at this time of the year.

The profits from the wool were essential to the abbey as it was engaged in expensive building works, for instance owing 3,000 marks (£2,000) in 1251. Though by 1284 this debt had been reduced to 1,000 marks (£666 13s 4d), and was then erased by the business acumen of John de Gamages (abbot of Gloucester in 1284-1306). He had increased the monastic flock to 10,000 head of sheep (Macray 1863, 39), so that 46 sacks (around 7.5 tons) of wool (or the equivalent of 13,800 woolfells) were available to be sold each year, which at 12 marks per sack gave a maximum annual income of £368, which was a huge increase in productivity. The heavy indebtedness of the abbey had been turned round, but only through making the wool business as profitable as possible. Concerns

15 St Peter's Abbey, Gloucester, now Gloucester Cathedral

obviously remained and new rules were introduced in 1301 by the Archbishop of Canterbury, which stipulated that the sale of wool should only be under the conventual seal (i.e. the individual monks should not use their own seals to complete transactions) and that the abbot and his senior monks should all know what had been transacted (Hart 1867, lviii). Clearly these new rules were set in place to correct monks who had previously succumbed to temptation during wool sales, and had either enriched themselves rather than their community, or had struck only poor bargains with the merchants, suggesting that debts had not only come about through spending on building works.

The Gloucester Abbey estate also included a borough with a market set up at Northleach (see below). This became a handy source of revenue when it developed into a central collecting point for wool and for visiting merchants. This monastic estate also shows well the extent of buildings required by the sheep. Gloucester Abbey kept sheep at Aldsworth and Coln Rogers, for instance, in the mid-thirteenth century, and had a sheep-house in the valley at the south end of Coln Rogers parish. The wool store was retained here in 1524, when the flock and its pastures with a sheep-house were farmed out. There were still two sheep-houses in the open fields in the seventeenth century, one belonging to the lord of the manor and the other to the rector (*Gloucestershire VCH* IX, 25). The sheep were clearly made integral to maintaining the fertility of the land by the constant turning over of the ground on which they had been kept in order to ensure that the dung was not washed away, and this arrangement was recorded in a set of instructions to the estate bailiff.

Hailes Abbey, Gloucestershire (Cistercian)
This abbey, founded in 1246 and dedicated in 1251 (*16*), derived much of its income from wool and by around 1300 was selling on average every year 20 sacks (3.75 tons) at a maximum price of £12 13s 4d per sack (Cunningham 1910).

Kingswood Abbey, formerly Wiltshire, now Gloucestershire (Cistercian)
Founded around 1150 this was a daughter house of Tintern Abbey, which was itself heavily involved in wool production. Kingswood Abbey seems to have been wealthy by 1230, and *c.*1300 it was averaging an annual output of 40 sacks of wool at 12–26 marks per sack. This represents a maximum price of £17 6s 8d per sack and a maximum income from wool of £693 6s 8d per annum. It imported some Lincolnshire rams in 1241, suggesting that breeding was very much a part of the Cistercian approach. This abbey had a total of eight granges in place by 1291 (Graham 1907), and these were presumably aimed at maximising its income from wool, and it sold sheep as well in the thirteenth century. However, business sometimes failed to keep up with the expenditure of the monks and in 1318 they had to lease out some of their properties to their Florentine creditors, the Peruzzi, who took advantage of an opportunity for profitable wool dealing (Dyer 2002a, 26).

16 Hailes Abbey looking across the monks' dining room towards its entrance with cloisters beyond

Llanthony Priory, Gloucester (Augustinian canons)

Founded in around 1108 Llanthony Priory at Gloucester managed extensive sheep pastures in the central Cotswolds (Rhodes 2002). In 1319 a Cirencester wool merchant, Geoffrey of Marston, specified that the 'Coteswolde' wool he was buying at Barrington from the priory must be 'good, dry, and well cleaned wool' (Hilton 1966, 180), and this is one of the earliest references to the wool of the area, as distinct from other wools. He bought at £7 13s 4d a sack. In the later fourteenth and fifteenth centuries the priory flourished, becoming as rich as Cirencester Abbey. There was a master shepherd who managed the Cotswold pastures at Great Barrington, Windrush, Aylworth, Sevenhampton, and Colesbourne, with Great Barrington being the gathering place for shearing where the prior had his own residence (Rhodes 2002).

Tewkesbury Abbey, Gloucestershire (Benedictine)

This abbey (*17*) had several estates in the Cotswolds. One of the largest was at Stanway, where the flock was so large in 1340 that the abbot complained that 1,000 sheep had been stolen. Stanway Hill long remained pasture for the local flocks, whereas the neighbouring manor of Great Washbourne, just below the Cotswold scarp en route to Tewkesbury, surely betrays by its name its function as a central collecting place for the abbey flocks, so that they could be washed and shorn. This practice may have been long associated with this area as the name goes back into at least the eighth century when the place belonged to Bredon

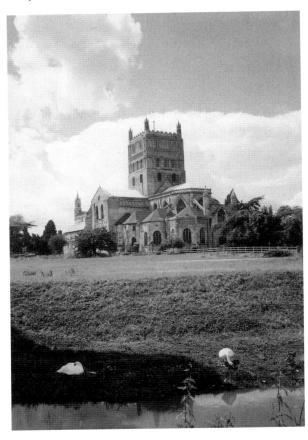

17 Left Tewkesbury Abbey, which owned extensive sheep pasture in the adjacent area of the Cotswolds

18 Below Stanway barn was built in the fourteenth century for the abbot of Tewkesbury. Storage facilities like this may have been partially used to store fleeces

monastery. As usual, investments had been made in sheep-houses, such as at Prescott, and the large barn built at Stanway in the fourteenth century may have included room for storing wool (*18*).

Westminster Abbey, London (Benedictine)
Despite its limited possessions in the Cotswolds, at Todenham, Sutton-under-Brailes and Bourton-on-the-Hill, this abbey managed to rapidly increase its annual earnings from wool from around £68 in 1305-6 to £153 in 1364-5 (Harvey 1977).

Westwood Priory, near Droitwich, Worcestershire (Benedictine)
This priory, a house of the order of Fontevrault, held land at Little Aston perhaps as part of the trend for west Midlands ecclesiastical estates to have access to some Cotswold upland (Dyer 1987, 174). However, this settlement remained poor and from the early fourteenth century was being abandoned. This seems to reflect the failure of a small hamlet to integrate sheep with the arable so as to maintain fertility of the land. Further up the valley of the River Windrush on the Knights Templar estate at Temple Guiting it was assumed that three or four sheep were required per acre, and that extensive access to meadows was also necessary to provide winter fodder for the sheep (Dyer 1987, 178). The fate of Little Aston indicates that careful management was key to the success of medieval sheep husbandry, which in turn led to success in arable. Where this mixed farming was practised the opportunities of wealth that wool offered could then be realised.

Winchcombe Abbey, Gloucestershire (Benedictine)
This was an ancient foundation of 811. By 1194 a half-yearly account puts the abbey's annual income as £9 10s 8d from wool, which was about half of its total income. The production and marketing of the wool was almost entirely controlled by the abbey, but it does not seem to have quite achieved the top quality of Cotswold wool found, for instance, at Hailes Abbey. Dealings with the Italian merchants did not always end in the abbey's favour, as in 1293 the abbot was £20 in debt to Frederick Ventowe and other merchants of Lucca (Haigh 1947, 51). By *c.*1300 the annual wool production was 40 sacks, being sold at 13 marks (£8 13s 4d) per sack. This made it one of the largest producers of wool at this time and it concentrated on quantity not quality. However, in 1329 this monastery was in dire financial difficulties, and its officials were being ordered not to sell any wool, wood, or pensions without the consent of the chapter (Graham 1907, 69).

The abbey seems to have encouraged the clothing industry locally. Sherborne, one of its properties, had four mills in 1086, and a fulling mill is mentioned in around 1200 and in a rental of 1355. A charter, possibly of late twelfth-century date, recorded the transfer of mills to the lord of Farmington on the condition that he did not attempt to convert any to a fulling mill without the abbot's permission. This implied that the abbot did not want his monopoly of fulling to be challenged, and this monopoly was still in force in 1340, when several tenants were fined for taking their cloth to be fulled outside the manor (Hilton 1957, 102).

In the late fourteenth century the abbey's fortunes were again increasing, as its annual income rose from 800 to 1,000 marks (about £666; Donaldson 2001). In 1428 the bishop of Worcester found it 'out of debt … an example to other monasteries'. Sherborne was the central manor for sheep on the estate, and the abbot and shepherds regularly gathered there after Easter. Italian merchants sought out its wool by personally visiting Sherborne (see chapter 8), such as Lawrence Marconovo of Venice, who bought wool in 1443-44, his 40 sacks for a total of £40 being from Gloucester, Oseney (Oxford), and Winchcombe Abbeys, and the prior of Gloucester (Donaldson 1978).

Worcester bishopric
The bishop of Worcester in around 1290 had 5,650 sheep, which were concentrated in a few areas of his estate; for instance there were 1,300 sheep at Blockley on the common and other pastures and at Bishop's Cleeve (Dyer 1980, 134). Blockley manor specialised in wethers that yielded the best fleeces, and in 1299 there was pasture here for 500 ewes and 1,120 wethers, as well as for yearling sheep (Dyer 1980).

Worcester Priory (Benedictine)
The priory was involved in the wool business and the wool of its flocks was valued at £106 13s 4d (£5 6s 8d per sack) in 1315, when arrangements were also made for future sales to the same London merchant up to 1318, with collection being made at Cropthorne in Worcestershire on 24 June (Wilson 1919). Shearing could have occurred closer to where the sheep were kept in the summer, and one clue may be that some of the Overbury tenants owed sheep-washing duties (Vose 1953). This manor was on Bredon Hill, an outlying part of the Cotswold Hills, and the price achieved in the fourteenth century does suggest that the priory had access to Cotswold wool.

TOWNS

Towns in the region performed a host of useful functions, which made the local wool more valuable. Communities of merchants provided buying power and links to distant markets and consumers.

Bristol
The twelfth-century charters of Bristol mention wool, together with hides and corn, as some of the main commodities handled by the Bristol merchants.

Bristol was acting as a collection point for the wool of south Wales in the early thirteenth century, and the abbot of Tintern, as a member of the Bristol Staple and also able to conduct his business free of tolls in the town, was a promoter of this trade (Carus-Wilson 1933). Most Cotswold wool was, however, exported via Southampton, rather than the much closer port of Bristol.

By 1337 Bristol had become the wealthiest provincial town in England (Sherborne 1971). Bristol was very exclusive and strangers were not allowed to trade there except at the fairs. Cloth making was a major local trade signified by Tuckers Street in the Redcliffe area in the thirteenth century (Latimer 1903), and the presence of merchants from Picardy (e.g. Amiens) who were trading in woad. Thomas Blanket was a notable manufacturer, who tended to contravene the local regulations in the pursuit of profit. By the late fourteenth century there was a guild of weavers here – the Guild of St Katherine with a chapel at the Temple church – and a separate guild for fullers (Fox and Taylor 1889). Temple church in Bristol has the earliest wool-related brass memorial, dated 1390. The exporting of cloths was a major business in the mid- to later fourteenth century, and by 1365-70 over 5,000 cloths per annum (double what it had been only 10 years before, and now 40 per cent of national exports) were being exported via this port. This all changed during the fifteenth century when London asserted its position, and Bristol's share in exports fell to 11 per cent, as London's increased to 60 per cent of national cloth exports (Sherborne 1971). It is likely, therefore, that much Cotswold cloth was being exported via the port of Bristol (Carus-Wilson 1933).

Chipping Campden

A 1273 survey of the lands of Roger de Somery, who was Baron Dudley but also lord of Campden, includes a reference to large numbers of sheep being kept on 'a common pasture called the Wold, where the lord can have 1000 sheep of his own, and it is worth 20s' (Madge 1903). At least four mills are also mentioned in the town, though it is unclear whether any of these was engaged in fulling. A large area by the town was called Sheppy, and so was a sheep walk. The tenants must also have had the right to run sheep on the commons, and the doubling of the size of the town between 1086 and 1273 was possibly due to the burgeoning wool industry (Whitfield 1958). Part of the manor eventually in the late thirteenth century descended to Edward de Ludlow, who may have been related to Nicholas and Laurence de Ludlow of Shropshire, who were some of the wealthiest wool merchants in the Welsh Marches.

In the late thirteenth century, when half of royal income was coming from wool, Campden was beginning to function, as were several other places in the Cotswolds, as a local collection point for wool. As the trade became more specialised and substantial, it drew in more important merchants who had the resources to develop the trade to a flourishing condition, for example the families of Weoley and Calf in around 1300. In 1356 a large amount of wool was stolen from John Weoley – 32 sacks worth £300. Foreign merchants also frequented the town, such as Godekin de Ryvele, merchant of Alemain, who in 1338 was on his way to Boston (Lincolnshire). Clearly some wool leaving England by eastern seaboard ports could easily, therefore, have come from the Cotswolds.

The medieval continental links of Chipping Campden are today well concealed, despite there being some surviving buildings and other reminders of this notable period in its history. These comprise a medieval wool merchant's house, the Woolstaplers Hall and memorial brasses to two wool merchants, William Grevel and William Welley, in the local parish church. All these relate to a period in the fourteenth century when Chipping Campden was the haunt of wool dealers eager to buy up the wool from sheep grazing the surrounding hills.

William Grevel was an outstanding wool merchant, who was described as formerly of London (*19*), and both he and his father Richard had links with Coventry. Looking to settle down he bought property in Chipping Campden in 1367 and in 1380 he was living there with five servants. He paid a high tax of 13s 3d in around 1377 when his servants were only paying 4d each (Rushen 1899, 21). His new house in Chipping Campden was originally a hall house and still survives, its broad frontage probably occupying several former burgage plots (*20*). The history of the house seems to be uncertain, as some have claimed this to be a barn only converted into a house in the sixteenth century (DoE undated). But large houses occupying wide plots are a feature of some medieval towns and reflected the wealth of some citizens. Therefore, it is entirely in keeping with William Grevel's status that he would have a larger than normal stone-built house. Undoubtedly the house has gone through a complicated series of alterations since its fourteenth-century construction, especially, it seems, in the sixteenth century.

William Grevel and his son John were pardoned for transgressing various wool laws, as they were far too important to the Exchequer to receive any sterner punishment. His connections were made clear in 1397 when he was lending King Richard II 300 marks (£200) on a promise of repayment at the following Easter (Rushen 1899, 20). As proof of his enormous wealth, at the same time he was buying the manor of Milcote near Stratford. In October 1401 he died owning 14 properties in Chipping Campden and properties in Mickleton, and left a bequest of 100 marks (£66 13s 8d) to the local church of St James, as a contribution 'to the new work to be carried on there'. However, the principal work on the church, as it stands today, was done in the mid- to late fifteenth century (Verey 1970, 153), and so it appears that the intended works were severely delayed.

The Woolstaplers Hall (*21*) was also built about the same time as Grevel's house, and was a building for the wool merchants to meet at in the course of their business. Wool was still passing through the town in the mid-fifteenth century (Whitfield 1958, 45). William Weoley, another wool merchant who was buried in Chipping Campden church, obtained the assistance of King Henry VI (1422-61)

19 Right Memorial brass of
William Grevel (d. 1401) in
Chipping Campden church
inscribed as 'of Campden,
formerly of London,
the greatest of the wool
merchants of all England'

20 Below The house at
Chipping Campden built by
William Grevel in about 1367

21 The Woolstaplers Hall at Chipping Campden built for the wool merchant, Robert Calf, in the late fourteenth century. This may represent the solar wing (private quarters) of a larger house, where the hall (living area) was situated to the right-hand side

when the Albertine Wool Company of Florence defaulted on £1180 owed to him, and this sum shows the extremely large scale of some wool deals. Chipping Campden was also one of the two main towns (the other being Northleach) that the Cely wool merchants visited to buy large quantities of high-quality wool in the fifteenth century (see chapter 8).

The Grevels of later generations seem may have turned to sheep farming rather than remaining as merchants, as in 1513 a William Grevel left money from his sheep for the rebuilding of the south aisle of Todenham church and for Winchcombe Abbey and Llanthony Priory (Rhodes 2002).

Cirencester

Richard I had originally alienated this manor, where a 'new' market had been created by 1086, to Cirencester Abbey. By around 1260 Cheping Street had been renamed as Dyars Street and there were six fulling mills in the medieval town (Gerrard 1994), which clearly indicates a substantial cloth manufacture in the area. Several wool merchant families also resided in the town (Baddeley 1924). The town failed to retain its independent borough status, as it came under the control of the abbot, who stole the borough charter and burnt it (Finberg

1957b). However, the position of the town as a natural centre ensured that it still flourished as a market centre. Major rebuilding of the nave of the parish church commenced from 1514, and wool will have played a part in generating the resources for this.

Gloucester

Gloucester does not seem to have figured much in the wool trade. One woolmonger is known (Patterson 1998), and he was based at Newland near Gloucester in the mid-thirteenth century. Gloucester became a cloth-making centre in the thirteenth century (Miller 1965), and remained as such into the fourteenth and fifteenth centuries, but thereafter lost out to rural competitors (Holt 1985). Woad, madder and alum deliveries from Southampton (Holt 1985) are some of the best evidence for its participation in the textile trade, but nearby Cotswold wool does not feature in return, as Southampton merchants were personally buying on the spot and then sending the wool southwards for immediate export.

Moreton-in-the-Marsh

Westminster Abbey established a new settlement here in 1222-46 in an attempt to take advantage of the Fosse Way, a Roman road, which remained in use as a major medieval route along the length of the Cotswold Hills. Their main rural estate in the region centred on nearby Bourton-on-the-Hill, which certainly specialised in wool production having 1,730 sheep in 1301 and employing six or seven shepherds. The extent of pasture attached to the new settlement at Moreton indicates that sheep were important to the new urban venture, and this is also reflected by a wool-house for wool storage being attached to the manor house by 1497 (*Gloucestershire VCH* VI, 247).

Northleach

Northleach was founded as a borough in 1219-20 by its landowner Gloucester Abbey, its market being granted in 1227. It also came to have a three-day fair (28-30 June; Finberg 1957b), which would have been just after the annual shearing, so that the new wool was probably the main commerce. By the late fourteenth century Northleach had become a principal market for local wool. This would have involved the wool of the Gloucester Abbey estate, and also of Winchcombe Abbey, which had centralised its own wool gathering at the nearby manor of Sherborne, as well as the wool of the lay wool growers in the region. Sheep were also driven to Northleach from nearby Cirencester for shearing (*Gloucestershire VCH* IX, 127). In the late 1300s Cotswold wool dealers came from Chipping Campden, Burford, Cirencester and Stow-on-the-Wold to Northleach to buy wool, and wool merchants were also attracted from much further away. Large amounts of wool will have poured into the town, and the dealers must have had considerable storage capacity in their houses. This wool will have left for London and later for Southampton as well. There is little sign of the wool being worked locally, though some local weaving occurred by 1266 as there was a local dyer called Cecilia.

Northleach church (*42*) can boast the best series of memorial brasses to wool dealers and merchants to be found in the Cotswolds. The town was clearly the base of some of the major later medieval dealers in Cotswold wool. The best-known were the Forteys, whose brasses survive in the parish church: Thomas Fortey (d. 1447) and John Fortey (d. 1458, see *35*) who is depicted with one foot on a fleece and another on a woolpack. The Bushes and Midwinters were Cotswold wool dealers with whom the Celys did business (chapter 8), and they inter-married and prospered. William Midwinter (*44*) left £600 and land in Northleach at his death in 1501. Thomas Bushe (died 1526, see *54*) left his family large sums of money (inlcuding £400 to his wife) and land in Oxfordshire, Wiltshire, Gloucestershire and Berkshire, all wool-growing counties, where property was being let stocked with sheep (Power 1926, 24). He had now clearly become a major grazier and grower for himself, as well as being a wool dealer. These local families had dealt with the exporters of wool, whose lives are illustrated especially by the Cely letters of the fifteenth century, where the younger merchants are apparently often distracted by hawks or horses, or the arranged viewing of a prospective wife (chapter 8).

One medieval inn known as Le Pyke, later as the Crown Inn and now as the Tudor House (*Gloucestershire VCH* IX), has survived intact (*22*). This building is likely to have served many wool buyers of the high period of wool buying in the town. The large houses built by the successful wool dealers in the town have not fared so well. Northleach remained an important staging point for travellers through the Cotswolds, and these large houses were usually converted into inns by the sixteenth or seventeenth centuries, and have subsequently been much altered. Unfortunately Bushe's Great House, which was presumably where the wool merchant Thomas Bushe (*54*) lived in the early sixteenth century, was largely demolished in 1936. A rare photograph shows this as a building with a large frontage, and traces of its medieval origins are just visible under its eighteenth-century façade (*23*). Its broad frontage displayed the wealth of its owner, as space on the road would have been at a premium in this successful late medieval town.

Stow-on-the-Wold

The abbot of Evesham established a market here from 1107 and there was also a fair from 1330 (Johnson 1994), with a second being instituted in 1476. Though not ideally located given the abbey's estates, it had good road links, mainly thanks to the Romans. Gloucester Abbey had large pastures at Evenlode close to Stow, and may have taken advantage of this market. In later days the Stow fair was famous for the number of sheep being driven in from the surrounding countryside (Johnson 1994), and Sheep Street is supposed to be where the sheep

22 Right Medieval inn known as Le Pyke (later the Crown Inn) overlooking the market-place at Northleach. Presumably a haunt of late medieval wool dealers from far and wide

23 Below A rare photograph of The Great House in Northleach in about 1900. It was known as Bushe's Great House in 1575 and had belonged to Thomas Bushe in the early sixteenth century. The main chimney stacks may represent the ends of the medieval building, and a probable medieval doorway is visible towards the left-hand end of the building. This house was largely demolished in 1936, though the bay to the right still survives today and was probably a later (possibly eighteenth-century) addition. *Photograph by courtesy of Joe Stevens*

flowed. The almshouses were the fifteenth-century gift of William Chester, a member of the only merchant stapler family known at Stow, whose father had previously presented Stow with its market cross (Johnson 1994).

Tetbury

Benefiting from being on the road from Cirencester to Bristol, a market and fairs at Tetbury had been established by the end of the early fourteenth century for the sale of wool from the surrounding area (Garner and Ingram 1973). When Edward III licensed the Peruzzi to export 500 sacks, they bought about one-fifth of these in Tetbury. In the mid-sixteenth century it was still considered one of the best wool and yarn markets in Gloucestershire and was busy providing raw materials for Stroudwater and Midlands manufacturers, such as in Kidderminster (Worcestershire). Though there were many weavers based here, it eventually faded because of its lack of water-power (Hodgson 1976).

Winchcombe

Wool was a principal trade in this royal borough, where business was dominated by the abbey while the absence of large merchant houses in the town reflects the abbot's primacy in the conduct of the wool trade in contrast with Chipping Campden (Donaldson 2001, 25). In 1327 taxes were raised in the town for the purpose of improving the streets and, along with the usual items of trade to be expected in a town of the period, there were tolls levied on wool by the sack (2d), and on teasels, which were used for finishing cloth, *by every hundred bunches* (2d). In 1377 tolls were also being levied on alum and woad showing the continuing extensive involvement of the town, and its environs, in the wool and textile trades.

VILLAGES

The early histories of only a few Cotswold villages have been studied in any detail. The success of the Cotswold sheep was tied up with the local village economy, often in the more remote parts of the countryside where small villages and hamlets were the norm. A village like Bishop's Cleeve sometimes served a special function as the centre of a large, mainly pastoral, estate. Most villages were, however, mixed arable and pastoral concerns based on two large common fields where one field was left fallow each year. It seems that the sheep may have paradoxically had a key role both in underpinning the survival of some villages, and in leading to the demise of others. In some locations, such as at Little Aston (upstream of Bourton-on-the-Water), the lack of sheep may have impoverished soil fertility preventing arable cultivation from being sufficiently productive to save the settlement from decline in the early fourteenth century (Dyer 1987). On the other hand, conversion to sheep pasture subsequently brought many owners of such deserted sites a handsome income in later years.

Bishop's Cleeve, Worcestershire

Bishop's Cleeve was part of the very large estate of the bishop of Worcester. The bishop kept large flocks of sheep here, and his tenants also followed suite, as more than 1,000 lambs were born annually in the later fourteenth century to the villagers. Wool production at 14 sacks suggests between 3,000 and 4,000 sheep in a single parish (Dyer 1980).

Minchinhampton

The fortunes of the medieval villagers of Minchinhampton were bound up with Caen Abbey in Normandy. The profits from wool were transferred to Normandy with the help of various tenants whose job it was to assist, and no doubt provide some protection during the journey. The occupation of some inhabitants of the manor as fullers by the later twelfth century (*Gloucestershire VCH* XI) also implies that some cloth-making was already underway, and this is likely to have used the local wool. The town was mainly a seventeenth-century development, though this was also tied up with the wool and yarn trades (*Gloucestershire VCH* XI).

Roel near Hawling, Gloucestershire

Hawling manor had been held by Flemish incomer Sigar de Chocques in 1086, and its upland village of Roel came into the hands of Benedictine monasteries, firstly St Évroul, and then Winchcombe Abbey after 1318. Hawling with Hazleton and Yanworth had been sold to Winchcombe Abbey in 1201, with the abbey finally buying Roel later (Aldred and Dyer 1991). Sheep were entirely integral to the local economy. The Roel demesne kept 200 sheep in 1294 and peas were grown for overwinter food for the sheep, and under a two-course rotation 600 acres of land would have been fallow each year. By 1390, 300 sheep were being kept by the farmer, and Winchcombe Abbey had a flock there as well. Common pasture would have been an important resource, and this was probably the uncultivatable steeper land.

A survey by Winchcombe Abbey in 1355 shows that only one-third of families at Roel were the same as they had been in 1327. One tenant was taking advantage of the unstable situation by taking several properties in his tenancy, and was accused of over-burdening the common with 200 sheep in 1379. But by the mid-1400s even the engrossers were giving up their enlarged holdings. It is evident that the abbey was working closely with its tenants to try and make a go of the land, but eventually the Roel land was given over totally to sheep and a sheep-cote established which was leased by a Londoner in 1541 for 21 years for over £23 (Aldred and Dyer 1991).

Upton

The bishop of Worcester's manor at Upton (near Blockley) was populated by families who made a living from ploughing and shepherding. Two of the poorer inhabitants were shepherds, whereas others with larger resources could have owned sheep and concentrated on arable, the sheep being an important component of the arable farming (Hilton and Rahtz 1966, 81). There was also a sheep-cote nearby (Dyer 1995). For once, archaeology is able to contribute something to the picture, as excavation of part of this medieval settlement has revealed a community that seemed quite prosperous, and one involved in wool production. The latter was evidenced by a high proportion of sheep in the animal bone assemblage, but more significantly by the age of sheep at death. They were mostly over two years old (Yealland and Higgs 1966, 140). More tantalisingly Upton also produced evidence of Roman and Saxon activity (Rahtz 1969), suggesting that this upland settlement at *c.*750ft (229m) had had a long history, and had perhaps always been engaged in wool production given its remote location.

TRANSFORMING COTSWOLD WOOL INTO CLOTH

The dealer/middleman was the *woolman* or *brogger*, and was most likely to have the larger quantities of wool that the merchants required for foreign trade (Power 1926, 24).

Types of wool
There was a basic classification into 'good', or 'middle' quality wools with younger wool being worth less. Inferior wools were *morlings* (skin of a sheep found dead) and *shorlings* (skin of a sheep recently shorn), *brecklings* (fragments), *pellwool* (plucked from a dead sheep), and *locks* (what was left after the fleece had gone, e.g. from the legs). This inferior material was usually classed by the wool-packer as *refuse* but still exported.

Packing
The wool was sampled at a collection point close to the production area and, on the basis of this, an agreement was drawn up about providing a set quantity and quality of wool at a specified price (Power 1926, 25). Typically, therefore, an Oxfordshire woolman agreed with a London mercer on 12 September 1478 to supply 25 sacks of young Cotswold wool, which was to be packed and wound at the woolman's house by 'an indifferent persone' of the fellowship 'of the Wolpakkers of London' chosen by the buyer (Kingsford 1923). The expert wool-packers were so skilful that when wool from elsewhere was passed off as Cotswold wool, this fraud could not only be seen through, but the bogus wool could even be identified as originally from another specific area (e.g. Buckinghamshire; Power 1926, 27). These skilled valuers had a guild of their own, and had been strictly forbidden from 1473 to deal in wool themselves (Power 1933). This restriction had become necessary because of increasing fraud involving packers such as William Breton, who had been caught in the 1450s, but who later became the Celys' trusted packer. The knowledge of the packers was

essential for the conduct of the trade, but obviously the more unscrupulous had found it easy to abuse their position.

Traditionally during the packing a set of weights was used comprising two of 7lb and three others of 4lb, 2lb and 1lb. At the farm a 14lb stone was manufactured to balance the two 7lb weights, so that these combined together made up the 28lb *tod* (Shilson 1944). The smaller weights could be used then to establish how much under or over 28lb any set of fleeces weighed, so as to establish the weight of wool fairly accurately (Shilson 1944). This method of weighing wool survived into the early twentieth century when it was regarded as a direct link with the Middle Ages. Only good wool was put on the scales initially and any of lower grade was cast aside, presumably the source of the medieval phrase for this stage as 'to cast a sort'.

The wool was finally packed into sarplers (usually equivalent to a weight of between two to three sacks) before the journey by wagon to a port and part of the deal was that the woolman delivered it all to the 'king's beam' at Leadenhall in London, which was the usual place for delivery as the appointed place for the weighing of wool. The sarplers would be carefully labelled with the merchant's mark (*24*), and other marks showing the source and quality of the contents, as well

24 Merchants' marks of wool dealers: 1 William Grevel (d. 1401; Chipping Campden); 2 Robert Page (d. 1440; Cirencester); 3 Reginald Spycer (d. 1442; Cirencester); 4 John Fortey (d. 1458; Northleach); 5 William Midwinter (d. 1501; Northleach); 6 Thomas Bushe (d. 1525; Northleach)

as a unique batch reference (56). The dealer and the wool-packer accompanied the sarplers to London, with each wagon-load of two to three sarplers costing about 18s 9d to cover the expenses of hire on the journey from the Cotswolds (Hanham 1985, 119).

Large sums of money were involved in the purchase of so much wool. In the deal of September 1478 mentioned above a total cost of £140 was to be paid to the woolman, who received a first instalment of £81 17s in hand when the deal was first struck, the balance to be paid the day after the delivery of the wool in London. Often the balance would be paid off in three instalments, firstly one at the weighing, then two payments at intervals of four or five months. This is the way that the Celys made contracts with the local Cotswold wool dealers, such as Bushe or Midwinter, in the 1470s-80s (see chapter 8). Additionally there were the incidental payments, to petty officials such as the weighers (4d per sarpler and 3d per 100 woolfells).

If the wool was taken to Southampton for export, there was a similar procedure involving another king's beam. This weighing apparatus was located in the Weigh House, known as the Poysage House in 1454 when it belonged to the earl of Warwick (Burgess 1976, 79). This building still stands today (51), just up the street from the main wool warehouse (52) on the medieval quayside. Surviving records from the Southampton Weigh House list payments made for hiring the official town weights, and record Cotswold wool dealers, such as Thomas Bushe, finally delivering their wool into the hands of the exporters (56).

Merchants' marks were an integral part of this system, as each sarpler would need to be clearly identified with the mark of its originating merchant and an individual number in that year's account. The design of the mark usually followed a familiar pattern of a pendant or flag surmounting an emblem, which often incorporated the individual merchant's initials (24). Merchants' marks were used to advertise, and some merchants used them to broadcast far and wide, as in the case of John Tame who put his mark on the outside of the tower of Fairford church for all to see (25).

Wool-fleets

The wool often left England for Calais in sea-borne convoys where the ships were less vulnerable to piracy, while this system also enabled merchants to easily spread their precious cargoes across several ships. Sailings usually happened in spring, summer and autumn, and were organised by officials of the Calais wool staple. The complete London custom record for 1478-9 shows that that year the first convoy set sail on 20 July and consisted of 38 ships carrying 1,160.5 sacks, 12 *nails* of wool and 268,227 woolfells. The Cely and Stonor companies all had cargo aboard and it was quite usual for between five and eleven merchants to be sharing a ship. Small fleets of between two to five ships then occurred until February, and the next large wool-fleet out of London was in the following spring (27 March), when 24 ships sailed carrying 945.5 sacks, 24 *nails* of wool

25 Fairford church tower, showing the merchant's mark of John Tame (top left)

and 111,767 woolfells (Power 1926, 28). Overall it has been estimated that the
freight charge for each sarpler across the Channel to Calais was in the region of
5s (Hanham 1985, 124).

Provincial ports on the east coast could also mount considerable fleets, for
instance on 15 October 1466 a fleet carrying 1,886.5 sacks of wool and nearly
35,000 woolfells left Boston. The picture was similar on the south coast where,
for instance at Southampton in 1443, most wool was brought into the port in
the autumn for sailings in October to December (Coleman 1960). In earlier days
much of this trade would have been carried in cogs (26), after which the larger
carrack became the main vessel type (31).

Examination of the wool at Calais
Part of the purpose of the staple system was to guarantee the quality of the
goods through checks, and so a Calais staple official appraised a sample of each
consignment. Fraud could occur, such as when wool from another sarpler was
knowingly substituted for sub-standard wool, and the Celys were guilty of this
practice at least once (Power 1926, 28). There were frequent complaints by the

26 A thirteenth or fourteenth-century cog (a half-size replica) alongside the medieval quay at Southampton. This was a broad-beamed flat-bottomed cargo vessel of clinker construction

foreign buyers about fraudulent declarations of quality and weight. Only after this stage could the wool be taken away for sale and warehoused in Calais. When sold, its weight was calculated by the lesser unit of the Calais sack, with 49lb less wool than in the English sack (Hanham 1985, 133), which increased the number of sacks for sale! As the buyers had to come to Calais, all the English merchants had to do was to await their arrival. Usually the Dutch buyers, for instance from Leyden and Delft, came after selling their cloth in Antwerp or at Bergen op Zoom, and they were particularly interested in the woolfells. Otherwise most of the buyers were Flemish.

Credit

The granting of credit was an essential part of the trade in wool at all stages. Having bought the wool from the grower, and made only a part payment, the wool merchant usually sold the wool abroad by dividing the cost into three, with the first (up to 50 per cent) being payable up front, and credit notes usually being issued for the other two for payment at the next two fairs (which occurred roughly quarterly). Credit was issued to maintain a steady price, and, if the value of the wool declined, then the loan could be over a longer period. Richard Cely senior constantly wrote to his son in Calais about these terms of business rather than the price of wool (Power 1926, 32). This system allowed large transactions to be undertaken without having large sums of cash, as the credit notes themselves became a form of tender whose legitimacy was only guaranteed by the common knowledge of transactions. Cash sums of foreign money could be converted to other goods of equivalent value for the return journey, and the mercers were often employed at this point. English mercers wanted Flemish money with which to purchase goods abroad, and so by lending them the money that the wool sales had generated, the wool merchants facilitated their trade as well. Subsequently they only saw their return from foreign wool sales once the mercers had imported their goods into England and sold them. Chasing debtors was a regular outcome of this system, though fortunately it generally worked.

As usual, unstable currency was the enemy, and in the fifteenth century there were official attempts at the Calais end to reduce this reliance on credit, as the English government attempted to divert foreign coins to the Calais mint. For instance, the 1429 currency statutes disrupted this system damaging the wool trade (and probably opening the market to Spanish wool), while in the meantime the cloth trade prospered which brought little gain to the English Crown (Munro 1979, 196).

It was also common practice for wool merchants to pay in advance for next year's wool from monastic estates, and sometimes the next several years' wool could be bought, and this could be up to 12 years in advance (Postan 1973). The advance would only be part of the price, but on other occasions additional money was offered as a loan partly repayable in wool. Sometimes as well the monasteries took advantage of this system by selling the wool of others they had bought (the *collecta* in which case the monasteries were acting as middlemen). This worked as long as the demesne was being directly farmed, but when this collapsed, especially in the later fourteenth and early fifteenth century, then the stage was set in favour of the wool gatherer, whose local knowledge became particularly valuable to the more substantial merchants.

Spinning and weaving

The wool was first sorted and washed, and then prepared for spinning, by carding if it was short-stapled wool, or by combing if it was long-stapled. The wool was next oiled and spun into yarn. Warp threads needed to be set up on the loom before weaving could commence, and it took 2–3,000 warp threads, each about 30yds long, to produce a broadcloth, and it took about 12 days to weave a single cloth. In the case of woollens fulling was next applied and this was an arduous business, often with the fullers working in threes to tread the cloth, though by the twelfth century, at the latest, water-powered mills were being used. After fulling the cloth was hung out on tenters to stretch it to the right size. Finally the cloth was finished, while still wet, by raising the nap with teasels set in rows in a frame, and by then shearing it, when dry, using large 3–4ft long shears. The latter two processes were repeated several times for the best cloth, and supplemented by careful scrutiny and mending to remove flaws.

Cloth making in Flanders

Cloth making was the chief impetus for wool production, but above all it was the high-quality cloth that was first produced on the Continent that coincided with the heavy demand for English wool. From at least the thirteenth and up to the fifteenth centuries, the most valuable and desirable cloth type manufactured in the Flemish towns was the *scarlet*. The nature of this cloth has been disputed, but study of the local town regulations, especially for Brussels, has shown that *scarlets* were made from only the finest English wool, which, for instance, in the fifteenth century were specified to be *Maertscher* wool (from the Welsh Marches, i.e. Herefordshire and Shropshire), the best *Cudzewoutscher* (Cotswold) wool, or the best *Linderzee* (Lindsey, Lincolnshire) wool (Munro 1983).

The economy of Flanders became completely dependent on this one major industry and the acquisition of wool was all-important. Some wool was available on the Continent, for instance through the Champagne fairs, but the greatest quantity and most high quality of medieval wools came from England. The system required Flemish agents to be based in the ports, especially of London and Dover. These belonged to the Hanse of Bruges which at its largest was an organisation representing the guilds of fifteen Flemish towns engaged in using English wool.

Conditions for the Flemish cloth makers were not necessarily very good. Wages were set by local statute and local authorities also had inspectors to maintain standards. Even the hours of working were specified, which were usually daylight hours with a lunch break of 1.5 hours. For instance, the bells of the belfry over the Cloth Hall of Bruges rang out the workday (*27*), making the whole town work like a single factory.

The influence of the large wool-consuming towns extended far beyond their walls for they were able to prevent cloth making over large surrounding regions. Hence Ghent in 1314 was able to ban cloth production outside the town (Thoen 1997, 79). The raw materials, and especially the wool, were controlled by the great guildsmen who handed out these materials as part of the piece-work system. These capitalists divided up the wool amongst master weavers, who sold the finished product. The wool and cloth merchants controlled not only the economy but also the local government and so laws were passed to increase the power of their guilds and to further repress the workers. Conditions for the workers became so oppressive that riots were eventually threatened, and so any gatherings by workers were restricted to seven, and they were not allowed to bear arms. In 1280-1 riots duly became widespread, including in Bruges. The wealth created was, therefore, confined largely to a privileged few (Thompson 1931, 63), who became wealthy enough to carry out many public works, such as the town hall of Bruges, with the principal motive presumably being self-glorification.

27 Wool Street in Bruges, Belgium, with the tower of the belfry at the Cloth Hall in the background, from which the working day was rung out across the whole of the city. The lower part dates from 1282-96, and the octagonal upper part from 1482-7

7

The fourteenth century

Wool ... the sovereign merchandise and jewel of the realm
(From an English ordinance of 1353)

Wool had generally risen in price during the previous century and this trend continued into the fourteenth century, though royal taxation eventually took its toll by reducing profitability, especially for the wool producers (Farmer 1988, 756). Annual wool exports now reached their peak at over 46,000 sacks (Donkin 1973). Cloth imports were high at 12,000 cloths per year (Bridbury 1982), but the home cloth industry was now mobilising on a large scale, and its growth was stimulated by the periodic bans on wool export and cloth imports during this century, so that home production rose drastically from 16,000 cloths in around 1360 to 40,000 in the 1390s (Carus–Wilson 1950). The number of sheep may have reached over 15 million (Postan 1973) to sustain this degree of trade.

This is the period during which the woolsack took up its position at the heart of government, as the place where the Lord Chancellor sits as the Speaker of the House of Lords. It is uncertain how this came about, but traditionally Edward III is thought to have introduced the woolsack (Fell and Mackenzie 1994). If so, then at this time it would certainly have acted as a reminder of the importance of foreign trade in general, and particularly of the wool trade.

THE PEGOLOTTI LIST

Francesco Balducci Pegolotti was a member of the merchant house of Bardi, which was well known in England for its wool dealing (Lloyd 1973, table 5). A detailed list (*La pratica della mercatura*) has survived which he presumably compiled while working for the Bardi in England in 1318-21, and which has survived as a fifteenth-century copy. It records 194 wool-producing, mainly Cistercian, monasteries confirming how heavily this monastic order was involved in the wool business, which very much fitted with the preference of this order for remote rural locations. It seems that in their case this type of property was not sought merely for purposes of seclusion, but also as a potential source of revenue. The Pegolotti figures for the price of wool include the cost of carriage from England to Flanders, and an assessment of the profit made by the merchant. The prices cover a range of qualities with 'middle' being the term commonly used then to refer to the average product.

The Pegolotti list suggests that the Cistercians got better prices than others in the market, and this may reflect their specialisation in the trade, which produced a better-prepared product from particularly well-managed flocks. Pegolotti defined some of the terms he used and these include references to the cleaning of the wool and neat packaging of the individual fleeces, suggesting that these may have been some of the refinements perfected by the Cistercians.

The Cotswold (mainly Gloucestershire) monasteries in the Pegolotti list are as follows (based on Cunningham 1910):

Cistercian houses (*Di cestello*):

Chinchesulda (Kingswood Abbey, Gloucestershire): 26 marks (£17 6s 8d) for the best and 15 marks (£10) for middle. Produced 25 sacks per annum.

Labriuiera di Ghontisgualdo (Bruern Abbey, Oxfordshire): 25 marks (£16 13s 4d) a sack for the best, 16 marks (£10 13s 4d) for middle, 13 marks for locks. Produced 12 sacks per annum.

Brondislea (Bordesley Abbey, Worcestershire): 19 marks (£12 13s 4d) a sack for the best, 11 marks (£7 6s 8d) for middle and 11 marks for locks. Produced 10 sacks per annum.

Eilesi (Hailes Abbey, Gloucestershire): 19 marks (£12 13s 4d) a sack for the best and 10 marks (£6 13s 4d) for middle, 7 marks for locks. Produced 20 sacks per annum.

Benedictine houses (*Dell'ordine nero*):

Guiccichonbo (Winchcombe Abbey, Gloucestershire): less good quality wool 13 marks (£8 13s 4d) the sack. Produced 40 sacks per annum.

Euesamo in Chondisgualdo (Evesham Abbey, Worcestershire): 12 marks (£8) a sack. Produced 10 sacks per annum.

Persore (Pershore Abbey, Worcestershire): 12 marks (£8) a sack. Produced 10 sacks per annum

Chausberi (Tewkesbury Abbey, Gloucestershire): 12 marks (£8) per sack and 8 sacks per annum.

Lofusfeltro in ghondisgualdo (possibly Gloucester Abbey): 13 marks (£8 13s 4d) a sack and 5 sacks per annum.

Osnea in Chondisgualdo (Oseney Abbey, Oxfordshire): 13 marks (£8 13s 4d) per sack. Produced 25 sacks per annum

Cistercian Cotswold wool from Kingswood and Bruern Abbeys was the most valuable wool produced in England, except for that produced by a Benedictine nunnery at Stanfield in Lincolnshire and the Cistercian abbeys of Thame in Oxfordshire, Dore in Herefordshire and Tintern in Monmouthshire

(Cunningham 1910). The Cistercians were outstanding for their graded wool, while other orders rarely came up to this standard. The Cistercians, however, relied almost totally on wool for their income, though in the Cotswolds this was not generally the case (C. Dyer pers comm). Likewise Worcester Priory, for instance, only had a modest part of its income from this source in c.1300, so some institutions passed over this particular financial opportunity. The Pegolotti classifications of the wool were based on how it was prepared and presented, without reference to staple length and fineness, probably because only the better quality wools are included in the list due to the fastidious requirements of the Italians.

The Cistercians also enjoyed certain advantages over others when it came to selling their wool, as they had very large flocks and were in a position to make long-term contracts of sale. They could even, if necessary, take advantage of their special dispensation from tolls and their access to unsalaried lay brothers to take their products to a convenient rendezvous-point with the merchant without incurring any additional expenditure such as tolls. There may also have been a belief that in dealing with the monks there would be less resort by the seller to underhand practices. As the monks were also responsible for cleaning the wool, grading and packing it, this belief in their honesty was an important consideration to the buyer. Dealing with the Cistercians, therefore, had considerable advantages (Donkin 1958) worth paying a premium price for.

TAXATION OF WOOL IN THE LATER THIRTEENTH–FOURTEENTH CENTURIES

While on a visit to Sicily in 1275, King Edward I had encountered systematic taxation of trade, and was clearly impressed with the idea of introducing a similar system in England. On his return he secured the agreement of merchants and magnates to tax wool and leather, the latter being worth less than 4 per cent of the wool trade (Carus-Wilson and Coleman 1963). This was the first time that previously free English trade had been subjected to this type of charge. The effect was to give the king an annual revenue of about £8-£11,000, and he also had the possibility in addition of being able to borrow against the security of future customs, as this was a steady revenue stream. This first wool custom (tax) was imposed in 1275, and was half a mark (6s 8d) per exported sack of wool (Rothwell 1975, 410), and the same again for each 300 woolfells ('which makes one sack'). This system rapidly became known as the 'ancient custom' sometimes also known as the 'great and ancient custom' (Rothwell 1975, 410, no.48) to distinguish it from newer taxes that were soon to be introduced, as the king sought to increase his revenues even further from this lucrative source.

The penalties for evading the 1275 customs duty were severe and involved forfeiture of all possessions and being 'at the king's pleasure', and the incentive to expose fraud was that the resident lord, wherever the crime was detected, would be given the forfeit property. As usual in medieval England the system of policing relied on informers looking to their own advantage. The system that the king set in place was the source of some resentment to the English as it had foreign merchants at its core, for specific companies of Luccan and Florentine merchants were identified to collect the customs from the port officials on the king's behalf (Rothwell 1975, 410). This was presumably part of a deal by the king with his bankers, who were being paid back via the profits of the wool trade and at the expense of the wool growers in particular, on to whom the merchants passed as much as they could of the taxation by holding down prices as far as possible. The native English wool growers and traders would certainly have disliked this arrangement.

From at least 29 July 1294 until 23 November 1297 the 'evil toll' or *maltote* was levied which penalised exported English wool much more heavily than Irish wool, though it was presented as a voluntary gift to the king from the merchants specifically to aid the war effort against France! The levy, called a subsidy, was 5 marks (£3 6s 8d) on a sack of 'dressed wool' (*lana fracta*) and 3 marks (£2) for each sack of other wool or woolfells (Rothwell 1975, 469). Though removed in 1297 (Rothwell 1975, 469, no.68), it was revived in 1336, after which it was soon to become a regular parliamentary levy on the wool trade.

In 1303 there was additional taxation on alien (i.e. foreign) merchants buying wool to export, and this added 3s 4d per sack, representing about 6 per cent of the alien merchants' costs. This was known as the 'new' or 'petty' custom (Platt 1973). Though alien merchants were let off some taxes (e.g. the 1317 tax on moveable possessions), they ended up paying 10s per exported sack of wool compared to 6s 8d paid by the English merchants (Lloyd 1982, 31).

Government interference in the wool trade not only extended to raising money from its business, but also to the whole conduct of the trade, especially with Flanders. This was accomplished by directing that the wool merchants had to transact their business in certain places where they could be closely monitored. So in 1313 (–1325) a compulsory staple was set up at St Omer, 19 miles (30km) south of Calais, for wool destined for northwest Europe. This also had the advantage that it stopped the most successful foreign merchants from taking over the wool trade, and instigating their own monopoly.

The staple acted like a cartel, keeping the prices high and thereby benefiting the royal Exchequer (Power 1941). Though its location was inconvenient to English merchants they had to go along with it. The staple provided a continuous mart and concentrated a commodity so that controls could be set in place more easily, and the foreign wool trade milked more effectively (Lipson 1953, 20-21). *Collectors* were the staple officials who oversaw the payment of customs charges and levies, registered the import of wool to Calais, and thereby put money into the king's coffers. Politically the official reasons for this system were declared to be the maintenance of standards and of more effective administration. The highest possible profits for the king were, however, the main reasons for this highly regulated system of foreign trade.

It has been estimated that Edward III made an average of £13,000 per annum out of English wool towards his total annual income of £30,000. From 1336 he raised wool export tax to £1 6s 8d, then to £2 6s 8d a sack for denizens, and £3 per sack and more for foreigners (Munro 1978, 164). Clearly the king had in mind making the wool trade pay for the war with France, and so on 12 August 1336 an embargo on exporting wool was set up to deliberately create a wool scarcity abroad and thereby stimulate higher prices in the Low Countries, combined with a glut and lower prices at home (Munro 1978, 135). This suited his purpose perfectly as long as the situation was not maintained so long as to cripple the trade permanently.

The tax situation changed drastically in 1337 when Edward III established a new monopoly of wool exporting, in order to raise even more money for the royal Exchequer. He did this by creating a syndicate of English exporters who were invested with compulsory powers of wool purchase in England, as well as their monopoly of export. Preparations for war with France were being made with a loan of about £100,000 from his usual Florentine bankers, the Bardi and Peruzzi, and from the richest merchants in England, the de la Poles of Hull. The king may have been hoping to make £200,000 out of his 1337 scheme, together with half the profits of wool sales (Munro 1978, 136). He dismayed the wool producers by setting a maximum price, apparently as the prices attained were regularly lower (Munro 1978, 136). And it soon became clear that the producers would not even be paid until the merchants had recouped their loan, which was to be recouped by a farm of the custom and subsidies raised to 40s a sack in May 1338 (Munro 1978, 136). This situation, therefore, bore down extremely heavily on the wool growers again, who were forced to provide extended credit.

The new 'English Wool Company', headed by William de la Pole of Hull and Reginald de Conduit of London, undertook initially to find 30,000 sacks of wool in the kingdom for export, and, in exchange for their having a monopoly, these merchants agreed to advance £200,000 out of the proceeds of their business, thereby for the first time rivalling the Italians as lenders to the king. They would be repaid in effect out of the customs normally due to the Crown, which were now not being charged, i.e. customs relief. With wool costing an average of £5 per sack, or £6 if the costs of collecting and exporting were included, the merchants were expecting to clear £2 per sack in profit. This amounted to 33–40 per cent profit on money that was not actually expended by the merchants but was in the form of (virtually forced) loans given by the wool growers themselves. No wonder some medieval merchants became fabulously wealthy, though in this case they had to make a staggeringly large loan to the king at the same time, which would have had to have been from their own assets, as the sale of the wool was also heavily dependent on credit provided by the sellers.

These monopolist merchants sent 10,000 sacks of wool to Dordrecht (Netherlands) in November 1337, but the system collapsed in 1338 when the merchants fell out with the king – not a very wise move on their part. The two leading merchants were subsequently arrested in 1340 and charges of widespread smuggling were eventually upheld. Individual wool merchants continued personally, however, to significantly fund the king's ventures (Fryde 1952).

At least one of the principal merchants in the English Wool Company by the name of Conduit was largely dealing in Cotswold wool and wool from the other high-quality regions in the west. For instance, he bought 50 sacks of Cotswold wool at £6 5s 8d a sack, and only the Herefordshire wool was more expensive. Once abroad the Cotswold wool was worth £11 per sack. The special circumstances of the trade at this period, namely the need for a military escort and landing in Dordrecht where there was insufficient warehousing, obviously increased the normal handling charges incurred in the trade to £1 12s per sack. Normally now the custom and subsidy was £2 per sack, in which case the normal profit would have been reduced to just over £1 per sack (Fryde 1964, 15).

At the source of the trade the effects of the royal manipulation of trade and customs on the domestic wool market were also severe, driving down the average price in 1335-7 of just over £5 a sack for better wool to just over £4 in 1339-41 (Munro 1978, 136) or over £6 for Cotswold which was sold at £11 in the Low Countries (Munro 1978, table 6). When the king delayed his invasion of France in 1339 awaiting adequate loans from the merchants, this brought about a glut of wool on the markets in Bruges and Antwerp and this hit prices extremely hard. For instance, a merchant known as Paul de Monte Florum, who was acting as a royal agent, sold his Cotswold wool in the summer of 1339 at only £7-£8 per sack at Bruges (Fryde 1964, app 8 and 11). The Bardi and Peruzzi were also beginning to default on payments because of the depressed market (van Uytven 1983). But it was the taxes and loans on wool that made possible this war and later much of the finance that bankrolled the battles of Crécy (1346) and Agincourt (1415) was again derived from the wool growers and merchants (Postan 1973, 342).

Until 1342 the English king was again relying upon his foreign merchant bankers, including the Bardi and Peruzzi companies, for money, but parliament complained that this meant that they were being granted favours, so in 1343 a movement was started to reduce the role of the foreign merchant and their command over English customs dues. Instead English wool merchants again struck a deal with the king so that they accounted for the customs themselves, and paid them to the king, though this also put them in a good position to negotiate for some recompense for their losses as a result of the king's aberrant actions in the past, which had left them out of pocket. A minority of merchants sought to use this situation to their own private benefit. So in 1346 the king again made an agreement with two prominent merchants, Walter Chiriton and Thomas Swanland, whereby they took over the farm of the customs and subsidies in return for £50,000 per annum paid to the king for two years, of which £4,000 was to be immediately made available. This enabled the king to pursue the Crécy campaign. The extension of this was then disrupted by the onset of plague (the Black Death) in England in the summer 1348-9, which stopped normal business in its tracks, and the king responded by again suspending the export of wool (Sayles 1931, 180). Other merchants became involved to spread the debt and grant the king his payments, but this only served to spread the problem.

In 1347 a 'cloth custom' had been imposed as well, so that both wool and woollen cloth were now the basis of medieval royal taxation, and these products accounted for about 50 per cent of royal revenue up to the end of the fourteenth century. In 1353 several English ports became staple ports, and aliens were given the sole right to export, a monopoly that was only abolished in 1362. A cloth tax – the ulnage – was also introduced in 1353, collected at 4d per woollen cloth (cloth of assize) plus ½d for measuring to ensure it was 26yds (23.7m) long and 45in (1.14m) wide. Cloth could be seized if it was sold without the seal to show that it had been checked.

In 1379-85 there was civil war in Flanders (Bolton 1980, 300), and in Richard II's reign (1377-99) the staple was moved to Middelburg (north of Bruges), and then sometimes switched to home staples in the 1390s. But with the accession of Henry IV (1399-1413) a company of about 200 wool merchants was finally settled at Calais (Bolton 1980, 296). This was destined to be the home of the wool staple for a long period, and the Crown was able to continue relying on the Calais staplers for loans entered into against future customs income as security, which gave a long-lasting stability to royal income.

The history of wool taxation since 1275, therefore, shows the erratic and arbitrary nature of early trade practices, as governed by royal whim and command, which must have done much to undermine the confidence of both producers and merchants, unless they were particularly close to the king. In the late fourteenth century the wool staple had been finally established at Calais, which had been captured in 1347 and remained in English hands until 1558, and where it was to stay for a long time, introducing a greater level of stability in the trade. However, the price of this was that the wool trade came under the close control of the English merchants who constituted the Fellowship of the Staple. Contrary to previous wool export monopolies this one was formally constituted and involved a large number of merchants (probably up to 300 in number). The only foreign wool exporters to survive this change were the Italians who still had royal licences to sail directly to the Mediterranean ports without having to go via the staple port at Calais. By the later fourteenth century additional subsidies on wool, as a result of the Hundred Years War, saw taxation on wool amounting to about 25 per cent of the merchants' costs, and this must have made it tempting to resort to smuggling despite the obvious difficulties of hiding something as bulky as wool.

COTSWOLD SHEEP FARMING

During the fourteenth century a more detailed view of local sheep farming and wool production in the Cotswolds comes into focus than previously. This shows that sheep were valued for their milk and dung, as well as their wool and meat. Sheep's milk was made into cheese, and the two dairies at Minchinhampton and Lowesmoor produced 445 cheeses weighing 2-3lb (about 1kg) apiece (Watson 1932, 335). Clearly cheese making should not be underestimated as a source of additional income. Folding was another income available to some tenants if they kept any sheep, where it was not a right of the lord of the manor. At Temple Guiting in 1326-8 it was worth 2s per acre, and £11 was spent by the lord of the manor on enriching the soil of about one-third of his land (Dyer 1988, 377). Such expenditure suggests how critical the folding was for the maintenance of soil fertility on the uplands. Contemporary landlords estimated that each acre of arable took three or four sheep to maintain its fertility (Dyer 1987, 177), and in parts of the Cotswolds where arable was so dominant that it reduced available pasture too far, then there was a problem in sustainability. This brought about desertion of remoter settlements even before the Black Death (Dyer 1987), and provided opportunities for landlords to increase the number of sheep runs, and the supply of wool.

A broad view of the state of sheep farming in the south-west Midlands emerges from the grant by Parliament to Edward III in 1341, as this can be used to assess the relative density of stocking with sheep in each county. Oxfordshire was the most densely stocked after Norfolk and had almost twice the stocking rate per acre as Gloucestershire (Trow-Smith 1957, 141 based on Rogers 1866). But given the higher value of Cotswold wool, the wool value per acre in Gloucestershire was amongst the highest in the country. During this century Oxfordshire became one of the wealthiest counties (Sherwood and Pevsner 1974), and wool must have played a large part in this affluence. As elsewhere, across the Cotswolds in Gloucestershire and also in Wiltshire and Oxfordshire, the new-found wealth of these regions was now beginning to be reflected in new church building, which continued into the following century.

Not only were sheep numerous, but they were also relatively valuable, as generally the price of sheep reflected the price of wool in their region, and by 1350-1400 the best prices for English wethers were being paid in the Cotswolds and the upper Thames valley. These prices were an average of 2s each (*AgHEW* III, 463), which was at a time when the wool from the Cotswold region was averaging 4s 7d to 6s 4d per stone, and when the ordinary day labourer earned about 10d per week. The 2s price per head was equivalent to the shorn wool of about three sheep, so the return in a single year was a minimum of about 30 per cent, or over a sheep's lifetime about 120 per cent in the value of wool alone.

The shepherd was a local figure of some importance, wherever sheep were the source of significant income (Franklin 1993). Tax lists for Gloucestershire in 1327 feature many communities where 'shepherd' appears as a surname, reflecting the general prevalence of sheep farming, even if the current holder held the name by inheritance. Their skills were in demand as the large estates continued to organise their sheep flocks centrally, and to bring in sheep from other parts of the country. Transhumance was still the basic approach, for instance on the monastic estates of Winchcombe and Westminster Abbeys. Accordingly, the latter's sheep spent the summer at Bourton-on-the-Hill and were moved for the winter to Moreton-in-the-Marsh. Profits could be better achieved where much of the washing and shearing was done by estate tenants for free (Miller 1991). The monastic estates also jealously guarded their special trading rights, which allowed them to convey the wool across England free of toll, the lay brothers of the Cistercians being especially useful for this purpose (Farmer 1991, 350).

The wool trade seemed set to prosper, as demand remained high. However, nothing escaped the scourge of the Black Death, which wrought havoc across the country in 1348-9. One survivor reminiscing about the scenes of this period later in life described how sheep and cattle wandered about unattended and how the sheep in some flocks all died of disease (Lumby 1895), presumably starved as a result of not being tended. Prices of goods plummeted, but the price of labour increased, so that society was shaken to its core. Once the shock had receded this created an ideal situation for landowners and those with access to grazing to increase their flocks, and it was not long before the survivors started cashing in on their good luck.

The wool business seems to have remained remarkably unaffected by the Black Death, especially given that half of its customers for cloth had probably perished. This buoyancy can be seen in the estate accounts of some of the larger monastic institutions, which provide a detailed picture of the later fourteenth century. Large consignments of Cotswold wool were still being sent abroad within a generation of the first appearance of the plague. In 1389 the Worcester Bishopric estate was owed £465, of which £261 was the arrears of a single manor Blockley where the Chipping Campden wool merchant William Grevel (19) owed, for instance, £134 for the previous summer's wool clip (Dyer 1980). Blockley was the centre of the bishop's wool business, and, even if sheared elsewhere, in June the fleeces were carried to Blockley. This system kept the ewes and lambs on lowland pasture, while the wethers – 50 per cent of the flock – were kept on upland pastures, and the bishop's Cotswold flocks seem to have been expanding in this period, as Bibury in 1381-2 had 344 mainly wethers, but 600 by the following June, and then 327 in September (Dyer 1980).

Flocks were moved about, so, for instance, in late spring 1381-2 214 ewes and lambs were moved from Ripple in Worcestershire to Bibury in Gloucestershire for May to August. This was a distance of 28 miles (45km). Blockley had sheep from Fladbury and Kempsey (Worcestershire), Hampton (Lucy) and Stratford (Warwickshire) in 1384, while in April 1394 there were 127 Kempsey and 224 Bredon sheep from south Worcestershire moved to Withington in the central

Cotswolds, estate fleeces weighing at this time about 1⅓-2½lb (0.6-1.1kg; Dyer 1980). Clearly wool was the way to make money, so, for instance, Bibury yielded £11 13s 9d from its wool business out of a total of around £18 in 1393-4, and sheep rearing was widely practised as tithes paid at Bishop's Cleeve in the late fourteenth century show that 1,020-1,340 lambs were born each year to sheep kept by the tenants, with wool production being about 14 sacks from 3,000-4,000 sheep in the parish (Dyer 1980, 329). These figures suggest a healthy rural scene, at least in terms of livestock, which belies the devastation of the Black Death in the previous generation.

While some upland Cotswold settlements were being reported as deserted in 1380-1, investment in special buildings to house the sheep continued, especially on the higher ground. In 1384 the bishop of Worcester built a great sheep-cote of eight bays at Blockley rectory at a cost of more than £14. The scale of this work is reflected in the roof needing 28,700 stone tiles from the Snowshill quarries. In 1384, 1,110 sheep were sheared at Blockley and 2,014 sheep from other manors belonging to the bishop (Hilton and Rahtz 1966, 85).

The tendency to keep enlarging flocks was apparent throughout the century both before and after the Black Death. Even by 1341 there are indications that some Cotswold villages are failing to cultivate land and that the tenants were leaving (Dyer 1988). This process was probably being encouraged by actions of those such as Lord Berkeley, who in 1330 bought the Cotswold manor of Beverstone and then also bought out many freeholders who held lands (probably used for arable) intermixed with the demesne lands. He then stocked the new ground with 1,500 wethers (Finberg 1975, 85). Three years later he sheared (not personally mind you!) nearly 6,000 sheep from Beverstone and the adjoining manors. The land north of Berkeley, with the addition of Beverstone, had become an enormous sheep run in the early fourteenth century, which was shared with the abbot of Kingswood, and disputes arose between the two indicating that the abbot owed folding services to the Berkeley estate (Perry 1986). As a distant echo of this industry a scene depicting woollen manufacture once adorned Beverston church (Brill 1968, 140).

Monastic institutions may have followed the same plan to extend their pastures, either deliberately or by default of desertion. Examples may be Aylworth, belonging to Llanthony Priory where the village was made into a sheep run in the fourteenth century, and Harford (Aylworth), which belonged to the Knights Templar (Smith 1976). One consequence of the increase in sheep numbers seems to have been large-scale sheep rustling. Rustlers were reckoned, for instance, to have stolen 1,000 sheep from the Tewkesbury Abbey flock in 1340 (Smith and Ralph 1996).

Very large estates could operate complex husbandry arrangements. For instance, the Hungerford estate had culled stock from Colerne (Gloucestershire) being fattened at Farleigh Hungerford (Somerset), and in the 1380s it was receiving ewe sheep from Down Ampney (Gloucestershire) and elsewhere (*AgHEW* III, 293). The intention was to be self-sufficient, and outside sheep were generally only bought in after great losses from disease. But, even without this occurring that often, sheep clearly moved around the region in large numbers and there seems to have been little to indicate concern about breeds in the course of these movements. Close management of the sheep is more the theme that chimes with the sources. This management had the desired effect, as wool weight seems to have increased in this period.

SHEEP-COTES

The sheep-cote or sheep-house (Latin *bercaria*) was used in England and in parts of continental Europe (Dyer 1995, 136). In the thirteenth century Walter of Henley, who is the best known of medieval writers on agriculture, advised that 'sheep be housed from Martinmas until Easter', that is from 11 November. In the Cotswolds these buildings usually had stone foundations and, quite often, stone gable ends, and were generally long narrow buildings up to 210ft (64m) long, and 23ft (7m) wide internally (Dyer 1995, see *28*). Until the late fourteenth century they appear to have been thatched (cf *30*), but from then on there is documentary evidence for tiled roofs. There are sometimes smaller buildings and enclosures in association, and

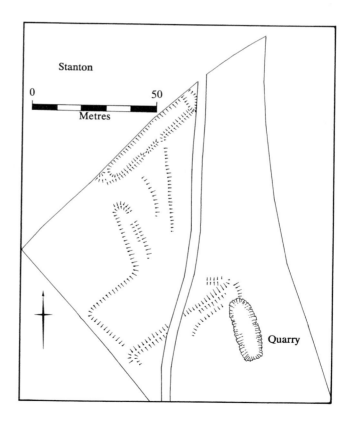

28 Plan of Stanton sheep-cote in the Cotswolds (from Dyer 1995). © *Society for Medieval Archaeology and reproduced by permission of the editor*

they could form part of the manorial farmyard, and on archaeological grounds the *bercaria* have been dated to the thirteenth–fifteenth centuries (Dyer 1995). They were generally set up in remote locations, often near upland pastures at above 600ft (183m), but in slightly sheltered positions, and both Church and lay manors invested in these structures. Sometimes they were used to keep sheep segregated from each other, for example at the 'hoggasters' sheep-cote' at Minchinhampton in 1329-30, as part of the management of large flocks. Sheep-cotes were particularly important for shelter, as it was thought that 'cotted' sheep produced better fleeces, and that the animals were healthier, and, when landlords leased out the demesne, but retained the sheep, the sheep-cotes were also retained.

Sheep-cotes were also lofted as they were used to store hay which was delivered to them in the summer and autumn, and the consumption over the winter is sometimes accounted for, with in 1380-1 30 wainloads of hay being consumed by 273 wintering hoggasters together with peas and oats (Dyer 1995, 152). Straw was also needed, and so much material may have required some of the auxiliary buildings sited next to the sheep-cotes in remote sites, and this also meant that the sheep-cotes would be sited near to tracks. Walter of Henley suggested scattering straw and marl on the floor every fortnight so that there would be a rich mixture ready for the fields at the end of the winter, and so the sheep-cotes were also a valuable source of manure. A gang of 20 workmen is recorded as removing the manure to the fields at Bishop's Cleeve in 1393-4 (Dyer 1995, 155) suggesting that a festering mountain of ordure was left by the cotting of the sheep. Folding continued this process of injecting manure into the ground in the better seasons of the year, and so it was handy to have sheep-cotes close to the arable as well. These buildings were also used for lambing when the shepherd was expected to stay at the sheep-cote overnight. Some ewes in the thirteenth century were milked in the summer, and so there may have been dairying facilities, and this may have been practised by the shepherds for their own use.

Sheep-cotes were, therefore, standard manorial buildings with many related applications. Sometimes there was more than one, as at Blockley where a tiled building of eight bays had been built as a second sheep-cote in 1383-4. They could also occur on peasant farms. Since one of their principal uses was for shelter, about 1m² should be allowed for each sheep. This tallies well with a standard flock being 300, though sometimes, as at Charlton Abbots, pasture could accommodate more sheep, i.e. 500 in the summer declining to 300 in the winter (Dyer 1995, 151). For instance, the earthworks of an upland sheep-cote at Stanton (*29*) suggest a floor area of about 350m² in a building probably 50m long, though damage at its east end introduces some uncertainty about its exact proportions. This would have been a large enough building to house the typical medieval flock of 300 sheep. A fifteenth-century French illustration shows how the sheep-cote may have looked in the winter (*30*), though this example suggests that ventilation was also necessary, at the same time as having the sheep packed together to maintain their warmth.

29 Site of Stanton sheep-cote. The rear of the building was where the field wall now stands to the right and the other side of the building is represented by the low earthwork running back into the field from the centre foreground

30 A sheep-cote as shown in the early fifteenth century *Les Très Riches Heures* of Jean, the Duc de Berry (month of February). *Illustrated by Carolyn Hunt*

Hay was in short supply in the Cotswolds and many manors had estate links to meadows along the River Thames in an attempt to maintain adequate supplies for livestock over the winter (Dyer 1995). Bibury had its hay from a meadow at Inglesham in Wiltshire (12km away), the Knights Templar at Temple Guiting from a meadow at Bourton-on-the-Water on the River Windrush (10km away), Daglingworth from Minety Salperton, Wall in Aldsworth from Latton, and Aldsworth and Coln St Aldwyns from Kempsford (Dyer 1995, 158).

The sheep-cotes of the fourteenth century were very high-quality structures presumably because this was a serious investment in a profitable business, where Cotswold wool had a high reputation. Each Cotswold fleece was heavier than average and was worth 8-12d to the producer (Dyer 1995, 156). A 'standard' 12-bay sheep-cote building in the late fourteenth century would have cost about £20, and this was nearly double the cash profit from Bibury wool in 1393-4. Bishop's Cleeve had most of Cleeve Hill for grazing and could have 1,000 sheep in the summer and 200 (usually hardier wethers) on the hills in the winter in 1299. Ewes and lambs had a shorter summer hill grazing the traditional end of which was 11 November and so sheep-cotes were needed both on the hills and in the lowlands as they were used to tend different parts of the flock. On the Gloucester Abbey estate the transhumance continued into the sixteenth century with the uplands sheep-cote at Aldsworth housing 360 wethers, while the 240 ewes were kept in the Severn Valley at Maisemore sheep-cote.

As the tendency for the lord to lease out assets increased, the sheep were also leased with their pasture, and this split up a previously integrated system, so that transhumance declined. Flocks were now maintained by purchase rather than by breeding from within the flock. In the fifteenth century sheep-cotes could be built to be leased out (e.g. at Dowdeswell). A lessee in Blockley may have established a second sheep-cote in the parish on the ruins of a deserted medieval village at Upper Ditchford (Dyer 1995, 158). Sheep-cotes were sometimes even established on the site of an abandoned peasant house (Dyer 1995, 155), probably using building materials from the abandoned property. With increasing pasture in the fifteenth–sixteenth centuries this was the heyday of the sheep-cote. They were implicated in the conversion to pasture from arable and the desertion of settlements that was reflected in mid-sixteenth century sentiments such as 'the decaye of England only by the great multitude of shepe' (Tawney and Power 1924a). But even sheep-cotes eventually had their day, and many were later converted into domestic dwellings by the seventeenth century.

Sheep-cotes formed part of a landscape-wide system that also included the lowland manorial centres where the sheep were gathered for the summer washing and shearing, such as Blockley for the bishop of Worcester, Bourton-on-the-Hill for Westminster Abbey, Sherborne for Winchcombe Abbey and Brimpsfield for the earls of March. These had comfortable accommodation for the officials, as well as being convenient places for them to get to with their baggage in contrast with the often remote sheep-cote which had few facilities, and was only regularly frequented by the hardy shepherd.

EXPORTING WOOL

It has been estimated that the wool of 8 million sheep was exported in the early fourteenth century (Campbell 1997, 243). This was the beginning of the heyday in Southampton's trade in wool, while some ports that might have been thought to participate in this trade were hardly represented (e.g. Bristol; Lloyd 1982, 226). In the early fourteenth century the king of France closed the Champagne fairs to the Flemish, and in 1307 and 1311 drove out the Italians on the pretext that they had contravened the canonical law against usury (Thompson 1931, 256). This may have had the effect of encouraging the direct supply of these countries from England, so that more foreign merchants descended on England. Southampton became one of the main beneficiaries, as it was a royal port far enough from London that the king was able to act independently. It was an entrepot that had an economic impact on a wide region reaching as far as the central Midlands, and Gloucestershire certainly fell within its area of influence (Platt *et al* 1975).

During the fourteenth century wool exports were reaching their peak, but this is also the period in which cloth production for export began to dominate the export trade from England. English wool prices recovered in the early fourteenth century, and this trade peaked at 40,000 sacks per year on average in 1304-9, only to recede again with the Hundred Years War of 1338-1453 (Hallam 1988, 730; Lockett 1974), so farming sheep at this time must have been a precarious business. Sheep were prone to disease and in the thirteenth and fourteenth centuries whole flocks could sometimes be reduced to under half their size, heavy rainfall being one of the worst enemies (Hallam 1988, 755). Taxes were serving to lower prices achieved by wool growers, and the heavy subsidy and tax of 40s per sack imposed in 1338 must have hit wool growers' profits hard, as the merchants will have passed on the tax as lower prices being offered to the wool growers. But the political situation was also important. The cloth trade of Flanders was being disrupted by wars and this gave English weavers a chance to increase their production, and even when the wool exports resumed they were now accompanied by a 33 per cent tax, again giving an advantage to the English weavers. Between 1350-1400 the amount of cloth produced at home may have increased seven-fold. This trade, once established, was profoundly important to the English economy right up until the nineteenth century, and, as it relied on homegrown raw materials, it was not so readily prone to foreign interference (Lockett 1974).

The wool trade was, in contrast, sometimes in a nervous state due to its precarious market abroad and increasingly the interference of the king and his merchant friends, who both saw it as an easy source of ready cash. A sign of this was when in 1306 William Combemartin, a London merchant, was accused at Gloucester of spreading a rumour at Northleach, Cirencester and Tetbury fairs that the king was going 'to take all wool', thereby pushing down prices (Hilton 1966, 180). These three places were presumably the chief wool fairs at the time.

The centralised methods of production favoured by the monasteries helped to streamline the export of the wool. As well as founding towns in the previous century, where trade could be organised, the monastic estates maintained their annual centralised gathering of sheep for washing and shearing. An example would be Llanthony Priory, which, as usual, gathered its sheep at Barrington for this major event in its rural calendar. The most highly assessed taxpayer of Great Barrington in 1327 was named Shepherd (*Gloucestershire VCH* VI), and this may have been the master shepherd. In 1319 a Cirencester merchant bought wool in Barrington from the priory, and specified that it must be 'good, dry and well cleaned' and from the priory's own sheep if possible, though, if not, it could be supplemented from elsewhere. Monastic wool was still at a premium, especially for export.

Local towns, and especially Northleach, were important as collecting points for wool, and the wool would often be stored there before being moved elsewhere. This must have provided work for carriers as well. In 1338 the rate for the carriage of the king's wool from Gloucester to London was 4s per sarpler, compared to 6s per sarpler from Hereford. Conveyance by water could be much cheaper and in 1388 part of the wool from Oxfordshire was assembled at Oxford before being carried overland to Henley, and then by boat to London at only 6d per sarpler (Willard 1926). Travel, however, could be hazardous, and valuable goods, such as wool and the cash involved in its purchase, could be tempting to thieves, as when a London merchant was killed on (Minchin-) Hampton Down and robbed of £40 in about 1372 (Watson 1932, 281).

Wool obviously remained important for the rural economy, whether it was exported or used at home. Across the Cotswolds the producers of the previous century continued to see good profits, and sheep featured prominently in the plans of large landowners. Successful wool merchants sometimes retired to the Cotswolds from London, having got to know the area well in the course of their travels, and William Grevel is the most famous example of this.

CLOTH MAKING IN THE COTSWOLDS

The making of cloth in England was being increasingly regulated in the fourteenth century, a sign that it was becoming a valuable industry, since the authorities were becoming interested in it as a source of revenue. Once under way it will have absorbed much of the local Cotswold wool, though without leaving the same degree of historical documentation that was associated with exported wool. This could lead to a misconception that home wool production was in decline, when it is more likely that wool had simply been diverted to home cloth manufacture. Since the Cotswolds was one of the chief areas for this development, it also seems likely that Cotswold wool was one of the main ingredients in this rising industry.

Cloth production now became a major occupation in some West Country towns such as Bristol, Winchester and Salisbury. Cloth was also coming into Bristol for export though it is less easy to tell whereabouts in the countryside it was coming from. When Thomas atte Hay, one of the founders of the Bristol Guild of St Katherine (the weavers' guild) left £20 for repairing roads from Bristol to Gloucester and from Bristol to Almondsbury, this probably suggests some of the main routes he had plied when buying cloths outside Bristol (Brill 1968, 140).

Fortunately the guild system is well documented for Bristol from 1346, and so the workings of an English cloth-making town in the West Country are more evident. The guilds as usual insisted on a high standard of workmanship, which, if infringed, led to an extreme penalty, the destruction of looms and cloth (Ponting 1957, 12), or, in the case of the fuller, being banned from working for a year. Daily wages were set, such as 4d for the fullers, 2d for those stretching the fulled cloth and 1d for the 'wedestere' who dealt with minor cloth imperfections. The guild rules were designed especially to keep the work of spinning in the city, and in the latter case the use of oil and combing are specified (Myers 1969, 1053). The dyers had their own guild that regulated the sale, storage, and use of dye-stuffs, and the town was also on its guard against merchants trying to corner the market.

However, this was a period when restrictive practices in the towns encouraged cloth production in the countryside. For instance, the ban on urban weavers doing any night working (Myers 1969, 1053) must have seemed an imposition to an ambitious and industrious cloth maker. The towns also discouraged the setting up of fulling mills in the countryside, and so, for instance, a 1346 ordinance at Bristol forbade both the sending of cloths outside the town, or the import of rural cloths for processing. Relations with the countryside had deteriorated so badly by 1355 that Bristol weavers were banned from using yarn produced outside the town. Similar battles were being fought in the countryside where local landlords were insisting that cloth should be fulled at their mill, and so, for instance, at Hawkesbury in south Cotswold 'Matilda' was fined in 1325-6 for fulling her cloth elsewhere (Carus-Wilson 1954). By the end of the fourteenth century Bristol dyers were also being closely regulated on the initiative of the local merchants who were concerned about their dwindling exports (Dyer 2002b), as the local urban industry declined.

The expanding foreign market for cloth, encumbered with only 2 per cent taxation as opposed to 33 per cent for wool (Carus-Wilson 1952), and the willing labour in the countryside made for a successful combination with the focus for this new West Country industrial growth being in the countryside, especially to the south-east and east of Bristol. So the main rural areas to expand cloth making were along the Somerset and Wiltshire borders, and in north-west Wiltshire, as well as the Stroud area of Gloucestershire. These new areas looked to London as the point of export rather than Bristol (Ponting 1957, 27).

Textile manufacture saw the emergence of wage earners in the fourteenth century paid by the piece, which was a move away from the ownership of the product as was practised by the urban guild members. These wage earners, however, owned their own equipment, and so it was not yet fully a factory system, though capital (of the clothiers) was necessary because of the complexity of the processes involved, and this capital was drawn into cloth making by the profits to be made (Lipson 1953, 69). However, there were early moves by some clothiers to gather weavers and others under their own roofs, such as by Thomas Blanket in Bristol in 1339 (Lipson 1953, 72), which produced a system far closer to a factory. Weavers from Flanders and elsewhere were also welcomed, for example at Stow-on-the-Wold (Carus-Wilson 1952). Sometimes the welcome was more coerced as when an invitation to Flemish weavers to settle in England was accompanied by an import ban on Flemish cloth, which was part of the diplomatic manoeuvring at the beginning of the war with France (Ponting 1957, 33). The home textile makers were, therefore, generally assisted by the foreign conflicts of the day.

With the general increase in cloth making the fulling mill continued to appear in the countryside along the local rivers. For instance, a mill, worth 4s 3d per annum, was built around 1300, at *Bremescumbe* in Minchinhampton, and this manor, which was in the hands of Caen Abbey (Normandy), had been heavily engaged in sheep rearing from at least the 1170s. Typically the customary duties of the tenants on this manor were the usual rural ones of haymaking and ploughing (Watson 1932, 295), but cloth making was also represented by rent for the digging of fuller's earth (for 20d), where seven persons were identified (of which four were named fuller). This suggests that the local demand for fuller's earth was on a considerable scale (Watson 1932, 323), and that cloth making was being encouraged locally. There was also a wool-house attached to the manor house from the early fourteenth century, presumably showing that wool was being stockpiled locally.

Winchcombe was also now building up its own cloth industry and indications of this are evident in the tolls being raised in the town. The town was profiting from tolls on wool, to which were added tolls on woad, teasels and alum (Royce 1892). Early in the fourteenth century Winchcombe Abbey also acquired yet another fulling mill belonging to Will Aderwyne at *Cotes iuxta Winchcombe* (Perry 1945, 52). St Kenelm's fair (28 July) at Winchcombe was an occasion for cloth sales (Perry 1945, 52–3), and this was another way in which the town gained from the industry. But the future lay with the rural cloth makers who were, for instance, setting up by *c*.1300 on the banks of the River Frome in an area later to be known as Stroudwater (Miller 1965). This was soon to become a rural cloth-making district famous for its cloth.

During the thirteenth century more allowances had been made for variable length and width of cloth, but this changed in the fourteenth century as greater standardisation was brought in. Accordingly the statute of Northampton in 1328 did away with the 2yd width for high-quality English cloth, and stipulated only two sizes of cloth: 'ray cloth' before fulling was to measure 28yds (25.6m) by 6 quarters (1.4m), and 'coloured cloth' 26yds (23.7m) by 6½ quarters (1.5m), though after 1336/7 length was left open. These regulations were cancelled in1353, and the king introduced a system for checking and sealing cloth at 4d each for every cloth sealed. From 1373 the regulations were again restored and into the fifteenth century there were many minor changes but cloth width was the primary concern. In 1464/5 this was set for broadcloth at 2yds (1.8m) or 7 quarters (1.6m), and the length after fulling at 24yds (21.9m), which was equivalent to a length of 28yds (25.6m) before fulling (Bridbury 1982, appendix A). Though the weight of cloth is never specified it has been calculated that one sack of wool stretched to making 4⅓ broadcloths (Carus-Wilson 1954).

THE ITALIAN CONNECTION

Traders in woollen goods were already prominent in Florence in the eleventh–twelfth centuries (Thompson 1931, 259), and the wool guild there was in existence by 1138, and the cloth guild by 1212. The elder Boccaccio, an agent of the Bardi, and Giotto, the artist, appear in their records, the latter for renting out an 'English' loom for six months. By the mid-twelfth century the Florentines were present at the Champagne fairs in France buying foreign wool and *panni Fraceschi* (Flemish cloth), the latter for resale once it had undergone more specialised processing back in Italy to enhance its eventual value (Thompson 1931, 260). Florence achieved all this, despite not having its own port or ships until the fifteenth century (Thompson 1931, 277). The Florentines were particularly in favour of the wool industry, and the Datini company moved there from Prato for this reason, but the industry was ruthlessly controlled so that the urban worker, as in the Flemish towns, was quite oppressed (Origo 1957).

However, the Italians were above all bankers whose businesses stretched across Europe. In the thirteenth century these Italian businesses kept *fondachi* (trading posts) in Italian cities and beyond, which were used for storing wool trade items, and which doubled up as banking halls and lodgings for merchants. For instance, the Velluti had such buildings in Paris and in London, as well as in Italy. Their speciality was loaning money to kings, and so the firm of Berto Frescobaldi borrowed 200,000 gold florins for Edward I in 1295, which was money raised partly in Florence. But the Italians also had a keen eye for where money could be made, and as the king's creditors they were no doubt in a position to win favours such as lucrative export licences. They were on such good terms with the English king, who was in their debt, that sometimes they could even make use of the king's own ships when sailing from Southampton, much to the chagrin of English merchants.

Italian merchants had long had an interest in acquiring English wool, which even in the eleventh century had been reaching Florence (Ruddock 1951, 15).

In 1200 English wool was making its way to Italy amongst other wool bought by Italian merchants in Flanders. Papal tax collectors travelling in England will have seen, especially when they visited the monasteries run by the Cistercian monks, that sheep were being farmed on a large scale, and that wool was available. In their travels they were also able to spot opportunities for purchasing raw materials in bulk, and were able to take over the delivery of important raw materials across Europe as an outlet for their banking activity. Papal finances benefited from some of the high prices that Italian merchants would pay, and it is possible that the Italian purchase of English wool was even encouraged by the papal officials.

Trade with Italy was also certainly encouraged by the English Crown from at least 1224. The English kings, such as Edward I, had to borrow money to maintain their spending, and these wealthy Italian entrepreneurs were a convenient source of cash. The Florentines had been given the general right in c.1250 to travel and trade in England, and under Edward I the Florentines became the most prominent of the Italian merchants. Throughout the thirteenth century the Italians were shipping out wool, but mainly from eastern England, and especially from the port of Boston. The Florentines were prominently active at this time, while the Italians as a whole had about 10 per cent of the total wool export trade from England in 1274, specialising in the high-quality end of the market (Fryde 1974).

The port of Southampton was doing some trade in wool from the late thirteenth century when 1272 Peter de Lyon and Henry le Fleming were exporting wool by licence (Platt 1973). Both foreign (mainly Italian) and English merchants were involved, and by 1287-8 the wool custom from Southampton was worth over £696 showing the rapid growth in wool exports from this port. However, up to the 1290s the Florentines, and occasionally the Lucchese (from Lucca), do not seem to have looked much beyond the nearby abbeys of Beaulieu and Netley from their base in Southampton. Perhaps they already had sufficient wool from eastern England not to look further afield. But they were venturing as far inland as Winchester in c.1300, and, once the quality of wool from this area was appreciated by the Italians, they overcame their fears and switched all their efforts away from eastern England to Southampton. This change was under way in the fourteenth century, and it was also convenient for vessels returning from Flanders to put in at Southampton on the way back to Italy.

After the expulsion of the Jews in 1290, the Florentines took over the domestic banking system of England. Their wool interests were also thriving, and in the later thirteenth century the Ricomani family, for instance, had fixed contracts for future shearings with 33 clients of which 25 were monasteries, so that at this time around 25 per cent of all the wool exported from England was exported by the Italians, half of which was by the Florentines (Thompson 1931, 265). The Florentines specialised in making contracts covering several future years, as opposed to the one year of future wool which most merchants dealt in. As buyers they were, therefore, welcomed by the wool growers, though they will have tended only to deal with the largest producers, such as the English monasteries. This may have limited their appeal, but their business must have helped to maintain the wool price.

Throughout most of the thirteenth century the Florentines had also been particularly privileged traders in France (Thompson 1931, 262), though eventually the king of France overtaxed the Flemish traders and thereby disrupted this lucrative trade route in around 1300. Then the Italians had chosen to go directly to Flanders and England (Thompson 1931, 262), especially via the port of Marseilles, where several Italian firms were established in the mid- to late thirteenth century, including the Medici, who became the leading merchants of the region. The Florentines had, therefore, been successfully manoeuvring throughout the thirteenth century to protect their interests in English wool, and the means of transporting it back to Italy. This was particularly precarious as the Florentines, lacking control of their own access to the Mediterranean, were initially dependent on the Genoese as their main carriers, the latter bringing alum to English ports since at least 1298 (Harwood 2000).

Though Florentine cloth had an export market in the thirteenth century, it was of low quality compared with the cloth from north-west Europe (Hoshino 1983). The troubled markets in the Flemish cities in the early fourteenth century may have had beneficial consequences far away in Italy, where the disruption of Flemish cloth imports based on high-quality English wool stimulated the Italian cloth industry to higher levels of quality. But progress was not always easy. At the death of Edward I in 1307 most of the financial administration was in the hands of the Florentine firm of Frescobaldi, who had become the chief creditors of the English king after the bankruptcy of the Riccardi of Lucca in 1290. Their position was so strong that the Frescobaldi actually controlled the collection of customs in Southampton and at other ports, and took any monies accruing from these sources as repayment of English debt. Relationships with the English were eventually strained by the extent to which the king had become indebted to the Italians. Aware of this tension one Frescobabldi advised all Italian merchants in England to only wear drab cloths and to behave humbly (Holmes 1960). Though Edward II might have been keen on the Italians, state officials, not to mention the populace, resented them immensely, so that in 1311 the Frescobaldi (despite the drab cloths!) were expelled from England to great popular acclaim.

Dislike of foreigners, and especially of Italians, was now intensifying, but the wool trade carried on. In 1320 some Florentine merchants bringing wool to Southampton for export took the trouble to get royal letters of protection before entering the town. This had a serious effect on the Venetian trade in particular, as they tended to arrive in port in a grand way in their fleet of large ships. Much English effort went into trying to reverse this, but it was many years before it was overcome, mainly because the Venetians themselves did not at the time require English wool of high quality as much as the Florentines. So the

Venetians instead established a trading colony in Bruges, which was an outlet for their exotic goods (Ruddock 1951, 26). Any wool they needed was picked up in Flanders. Even the Genoese may have avoided Southampton, though the Florentines (mainly associated with the firms of Bardi and Peruzzi, who were taking over from the expelled Frescobaldi) still persisted in having wool delivered into Southampton for shipment out by sea.

From at least the 1320s a change in tempo becomes clearer. The rise in Florentine quality has links with the presence of Italians in England who were dealing in English wool, and sending it back to Florence. Francesco Pegolotti himself was a Florentine merchant working for the Bardi of Antwerp in 1315 (Thompson 1931, 263). He carefully categorised English wool in three qualities: 'best' (*buona*), 'middle quality' (*moiana*), and 'loose pieces' (*locchi*). Florentine documents used *lana lunga* (literally 'long wool') and *lana gentile* (soft wool) as terms for the best quality wool, and *agnellina* (meaning too soft for the processing needed for highest quality cloth) for the lesser quality cloth. The reference to long wool is tantalising and may suggest that some of the best wool included longer than normal fibres that were still fine.

The very best English wool in Italian eyes was the same as that sought after by the Flemish. It was identified by the Italians with particular parts of the English countryside: *Bincestro* (Winchester), *Contisgualdo* (the Cotswolds) and *Marcia* (the Marches; i.e. Herefordshire and Shropshire; Hoshino 1983, 194). These English wools continued to be imported even after the Bardi and Peruzzi companies had failed, as other Florentine merchants took over the trade in their place. The Florentine chronicler Giovanni Villani recorded that by 1336-8 English wool had transformed the wool industry in his city, as the cloths now being made were worth twice as much as before because of the fineness of quality that was possible with the new English wool (Mazzaoui 1981, 134). Fortunately the market was capable of absorbing these high-quality and therefore expensive cloths, as there was no shortage of rich people who wanted to display their wealth. Problems with the supply of English wool did, however, cause an influx of Spanish wool by mid century (Mazzaoui 1981, 134), and this was of comparable quality, and so the stage was set for the eventual eclipse of English wool, should its supply or quality ever prove a problem in future.

Meanwhile the attraction of the high-quality Cotswold wool ensured that the Italian merchants that visited Southampton in search of wool continued to visit year after year, despite the long and arduous journey involved. In the early fourteenth century they had mainly exported Lincolnshire wool via the port of Hull, but this was a more difficult journey to make as the fourteenth century wore on and the French became more of a danger to English allies. In 1337 Edward III instituted a great series of taxes to finance his war with France, and the success of the wool trade was fundamental to the royal income, as part of the finances rested on loans from the foreign wool merchants. The Italians were prominent in this arrangement and the Florentines in particular (namely the

Bardi and Peruzzi). When the Genoese eventually joined the French side, the Italian wool was then sent back to Italy in Spanish ships! (Ruddock 1951).

Into the second half of the fourteenth century the interest of the Florentines in English wool for their home cloth industry remained strong. One Florentine agency, the Del Bene company, acquired about 66 tons of English wool which was mainly *Marcia* and *Contisgualdo*. The customs situation in England may have contributed to the exporting to Italy of mainly the best wool after the 1330s, as the new tax brought in at the beginning of the Hundred Years War was raised on quantity not quality. By 1340 the Florentine cloth industry was so specialised that there were 200 cloth-related lines of business (Thompson 1931, 257). They were especially proficient at dyeing, and produced bright colours, which were favoured in the East, where some of their principal markets lay (Thompson 1931, 268), and guild regulations were enforced to ensure that dyes were permanent (Thompson 1931, 279). The best quality Florentine cloth of all, which was made exclusively from English wool in the mid- to late fourteenth century, was the *panno di San Martino*, named after that part of Florence where it was made (Hoshino 1983, 203).

The direct contact with Italy was important for England as a whole, as it brought the country in contact with the most advanced industrialised societies of the time, and also indirectly established trade contacts with more distant markets to the east, which in turn guaranteed supplies of exotic spices and other luxurious goods. England became part of this high-class trade by supplying one of the essential raw materials – wool – that some European states relied upon. The new sea route from Southampton to Italy avoided the dangerous overland route that had been used for so many years previously. The sea route was also now possible because of great improvements in the design of shipping, especially in Genoa, which allowed ships to undertake long voyages along the Atlantic coast. Indeed this was probably a step on the way to the discovery of America later on in the next century. Occasionally Genoese ships had plied this route in the mid-thirteenth century, but now a regular service was put in place at first with the intention of reaching Bruges (Ruddock 1951, 19), a main market for wool, and where cloth could be bought for distribution in the Mediterranean. Later Southampton became the main port of call for Italian shipping, where wool and cloth were the principal goods being sought. This foreign trade was made even more valuable by the bulk importation of alum and woad, particularly by the Genoese (Power 1926), who carried woad from Lombardy. Woad was also imported from northern France, and in 1308-9 this accounted for 30 per cent of Southampton imports and was alone worth £3,779, while it accounted for up to 48 per cent in 1310-11 (£5,756; Lloyd 1982, 31). These materials all aided the continuing improvement of English cloth production.

Southampton was the key port for the Italian wool trade, chiefly because of its links with the Cotswolds and major towns in a hinterland that reached into the central Midlands. Salisbury was a convenient and major market, which then could easily be reached from Southampton by cart. And by the same route beyond Salisbury roads went to Burford, Stow, Chipping Campden, Stratford and Warwick (Platt 1973), all places extensively engaged in the wool and cloth trades, and all places where deals could be struck. Southampton also had established road links with Gloucester via Oxford. The wool carts arrived in Southampton mainly in October to December, whereas cloth came in over the winter and into the summer (Platt 1973). The trade in wool, and in the luxury goods imported in exchange such as spices, all enlivened the economy of the towns in this region, and provided the opportunity for contact with some of the most sophisticated of contemporary Europeans who were on the verge of the many great achievements of the Italian Renaissance.

Advances in shipping and navigational enterprise were also key to this era. The new Genoese ships were mainly merchant galleys carrying three masts together with a complement of 150 oarsmen, three to each oar (Lockett 1974), which meant that they could deal with adverse winds, and were dependable even when the wind dropped (cf 31). This made them less vulnerable to pirates and, besides their large crews, were often supplemented with bowmen. They were, therefore,

31 Antwerp harbour scene of c.1520 by an unknown artist showing one of the last of the Venetian galleys (centre), which had regularly carried wool back to Italy, and the new tall sailing ships. © Koninklijk Museum voor Schone Kunsten, Antwerp

defensible against attackers, which was essential in a period when even state fleets were able to engage in piracy without any official sanction. They were also capable of very large payloads which made them very efficient carriers of bulk goods. The earliest records of Genoese ships in English ports place them largely in London, and they usually arrived in July or August, and left soon afterwards in order to avoid the winter storms. These voyages were undertaken in ships owned by the first Genoese venture capitalists, such as the Spinola, Lomellini, and Zaccaria families. These merchant galleys by the early 1300s had a choice of London, Sandwich or Southampton as ports. The first documented named Genoese ship to pick up wool at Southampton had been the *Sanctus Nicholaus* owned by Guidetus and Janotus Spinola in 1305, which collected 400 sacks of wool.

The city of Venice followed a similar path to Genoa, firstly sailing to Flanders and then tending to concentrate on Southampton (Ruddock 1951, 22). In 1319 five Venetian galleys drew into Southampton, and this was typical of a Venetian arrival as they sailed in small fleets, which were state-organised ventures, in contrast to the Genoese habit of enterprising individualism. The Venetian trade tended as a result to be on an even larger and more organised scale, which made it rapidly very successful. A regular Venetian state fleet visited Flanders, and this was magnificently attended by a priest, a notary, two doctors, four musicians, and each vessel had 170 oarsmen, with 30 bowmen chosen by public contest in Venice, so that each vessel had a complement of above 200. In the 1330s the Venetians were assisting the wool sales from their state galleys by declaring that any wool brought overland had to pay 25 per cent duty, unless it arrived at least a month after the galleys (Brown 1864, 7).

In 1337 Southampton became the main port for the Italian trade in wool, and most of this trade involved the Bardi and Peruzzi, as the English king took steps to raise large sums of money for the war with France. This led to great freedom for Italian merchants to buy wool freely in England, so that by *c.*1400 they had built up a business which involved Cotswold sheep farmers in supplying most of the high-quality wool leaving by way of Southampton, and amounting to about one-fifth of the total wool export trade. Cotswold wool was, therefore, now centre stage in an important national trade network which played a major role in sustaining the national economic system. The wool always arrived in Southampton by cart. There was a parallel increase in local cloth production as well, and a growth in demand for Italian imports, as more people became wage earners and could afford some of the exotic Italian imports off-loaded at Southampton, though London remained the chief market for these. Expansion of cloth making was a significant factor as it meant that the textile manufacturing supplies that the Italians specialised in exporting could now be offloaded at Southampton. Bristol may have been the logical port in terms of its proximity to wool and cloth production centres, but it was too inconveniently placed for the Italians, who, therefore, favoured the development of overland routes from

Southampton into the Cotswolds, though London also remained important for them as Cotswold wool could easily be sent down the Thames valley by river, and London was now beginning to assume its dominant position as a port (Table 1).

Date	From Southampton	From London
1279–80	4364 (709 tons)	5870 (954 tons)
1329–30	2575 (418 tons)	10,976 (1783 tons)
1364–65	2543 (413 tons)	17,225 (2799 tons)

Table 1 Average wool exports (in sacks) from major ports. After Carus-Wilson and Coleman 1963

Most of the Genoese consignments of English wool were bound for Florence or Milan (Fryde 1974, 298-9). The Bardi (of Florence) in return for loans to the king were able to export wool free of duty up to 1341, and for instance in 1339 this privilege allowed them to export nearly 8,000 sacks, around 9 per cent of the total exported English wool, but because of the political situation they had ended up using Catalan vessels. Cotswold wool must have been involved, as when Southampton was attacked by the French in 1338, the incoming wool was diverted to Bristol. When the Nardi and other Florentine firms became bankrupt in 1342-6, the Leopardi of Asti started exporting from Southampton. In 1353-7 only aliens were able to export wool, presumably because the king was so badly in their debt. So in 1356 the Malabayla of Asti, to whom the king owed over £18,000, were allowed to export over 10,000 sacks (27 per cent of the total exported that year) at favourable rates of duty (Fryde 1983).

Unfortunately the detailed picture of Southampton trade closes in 1342, and does not open again until 1370, as the customs records are lost for that period. English merchants were also now engaged in exporting cloth from Bristol, as shown by surviving Bristol records of 1347-70, much of it presumably made with Cotswold wool. It is assumed that the main destination was Gascony, until war with France re-erupted in 1369. By the time the Southampton records recommence cloth exports have become more significant here as well. Once more it is the Italians who are key as they led this new export initiative. Southampton was already a clearing ground for textile supplies on a large scale, hinting at the growth of textile production in south-west England. Some confirmation of this growth is the appearance in the 1390s of cloths from the Cotswolds shipped from Southampton, and put on sale at the Datini cloth shop in Pisa (Fryde 1976, 347). The Italians were, therefore, at the head of a new export industry in the later fourteenth century with their exports of cloths from Southampton rising to over

5,000 per annum in 1383-4, and so they were instrumental in building up the cloth industry of the Cotswolds and surrounding area.

The Southampton trade in cloth-making supplies certainly continued to prosper. For instance in 1372 a Genoese ship called *Christopher* landed 52 bales of woad, 26 of alum, 20 of madder and 6 of brazil (a type of dye-stuff from the East Indies). The Genoese had fully regained control of the alum mines at Phocaea in 1381, and they started to use the biggest available ships. These ships carried hugely valuable cargoes and one vessel, on departure from Southampton, carrying cloth, wool and tin, was reckoned to be in charge of goods worth nearly £30,000 (over £100 million at today's values). Incoming cargo to Southampton during six months in 1387 on four Genoese ships comprised 959 bales of woad (alone worth £1,198), 476 bales of alum and some scarlet grain dye. Charges for space varied according to the value of goods. Alum and woad paid freight charges of 7-8 per cent of their purchase price, while wool being exported paid only around 4 per cent, with tin that was useful for ballast only paying around 3 per cent.

Venetian state galleys (*31*) returned to England from the 1390s, and the Florentine state fleet arrived regularly from 1425 to 1478, with Italian shipping and commerce in England peaking in the period 1390-1460 (Fryde 1974). In the fifteenth century the galleys were still preferred to the newer carracks, as the former were faster and more manoeuvrable in port. Their large size was also a big advantage, as they could cope with heavy seas and their large crews were useful if pirates hoved into view. The expense of putting such a large ship to sea was compensated, to some extent, by reduced insurance costs, and the higher freight charges that could be set. The largest Florentine galleys were about 138ft (42m) long, 25ft (7.6m) wide across the middle, and 9ft (2.7m) high amidships (Mallett 1967). As well as two or three masts for sails there were around 150 rowers arranged in threes who manned the 30ft (9.1m) long oars weighing up to 120lb (55.5kg) each. No wonder there was a Florentine regulation in 1442 that decreed that each ship should carry over 20 tons of biscuits, to ensure the rowers had enough energy to power these vessels. The same regulations also stipulated 2,000lb of soap which may have been to overcome the whiff of 150 straining rowers, though perhaps the soap was used to lubricate the rowing tackle.

One Italian family that had direct connections with the Cotswolds in this period were the Datini of Prato and later of Florence, and they kept detailed business records that have survived in quantity (Origo 1957). Francesco Datini ventured into the Cotswolds (*Chondisgualdo*), and especially frequented Northleach (*Norleccio*), Burford (*Boriforte*) and Cirencester (*Sirisestri*). Perhaps he did business with the unknown wool merchant whose brass in Northleach church is dated c.1400 (*32*). However, Francesco largely depended on the Tuscan firms based in London such as the Mannini and Caccini that had buyers already roaming the area, and was importing wool in 1382-1410. In 1397 Datini listed 38,749lb of wool at his Genoese branch mostly ready for selling on, as his workshop at Prato was too small to use all of this quantity of wool. A letter of

32 Brass in Northleach church of an unknown wool dealer of *c.*1400

1403 to the Datini in Florence refers to 1,000 ducats (about £166) being taken to the Cotswolds to buy wool. It was still the custom to buy in advance, and occasionally this backfired as the quality was below par, and so the Caccini of London wrote to Datini apologising for some wool from Cirencester Abbey, but adding 'one must buy in advance from all the abbeys, and especially from this one, which is considered the best' (Origo 1957, 71). The Cotswold fairs at Midsummer were a prime time to buy wool (Origo 1957), and so the Mannini recommended to Datini that around St John's Day (24 June) was the best time to buy wool (i.e. immediately after shearing). Datini also imported some English cloth, including undyed cloth from the Cotswolds.

8

The fifteenth century

... [English] wool and fabrics, considered the best in the world ...
(Extract from a letter by *Andreas Franciscus*, an Italian writing in London in 1497; Williams 1967)

By 1400 the amount of wool being exported from England was dropping to around 19,000 sacks per year from a peak of over 40,000, while exported cloth was now rising rapidly to about 40,000 cloths from only 4,500 in the mid-fourteenth century (Carus-Wilson and Coleman 1963, see *33*). Exports dropped to 14,200 sacks on average in 1400-30, and by 1450 some of the better wool was only fetching £4 6s (Munro 1978). By 1450-62 the annual export of raw wool and cloth taken together represented 15,690 sacks of wool, a considerable drop from earlier in the century, but by the early part of the following century the

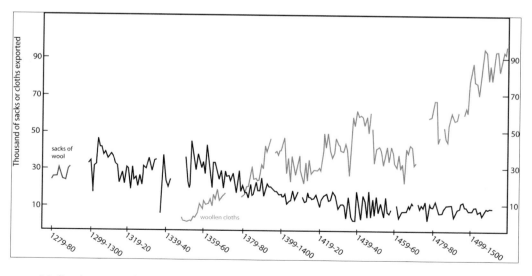

33 Medieval exports of wool and cloth based on Carus-Wilson and Coleman (1963, pp122-3, and pp138-9). *By permission of Oxford University Press*

same figure was over 30,000 sacks (Bowden 1967), and so the wool production industry obviously staged a strong recovery later in the fifteenth century.

Competition for the best wool could be keen and the freedom of the Italian merchants was to become a particular cause for resentment in this period, as is expressed in a political poem written in 1436/7:

> In Cotteswolde also they ryde aboute
> And al Englonde, and bein wythouten doute,
> What them liste, wythe fredome and fraunchise
> More than we Englisshe may getyn in any wyse.
> (*The Libelle of Englysche Polycye*; after Wright 1861)

TAXATION IN THE LATER FOURTEENTH AND FIFTEENTH CENTURIES

Government still took a keen interest in the wool industry. In 1390 the wool staple was removed back to English ports, and there was an attempt to revive an alien wool cartel as in the time of Edward III. A law in 1391 demanded that, for every sack of wool sold, the merchant was to bring an ounce of gold to the mint at Calais (Power 1933, fn 172). Strong opposition forced Richard II to restore the English wool trade and the Calais staple was re-established in 1392 (Munro 1979, 197). In the early 1400s there were laws to enforce a ban on the export of English coin or bullion. The use of counterfeit (underweight) English coins became a problem, and so in 1422 a mint was started at Calais to recoin suspect coin, and in 1430 the English king ordered that two-thirds of the wool price should be paid at the Calais staple in English coin (i.e. credit was denied) and the rest in bullion, where the latter was minted into English coin. This system was also intended to extort cash for paying the Calais garrison, where in return for full control over the wool trade a small clique of wool merchants provided a useful service to the king. This lasted to the 1460s and had the effect of ruining urban Flemish luxury cloth production, as it reduced wool imports from England to Flanders to 50 per cent of its level in the 1420s (Munro 1979, 116).

THE WOOL TRADE

Besides the taxation vagaries of the English king who was constantly trying to extract more income from international trade, any foreign merchants had the prejudices of the English to contend with. Disruption to the foreign involvement in the wool and cloth trade sometimes arose because of direct antagonism against foreigners. The early 1400s was a period when this had an impact, for in 1405 the Italian wool buyers dared not travel inland in England. Local uprisings also threatened foreigners in Romsey near Southampton, where cloths from the Low

Countries were being finished before being re-exported to the Mediterranean. Only the ability of Southampton to protect foreign merchants within its own jurisdiction allowed their continuing operation (Fryde 1991, 805), and the continuance of the profitable trade with Italy which this port thrived on. This was important for the Cotswolds as nearly all the wool exported via this port was from this region (Ruddock 1951, 89).

In 1421 wool was still contributing 80 per cent of customs revenue (Lipson 1953, 16). A fifteenth-century pamphleteer saw wool as the means whereby the English 'might rule and govern all Christian kings'. It is celebrated by the poet John Lydgate (*c.*1370-1450):

Off Brutis Albion his wolle is cheeff richesse,

In prys surmountyng euery othir thyng

Sauf greyn and corn: marchauntis al expresse

Wolle is cheeff tresour in this land growyng:

To riche and poore this beeste fynt clothyng:

Alle naciouns afferme up to the fulle,

In al the world ther is no bettir wolle.

(Extract from *The debate of the horse, goose, and sheep*)

But the amount of exported wool was now beginning to decline, and by the 1430s was at about one-third of volumes achieved at its peak (Bridbury 1982, 92). In contrast English cloth exports rose to new record highs, such as 46,748 cloths in 1401/2. Spanish wool, which also offered good quality, was now making inroads in Flanders to compensate for the poor value of English wool due to its heavy tax burden. Cotswold wool, however, went against this trend, and managed to increase its importance amongst English wools compared to that of other English regions in this period. There was also a switch to a greater emphasis on woolfells than shorn fleeces by the later fifteenth century, the tax regime being the main incentive for this (Lloyd 1977).

Despite advances by the Spanish wool importers English wool maintained its commodity status for the moment, and it still remained essential to the economies of some European cities. The Italians were again active by the 1440s buying wool from the abbeys raising sheep in the Cotswolds (Power 1933), and they were still able to enjoy long credit beyond the more usual two years, presumably as they still paid high prices. If the English wool failed to arrive, as at Leyden in 1445 and at Venice late in 1485 (Power 1933, 365), then whole city economies could be threatened with disaster. In particular the urban poor depended on the work provided by wool processing. With certain types of English sheep being so valuable steps were taken to prevent their export, as in 1425 (Read 1865), presumably in an effort to prevent any foreign competition from benefiting.

Wool remained so valuable that even moving it long distances did not noticeably alter its cost at the point of sale. On occasion that the wool was moved from Southampton to London in the later fifteenth century wagons were preferred for the trip at 18s 9d per load (the normal wagon load amounting to six sacks weighing about 1 ton), equivalent to only 2 per cent of the selling price. The normal weight of a sack (at 364lb or 165kg) was above the normal payload of a packhorse, which were largely reserved for only the more difficult routes from about the fourteenth century (Farmer 1991). This suggests that the wool trade required good roads and relatively easy access to the sea to be successful, and may have been an incentive for road improvements. Certainly the occasional mention of bequests for roads in wills suggests that this was a factor.

During this time the Cotswold wool in fact came to even greater pre-eminence. It did this by maintaining its reputation for excellence, as shown, for instance, by an ordinance issued to merchants of Leyden in 1415, which ordered them only to buy certain types of wool and *Colswout* (Cotswold) was at the head of the list (Power 1926, 23, and 1933, fn 52). One type of Leuven (east of Brussels) cloth also had to be made with Middle Cotswold, Lindsey, Kesteven or Middle Berkshire wools with 15 nappings in a 22.5-hour period (Munro 1983, 33), and other places (Brussels, Ghent) also had Cotswold wool specified for their staple high-quality cloth products (Munro 1983, 34, table 3.2). Cotswold wool may have benefited commercially by being available in sufficient quantities to meet demand, unlike Herefordshire wool, the other high-quality wool from western England, which was generally in much shorter supply. The staple sale price of Cotswold wool was approaching £14 a sack in 1475 and reached £15 a sack in 1499 (Munro 1978, 147). The only wool that was held in higher esteem was from the Leominster area of Herefordshire, which commanded a price of £25 a sack in 1499! Even the sale price of wool on the home market was almost 6d per lb, which made it one of the most valuable raw materials. This was at a time when a cow was worth 6–10s, and an oxen 10–13s 4d (c.1400; *AgHEW* III, 240).

The continuing success of the Cotswold wool industry is reflected by the bishop of Worcester continuing to invest in the business by increasing his flock in the Cotswolds. In 1412 his wool sales were just over 10 sacks (2,200 sheep; Dyer 1980), while in c.1450 the master shepherd was tending up to nearly 3,000 sheep. Pastures must have been coming under pressure, as the 1,000-strong flock of the previous century at Blockley had also increased to up to 1,760 head of sheep. Private pastures were being sought, and this was contemporary with a move away from transhumance. The latter meant that Kempsey in Worcestershire, for instance, ceased to be integral to sheep farming on the bishop of Worcester's estate. In 1449-50 five shepherds on this estate were looking after 4-500 sheep apiece, which was again an increase from the recommended 300 of earlier days. In the mid-fifteenth century deals are recorded with John de Leona (a Lombard merchant), and also with local merchants from Tetbury and Worcester. Bishop Carpenter (1444-76) cleared a new pasture at Dowdeswell and built a new sheep-cote for just over £40 (*Gloucestershire VCH* IX, 61), and spent £13 9s 6d on stocking it with 164 sheep. However, the late medieval bishops of Worcester were often absentee landlords of Italian extraction themselves, and this was a source of local resentment by the early sixteenth century.

The accounts of Winchcombe Abbey also reveal quite a lot of detail about wool production in this period. This abbey estate had a master shepherd and two under-shepherds based at Sherborne manor. However, there were hardly any sheep on the manor of Sherborne itself, and all the records point to it being a typical largely arable farm economy. Two sheep-cotes are also mentioned in the 1436 accounts as receiving pulse from Sherborne for feeding sheep, suggesting that sheep were kept in or near Sherborne, and maintained by that manor but without being part of the manor estate. Meadow was important for hay for winter feed for sheep and 80 cartloads were used in this way for the Winchcombe sheep in 1436 (Hilton 1957, 108), such quantities confirming again the centralised organisation of sheep rearing and wool production on the abbey estate.

Thus the village of Sherborne was central to the management of the abbey flock. The abbot and his servants moved from Winchcombe to Sherborne for a whole month (Finberg 1977, 88) after Easter each year for the shearing, which was in addition to their normal attendance twice a year to hold the manor court. This put a strain on the manorial larder and probably explains why this relatively populous and productive manor was chosen for its central role in the wool production. The extra labour would also have been available here, while Sherborne was conveniently placed to be reached from the manors where the sheep were kept most of the time and Sherborne was also close to Northleach which had a notable wool market. The local Sherborne Brook was also suitable for washing the sheep, while the meadow alongside was suitable for keeping 2-3,000 sheep. Most of the tenants of the village (i.e. 14 cottagers) owed wool-related services to the abbot, namely washing, shearing (34) and sewing up the wool in packs of 200 fleeces each, for which they were fed while at work, with a special feast at the end (Finberg 1977, 89). Wool storage must have been available as some wool from a previous year was also sometimes packed here.

The Italian merchants continued their habit of buying directly from the monasteries, and thereby heading off the local woolmongers. Sale bargains struck at Sherborne involved Felix de Fagnario and Alessandro Palestrett, merchants of Lucca, who paid £1,263 for 179 sacks of Cotswold wool between Michaelmas (29 September) 1441 and Easter 1443. Such large sums were not exceptional, as in 1442-3 Frederico Cornes and Carlo Cotarini paid £478 10s for 53 sacks of wool from the abbot of Cirencester and other Cotswold producers (Lloyd 1977). One of the visitors at the annual shearing at Sherborne in 1446 was Bernard Lumbard, an Italian merchant, who was provided with food and drink at the weighing of the wool. These buyers would all probably have taken the wool back to Italy via Southampton. The abbot also acted as a middleman buying up wool from his own tenants, and so this was a time when the locals could turn a pretty penny both from all the wage labour on offer, and from selling any wool

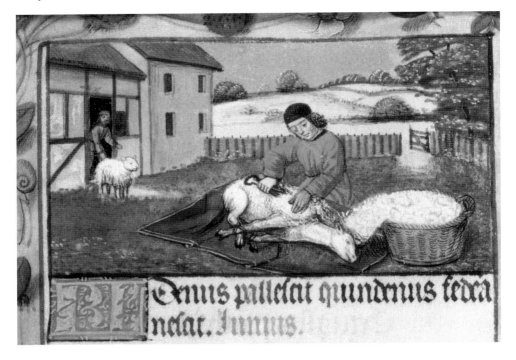

34 Flemish sheep shearing scene of 1425-50 from a calendar (June) – BL Add 17012, f6. *By permission of the British Library*

they produced themselves. In 1446 this extra wool was worth £5 13s, which at the rate of £8 per sack of 200 fleeces, indicates that the locals had about 150 shearable sheep.

A Winchcombe Abbey account of 1485 provides the following description, which goes a long way towards recreating the typical scene of a Cotswold sheep shearing event:

> And in victuals bought at the time of the shearing and washing the sheep, 29s 4d. And paid several men for bringing the sheep to the washing and shearing 2s 4d. And paid one woman for collecting the fleeces for 4 days, 6d. And paid one woman working in the kitchen, 4d. And paid 4 shepherds coming there to help at the shearing, 2s. And paid Richard Smith for sorting ('le tryndynge') 14 sacks of wool, 16s 4d. And paid for the packing of the said wool, with victuals and wages provided 14s 2d. And paid for washing and shearing 2900 sheep ... 67s 3d. Total costs £6 12s 3d.
>
> (Sherborne muniments 1900)

The manor of Sherborne had been farmed out to private hands since *c.*1474, and the sheep shearing was integral to this, as the farmer had to look after the horses of the abbot and his retinue (Finberg 1957c). In 1485 there were 2,900 sheep being processed in this way, when a monk was responsible to the abbey for the work, the whole operation taking four days and the wool being packed into 14 sacks (just over 200 fleeces to the sack). These production figures are, however, lower than in *c.*1300 when Pegolotti saw Winchcombe as capable of 20 sacks. Prices still made the effort worthwhile, and, besides, this was a traditional seasonal event that no doubt appealed to most of the participants. At nearby Barrington the prior of Llanthony, who held extensive estates in the vicinity, including Turkdean, attended a similar scene; while at Blockley the bishop of Worcester similarly presided (Smith 1976). But many monastic estates had been totally leased out by mid-century. For instance, in 1445 the Giffards leased Combe pasture near Chipping Campden from Bordesley Abbey to keep their 2,156 sheep (Dyer 1991a).

Other wool deals were being regularly struck in the towns, such as by John Lenard of Campden who sold John de Ponte 50 sacks and 6 *nails* of wool on 10 October 1457, payable as £111 8s 10d at the following Easter, and £111 8s 11d at each of the following Easters (Power 1933, fn 92). Lechlade and Henley-on-Thames also saw some large wool sales showing that the market for Cotswold wool was operating strongly between the Cotswolds and London. However, such easy and large profits did not last for ever, as presumably more and more people tried to capitalise on the business, and in some cases the existing business may have become too large, in particular for the monasteries, to run efficiently. Profits were declining after the middle of the century, and in the 1440s-50s the price of wool was so low that large estates sometimes held on to their wool for three to four years in the hope that the price would recover. The increasing tendency for demesne estates to be leased out was due to the difficulty of making profits. Even at the heart of the Cotswold wool region the flocks were being leased out, as at Bibury and Withington, where, in 1454, 2,500 sheep were leased out for £26, at 2½d per sheep. Here the sheep were later sold outright in 1458 (Dyer 1980).

The opportunities for wealth were still there as a new breed of sheep farmer came to the fore. This was the independent grazier, such as Thomas Bleke, who held extensive pastures in Blockley, Withington, and Bibury in the mid-fifteenth century (Dyer 1980). Another lessee of Blockley pasture was John Grevill (Hilton and Rahtz 1966, 86), presumably descended from the great fourteenth-century wool merchant family from Chipping Campden. Into the sixteenth century this was a regular way for great wealth to be amassed and was the foundation of many gentry families of this period. For instance, the Hornyolds, who were in a position to buy Blackmore Park in Hanley Castle (Worcestershire) for over £850 in 1559, had been grazing sheep on land belonging to the bishop of Worcester at Blockley in the 1540s (Hilton and Rahtz 1966, 86). This new breed of farmer, whether tenant or landowner, went hand in hand with enclosures from the 1450s, and their presence lent weight to the growing trend towards at least partial enclosure.

The continuing importance of sheep is reflected by pressure on traditional grazing rights on the common pasture. In the fifteenth and sixteenth centuries the numbers of sheep being grazed in this way would be carefully recorded.

There was a stint of 30-120 sheep per yardland allowed on the bishop of Worcester's estate where open fields prevailed as in the Cotswolds, and often it was at two or more sheep per acre. Many infringements of the local stinting regulations suggest that there was a lot of concern about the impact of having too little grazing to go round. The new tendency to take graziers' sheep in the summer reduced opportunities for fertilising the arable in the traditional way, as these animals were sent back in winter and were not then available for folding (Jones 1994, 78).

The tradition of folding in the common fields, where any fallow was open for grazing, was essential to the success of arable agriculture in the Cotswolds. The sheep also benefited and so this was a valuable right of the flock owners, as well as of those with folding rights. For instance, the rectory of Stanton was endowed with the right to graze 400 sheep on Snowshill common fields. The *Valor Ecclesiasticus* usefully lists sheep pastures that related to common land; for example Bruern Abbey had 500 sheep pastures, that is pasturage for 500 sheep in Hinchwick, and 400 in summer and 300 in winter at Guiting Power; Llanthony Priory had 400 in the Barringtons and 200 in Windrush; Winchcombe Abbey had 1,000 sheep pastures in the summer in Snowshill with 500 in winter, 500 in Charlton Abbots in summer with 300 in winter, and 600 in Hawling all year round; while Hailes Abbey had the right to graze 600 sheep in Lower Swell and 300 sheep in Longborough (Jones 1994, 79). This was also a way of bringing the sheep down to lower ground during the winter, and retaining a high number through the winter.

There are some signs that the increased amount of wool available as a result of the fifteenth-century expansion of sheep farming was depressing the wool price. It was also creating local problems when some graziers, as at Toddington, were erecting illegal enclosures and also exceeding their allotted quota on the common pastures (Dyer 1991b). In the 1440s prices were low and some flocks were drastically reduced in size, and it is at this point that there is the return to a greater emphasis on meat, so that grazing began to be directed more towards fattening (Mate 1997, 257). But this was probably reversed later in the century when wool prices showed a higher increase, especially in 1462-86 (Beresford 1971, 14). The wool prices fluctuated, but generally increased beyond mid-century as a long series of good harvests brought about a sense of prosperity, which increased the demand for clothing (*AgHEW* IV 636). Government in 1489 sought to channel much of the English wool into home cloth production by stipulating that foreign merchants were barred from purchasing it from shearing-time (June) until 2 February following (Tawney and Power 1924b). This reflects the ascendancy of English cloth with the wool merchants now being made to serve this industry rather than supplying their traditional foreign markets.

Major transformations in the shape of the English countryside were also being noted by contemporaries and this has often been attributed to the pursuit of growth of pasture by the landlords. A Warwickshire priest in around 1486 produced a list of 61 places, including Sezincote in north Gloucestershire, where there were abandoned villages (Aston and Viner 1984, 287). A documented instance of forcible removal occurred to the north of Hailes where the abbot of Tewkesbury evicted 30 villagers in 1491 (Beresford 1954a). At Middle Ditchford, also in the north Cotswolds, records reveal a sudden end to arable cultivation in the late fifteenth century (Dyer 1982, 26). This process, however, may have begun in the previous century, and with the loss of population and a deterioration in climate, Cotswold arable agriculture, with its difficult soils and lack of major markets, may also have been a factor leading to settlement desertion (Dyer 1982). However, where the integrated mixed farming of sheep and corn held firm, this may have conferred some protection (Beresford 1971, 16), unless the pressure from landlords became irresistible, or all the tenants had decided to leave of their own volition (Dyer 1982).

It is tempting to link this reduction in rural population with a period of increasing enclosure of farmland which clearly occurred in large parts of this region well before parliamentary enclosure of the eighteenth and nineteenth centuries. Though not commented on so much by contemporaries until the sixteenth century (Beresford 1971, 40), the early growth in enclosures may have been a factor in the changing nature of the Cotswold sheep, as a more enclosed landscape would have offered greater opportunities for breeding from an earlier date than in some other parts of the country. However, archaeological evidence in the Cotswolds shows no obvious change in sheep appearance at this time, and the general increase in stature, for instance, did not occur until later.

HEYDAY OF COTSWOLD WOOL SALES

Cotswold wool growers were now in a good trading position, as they had a good product in the Cotswold sheep, could supply in bulk, and also had their strong links with the Continent. Supplying both Flanders and Italy had meant over the years greater marketing stability regardless of the political situation abroad. The quality of wool from the Cotswold sheep was so renowned internationally that they were even chosen by the king to form part of diplomatic gestures, as when Edward IV presented four rams to Henry IV of Castile in 1464, and to John of Aragon in 1468, in the latter case supplemented with 20 ewes. Some have considered that the Spanish *merino* sheep were further improved as a result (*Gloucestershire VCH* II, 156), but this is disputed by others (Ryder 1983b), though it was commonly thought over 100 years later that these gifts had given away to the Spanish a great advantage (Smith 1747 quoting from a tract of 1603).

Much of the Cotswold wool continued to be taken to Italy, and a detailed account of around 1475 has survived, known as *A Discourse of Weights and Merchandise* (but commonly referred to as *The Noumbre of Weights*). This shows the costs involved in this international trade (Myers 1969, 1029):

The costs that run upon a sack of Cotswold wool before it is sold:

First, carriage to London or to Southampton, every sarpler	4s
Also for packing in the country, every sarpler	1s
Also for sheeting and serving at the cord, every sarpler	[1s 3d]
Also for the costs in riding, every sarpler	4d
Also every sarpler, 12 ells customs at 4d the ell	4s
Also for sewing and painting, every sarpler	4d
Also, for pack thread, every sarpler	1d
Also, for porters, every sarpler	6d
Also, for hostelage at the quay, every sarpler	2d
Also, for the weigher at the custom, every sarpler	53s 4d
Also, for the cocket, every sarpler	2d
Also, for petty custom, every sarpler	4d
Also, for the billet to the scrivener, every sarpler	2d
Also, for various galleys, every sarpler	8d

Cost of the galley into the port and to the time that the wool is sold:

First for freight of the galley, every sack	40s
Also, at the custom house of Venice, every sack is priced at 100 ducats and the custom on every 100 ducats is 3 ducats, and a ducat is 3s 4d; so the custom of a sack is	
	10s
Also, for brokerage, every sack	3s 4d
Also, for small costs, every sack	5d
Also, for the care of every sack	10s
Total	63s 9d

The first buying of a sack of Cotswold wool is worth according to the rate of the year, one with another, 12 marks	£8
The raising of the price because of the costs that run upon a sack unto the time that it is in the galley aforesaid	£3 6s 4d
Also, raising the price for freight of a sack, with other costs aforesaid	£3 4s 2d

This puts the costs of getting the wool to Italy at £14 10s 6d per sack, though the itemised account deals in both sarplers and sacks, and so the cost may have been slightly less. Cotswold wool was still equally valued at Calais, where the price of 'fine Cotswold' wool was 18 marks (£12) c.1475, and only exceeded by 'March', i.e. Welsh borders wool (Myers 1969, 1028). The stapler merchants continued to be assisted in their trade by the indebtedness of the English king. In 1469 leading members of the Staple at Calais redeemed jewels of Edward IV from Thomas Portinari, and were then owed £2,700 by the Staple, which would have given them a strong trading position, and so kept the trade through Calais in their favour.

Personal and business letters survive for the 1460s-80s that give an intimate account of how the Cotswold wool business was conducted between England and Calais, and beyond. By far the best series of letters is that of the Cely family (see below), and there are also letters of the Stonor family. Both families seem to have specialised in Cotswold wool. The Stonors were graziers in the Chilterns and Cotswolds. They were originally from Oxfordshire and were living at Stonor in the mid-fifteenth century (Kingsford 1919, xliv), where they had easy access to the Thames and London. The Celys (see below), though residing in London, also had family connections towards the Cotswolds, where they combined both family and business dealings. For both families travelling for business was also a social occasion when all sorts of luxuries from London or the exotic markets of the Low Countries could be sought out to satisfy the wishes of various relatives and friends, and most especially the close female relatives.

Both families were very substantial dealers. Whereas the Stonors operated the business through family connections including Thomas Betson, the Celys largely kept it within the family circle. Many incidental details of the trade are mentioned in their letters, such as the existence of the *wollkey* in London, and the need to pay 1d to the weigher for each sack, ditto the chalker, and 8d to porters (for moving each sack). It is clear from the tone of the letters that the business was not without worry, and the time of most concern was usually the sea crossing to Calais. Often there are letters sent straight back to say how the cargo had arrived safely in order to waylay these fears.

In 1460 Stonor sold 80 ewes at 12d per head in Oxfordshire, and in 1475 the wool of 140 sheep was sold by him for 46s 8d (Kingsford 1919). Stonor's business agreed in September 1478 to supply a London mercer with 25 sacks of young Cotswold wool, of which 20 sacks were to be fine wool, five sacks of middle wool, and 50 fleeces, the wool to be packed at the woolman's house by a member of the Fellowship of the Woolpackers of London as appointed by the buyer. The woolman then agreed also to transport this consignment to London before the Feast of the Purification of the Virgin (2 February; i.e. in about four or five months), and to deliver it at the King's Beam at Leadenhall, which was the usual place in London to officially weigh the wool. The purchaser agreed to pay £140, and the woolman received £81 17s in advance, the rest being paid the day after the delivery, and so little credit was given here which was unusual (Power 1926, 25). The supplier was a woolman called Robert Warner of Watlington, who was based to the east of Oxford, approximately half way from London to the Cotswolds, and not far from the River Thames which might have been the easiest way to convey the wool to London.

The flow of wool through Calais was still considerable. In 1472 about 7,800 sacks of wool and 416,000 fells passed through the town (Salzman 1931). In 1480 'good cotes' from the Cotswolds was worth 19 marks (£12 13s 4d) per sack and 'midde cotes' 13 marks (£8 13s 4d; Power 1933, 367, fn 57), and these prices remained fairly stable into the early sixteenth century (Hanham 1985, table 2).

Demand for Cotswold wool remained high, as it was incorporated into the luxury cloth which became the mainstay of the diminished textile industry in Flanders, and was even specified for addition to the Spanish wool used for the new types of cloths emerging at this time (Munro 1978, 153). Hence it was very important that the types of wool were clearly identified on each sarpler. 'Goode Cottiswolde' written on the protective canvas would have guaranteed a premium price. The temptation to deliberately falsify the wool description must been great, especially as the fine of £20 for fraudulently mixing wools seems not to be that harsh.

In the mid-fifteenth century there were numerous merchants in the Fellowship of the Staple at Calais, and documentary sources record more than 300 (Power 1926), and this number may have continued to increase as the staplers reckoned there were 400 'shippers' in the sixteenth century. But the staplers were now, for the first time, beginning to face competition. A merchant alliance, known as the Merchant Adventurers, dominated by London mercers (Sutton 2002), began to control the export of the undyed broadcloth with the establishment by the City, from the end of the fourteenth century, of Blackwell (formerly Bakewell) Hall in London as the main weekly market centre (Ponting 1957, 35). As usual this concentrated the business, and made it easier to control, and there were few other export outlets. Only freemen of the City were able to sell any cloth in the City, and so, in line with typical business practices of the time, these traders were able to control cloth exports to a considerable degree, though not as much as the staplers had previously been able to control wool exports (Carus-Wilson and Coleman 1963, 25).

Meanwhile the Italians were still active traders in England (see below). The Venetian merchants of the mid-fifteenth century were becoming keener to export cloth rather than wool. They were certainly starting to buy cloths from the Trowbridge area, and much of the cloth picked up in Southampton was eventually sold at Constantinople, after further processing in Italy. In 1440-42 Leonardo Contarini purchased cloth for £5,161, of which £248 was for Cotswold cloths, and these were some of the most expensive at £2 13s 4d each (Fryde 1976, 351). In the fifteenth century the port of Bristol was also handling some wool, though this may mainly have come from Wales as the abbot of Tintern was a member of the Bristol Staple and his monks were able to trade in Bristol free of toll. Bristol seems never to have been able to build up a wool business, and even the north Herefordshire wool seems to have been taken overland to Chipping Campden to join the main wool routes to London and Southampton rather than to Bristol. However, Bristol seems later to have had more success with Cotswold cloths, as these were being exported from here, in addition to its main trade, which was in wine from Gascony, and in woad (Carus-Wilson 1933).

Wills of this period also show sheep figuring in bequests to relatives. For instance, John Rogers (died 1498) of Compton Abdale gave away 64 sheep to various people. He was one of the new breed of expansive graziers who had acquired more grazing by taking over parts of the common field which carried pasture stinting, which was recorded in manor court rolls as a series of fines (Kosmala 1993).

CLOTH MANUFACTURE

> Clothmaking … the greatest occupation and living of the poor commons of this land
> (Parliamentary petition of 1454)

By the late fourteenth century the value of English cloth exports had probably exceeded that of wool (Bridbury 1982, viii; *33*). This was achieved at the expense of the towns where cloth making had suffered from being under close regulation. Rural workers took advantage of their greater economic freedoms following the Black Death, as well as realising the natural advantages of water-power and so this growth in cloth production was a great achievement of the rural worker. After years of benefiting from wool exports the Cotswolds next succeeded in becoming a cloth production area as well, and the easy availability of good quality wool will have been one factor in favour of this transformation (Baker 1973).

The increase in the English cloth trade, therefore, saw wealth being generated in the English village to offset (in a sense) any economic decline in the towns (Ponting 1957, 34), to which this transfer of industry may well have contributed. The new clothiers found greater freedom outside the towns. The quality of the native cloth was now much higher, and so in 1440 the green and red cloth of the Cirencester area cost, for instance, about 6s 8d per yard (Baddeley 1924), a valuable product. The colorants were all based on natural materials, yellow or green being produced with Dyer's Rocket or Dyer's Greenweed, and red from madder.

However, the English rural cloth industry was not going to escape regulation wholesale. Leaden seals had to be affixed to all bales of cloth (Phillimore 1894-5). But controls and taxes were light compared to the burden on exported wool, and the cloth industry continued to grow rapidly. In the 1480s England was exporting an average of 51,850 broadcloths a year and 8,511 sacks of wool (enough to make another 38,300 broadcloths; Szarmach *et al*, 1940). Towards the end of the fifteenth century cloth making was still increasing, and the main production areas were the south-west (Gloucestershire and Somerset), East Anglia and Yorkshire. Bristol according to the surviving ulnage accounts was one of the most prominent centres. This also had the effect that the north Cotswolds lost out to a more burgeoning south Cotswolds (Powell 1992), as water-power was now all important. In the days of wool dominance, it had been the north Cotswolds that had the greatest advantages in fine pastures, and the better sheep.

At both Bisley and Minchinhampton a number of scattered industrial centres grew up down in the valley of the River Frome and along the adjacent valleys below these upland villages. This district came to be known as Stroudwater. Wool was available locally, and any fuller's earth needed for processing the cloth was also available locally near Chalford, Rodborough and Avening. Bristol now became a useful port as a way in for dye-stuffs, and cloths began to be exported via this port, so that cloths of the region were often known as *Bristols*. The wonderfully clear water was perfect for applying the finest dyed finishes, especially the reds, and its quantity was great enough for driving many fulling mills.

In the fifteenth century there was much expansion of cloth production, in this part of the south Cotswolds. Fulling mills were at a premium and mills could be sublet at over four-times their manorial rent. The workers of a fulling mill at Bisley who had sublet without permission were fined 43s 4d, but in return made a deal for a new lease for three lives with powers to sublet. Fulling mills became very common in this part of the Cotswolds, and there were as many as four at Stonehouse by 1496 (Swynnerton 1923, 231). So great was the demand for water power that virtually every part of the watercourse was being let out for this purpose with higher rents being set each time. Equally the Bisley commons were being overstocked because of the large workforce that was becoming established here.

Cirencester weavers would send their cloth eight miles by packhorse to be fulled, dyed and shorn at Chalford in the mid-fifteenth century. The fuller was sometimes a man of substance who had many business interests beyond cloth making. Gradually these mill owners became cloth dealers in their own right, and then the industry became fully fledged, as in the case of John Grymer 'late of Rodbough', who was also described as 'alias of Stroudwater, clothman' in 1476. Cirencester cloth workers also tended to take up residence in the valley, such as John Benet who came to have water mills at Rodborough. He made bequests to the parish churches of Minchinhampton and Woodchester, and to chapels at Rodborough and Stroud. His friend was William Halyday of Rodborough 'clothmaker', who was the son of a fuller, and has a brass in Minchinhampton church. The terms *Stroudwaters* and *Castlecombes* were also known on the Continent by the late 1400s as trade names for fine cloth. Most of the cloth went for sale to the cloth mart at Blackwell Hall in London by packhorse.

Local lords of the manor seem, however, to have largely missed out on this boom. Comparison of taxes of 1334 and 1523 show that Gloucestershire was booming in comparison with, for instance, Lincolnshire, with a 62 per cent increase in wealth being recorded. Some individual places, such as Bisley, increased in size thirteen times, and ended up competing with Cirencester. Wage earners were much more common in Bisley in contrast with at the normal village, and here this category accounted for nearly half of the taxpayers. In the later fourteenth century Castle Combe in northwest Wiltshire had benefited from large military orders for cloth. Here fifty new houses were built in the first half of the fifteenth century, and four new mills. Servants also became new wage earners as weavers. There were attempts to deal with the drunkenness that accompanied these developments with taverns being ordered to close at 8 p.m. in winter and 9 p.m. in the summer, and gambling was also forbidden. As an outward sign of this prosperity the local market was revived, and an annual fair was instituted (Carus–Wilson 1959).

The role of the clothier was now being born out of the need for the larger merchants to have a regular bulk supplier, much along the same lines as the woolman had served for the Calais wool merchant. Initially this often came with having a fulling mill. In some cases former wool merchants such as John Tame of Fairford took this direction seeing the relative decline in wool. The fuller ended up buying and distributing the wool, and taking control of most aspects of the trade (Ponting 1957, 28). Sometimes clothiers from the small villages of this area made marriage alliances with clothiers from other famous textile regions such as Bradford (Ponting 1957, 30), suggesting that the trade was not as parochial as it might seem at first sight. The main product was probably undyed broadcloth, an export line, which was fulled but was only fully finished in the Low Countries (Ponting 1957, 31), or elsewhere. This circumvented the high price of English wool export as it was cheaper for the foreign buyers to buy English cloth rather than the English wool. And so from c.1500 to 1800 wool continued to be the biggest item in Britain's export trade, but now it was as cloth rather than raw wool.

WOOL MERCHANTS AND CHURCHES

The accumulated wealth of the local merchants had an enduring impact on several parts of the kingdom in the fifteenth century, with the large-scale rebuilding of parish churches, and the Cotswolds was one such region. This had the effect that it was the church naves and not the chancels that received most attention from the builders, as the chancel was the responsibility of the clergy rather than the parishioners. For instance, the parish churches of Cirencester, Northleach (*42*), Chipping Campden (*40*), Fairford (*41*), Winchcombe, Lechlade, Chedworth and Rendcombe all show signs of rebuilding at this time. Sometimes the building works can be explicitly associated with particular benefactors, such as at Northleach, Chipping Campden and Fairford, where the works were associated with the Fortey, Bradway and Tame families respectively (Verey 1970), and these were all people engaged in the wool trade.

Church towers became, in particular, confident statements of piety expressed through enormous wealth and affluence. The new Perpendicular style of building also introduced greater light into a church, and this effect could be enhanced by the addition of a clerestory, as, for instance, at Northleach parish church. Additional chapels, often swept away at the Reformation, once reflected even more obviously the prominence of the wool dealers.

Memorial brasses at several Cotswold churches bring us face to face with some of the wool merchants, who made major bequests in support of the church fabric. Probably the most famous was William Grevel of Chipping Campden (*19*), who died in 1401, and was described in Latin on his memorial brass as 'the flower of the wool merchants of all England', thereby staking his claim to be the greatest merchant of his time. He left in his will 100 marks (£66 13s 4d) towards the rebuilding of Campden church, possibly contributing to the work on the north aisle (40), where brackets integral with two later adjacent piers suggest an important benefactor's tomb. However, rebuilding occurred again at this church late in the fifteenth century, and was on a grander scale still, as it involved the nave and the tower. The addition of the clerestory was a particularly inspired part of this phase. Another Campden wool merchant, John Bradway, who made a gift to the church of 100 marks in 1488 (Finberg 1975, 89), presumably helped fund these later extensive works.

The brass of Robert Page, another woolman, who was buried at Cirencester in 1440, also asserts his worthy interest in the repairing of churches and roads, as also did that of Thomas Fortey who was buried at Northleach in 1447. His son John Fortey (35) continued this tradition by paying for the clerestory above the nave and amongst other benefactions, including giving each of 40 poor girls 20s as a wedding gift, still included funds for the mending of roads and bridges. He also gave £200 for making clothes for the needy. Some prominent merchants, though dealing predominantly in Cotswold wool, preferred to reside permanently in London, and so endowed their local London church instead (see the Celys, below). This flurry of rebuilding of churches in the larger towns and villages should not be taken as a sign that all sectors of society were enjoying

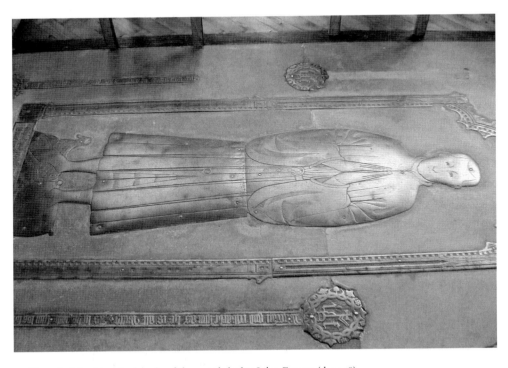

35 Brass in Northleach church of the wool dealer John Fortey (d. 1458)

an economic boom. For instance, it contrasted markedly with the depopulation and abandonment of many of the smaller settlements in the surrounding countryside.

Unsurprisingly, given the prominence of Northleach in the medieval wool trade, this parish church has the best collection of memorial brasses. They comprise, in order of date, memorials to: an unknown woolman (*32*), Thomas Fortey, John Fortey (*35*), John Taylour (*36*), William Bicknell, William Midwinter (*44*) and Thomas Bushe (*54*), ranging in date from the earliest in *c*.1400 to the last in 1525. And in some cases the wives of these Northleach wool dealers and merchants clearly continued the business following the decease of their husbands. The wills of John Forty and Thomas Bushe survive, and reveal details of their considerable wealth.

The Tames of Fairford were another eminent wool merchant family. John Tame, the famous woolman who died in 1500, had begun the building of a new church at Fairford, and this was finished by his son Edmund (Finberg 1975, 88). In his will he left money for the 'marriage of xxx poor maydenes within four myle of Fairford or else in the town of Cicetter' (Holt 1871). His son purchased the manors of Dowdeswell, Barnsley and Eastleach Turville, Nymphsfield and

36 Brass in Northleach church of the wool dealer John Taylour (d. 1509) and his wife (d. 1510). This brass dates to the 1490s

Tetbury, and he also made bequests on his death, but since the church was newly built he instead left silver ware to the abbot of Cirencester, and £10 for mending the road from Cirencester to Faringdon, suggesting where his main business had been transacted.

In other cases it can only be surmised that benefactors were local wool dealers or growers, such as the group who paid for the elaborate rebuilding of the north wall of the nave at Bledington church (*37*), whose names were Thomas ?Eyre, Willi Water, Thomas Andrewes and Thomas Smyth and their wives who were all called Agnes, a common name in this sheep-farming district, being derived from the Latin for lamb. The incising of a pair of scissors into the fifteenth-century tower of Cranham church (*38*) has also usually been taken as an indication that wool provided the funds for building, though scissors would be more in keeping with cloth working, than with sheep shearing where the traditional implement was the sprung shears (cf *34*).

37 Bledington church showing the north wall of the nave, constructed in the later fifteenth century, with stained glass dated 1476 in the upper windows depicting the benefactors Thomas ?Eyre, Willi Water, Thomas Andrewes, Thomas Smyth and their wives (all called Agnes). The striking quality of construction suggests that wool may have contributed to the work

38 Pairs of scissors incised into the tower of Cranham church. These are symbolic of the clothiers' trade rather than the wool trade, where shears were used

Though less obvious today, the appearance of new chapels was also a sign of affluence based on wool, and much of the wool was surely local until the canals and railways facilitated easier transportation. For instance at Stroud, which was a new manufacturing centre, a fourteenth-century chapelry of Bisley was established (Finberg 1975, 87). Rich merchants also endowed almshouses, such as at Burford (*39*) and Northleach. At the former the buildings were put up at the expense of Henry Bishop, a local wool merchant recorded making deals with the Italians for the export of Cotswold wool via Southampton. At the latter Thomas Dutton erected the almshouses in 1616, and his family had long dealt in wool, including with the Cely family in the fifteenth century, and finally acquired parts of the Gloucester Abbey estate after the Dissolution.

39 The Great Almshouses at Burford, founded in 1457 by Henry Bishop, a local wool merchant. The charity board in the south transept of the church records that permission for the almshouses was granted by Richard, earl of Warwick (the 'Kingmaker')

SOME COTSWOLD WOOL CHURCHES

St John the Baptist, Burford

This church was remodelled in the fifteenth century starting in *c.*1420, and the windows received a lot of attention from the builders. The tower and the porch were built in mid-century. None of the benefactors are known. Unfortunately the church was so heavy-handedly restored in the nineteenth century that it was the reason that William Morris founded the Society for the Protection of Ancient Buildings and, on hearing this criticism, the vicar apparently responded that the church was his, and that, if he liked, he could stand on his head in it (Sherwood and Pevsner 1974).

St James, Chipping Campden

William Grevel and his wife are depicted on a memorial brass, where he is described as 'the best of the wool merchants of all England'. There is also a more modest brass to William Welley (alias Weoley) dated 1450. There have been various claims about how Grevel's donation in 1401 to the church rebuilding project was expended, some claiming that it was used for the tower, and others that it went

40 North aisle of Chipping
Campden church incorporating
fourteenth-century work (Verey
1970, 153). This is the most likely
part of the church to have been built
with funds from William Grevel.
Major rebuilding work at this church
followed from about 1450

towards the north aisle (*40*). The major work of rebuilding this church has been
dated *c.*1450-1500, and similarities with Northleach have suggested that the same
masons were working on both churches (Verey 1970).

St John the Baptist, Cirencester
This was the largest parish church in Gloucestershire and it was further
embellished in the mid-fifteenth century by merchants. There are memorial
brasses to the wool merchants Reginald Spycer (1442), Philip Marner (1587),
Richard Dixton (1438) and William Prelatte (1462). A wool merchant family
named Garstang established a chantry chapel. In the early 1500s the nave was
rebuilt and merchants' marks are depicted to commemorate their contribution.

St Mary, Fairford
This church was completely rebuilt around 1490-1500 (*41*), the work being
carried out initially by the wool merchant John Tame and then by his son,
Edmund Tame, whose memorial brass of 1534 survives.

41 Fairford church, rebuilt by the wool merchant John Tame in 1490-1500

St Peter and St Paul, Northleach

This church of St Peter was almost entirely rebuilt in the fifteenth century (*42*). It contains a fine set of memorial brasses of wool merchants dating from *c.*1400 to 1525, the finest in the Cotswolds. The will of John Fortey (*43*) gave the enormous sum of £300 'to complete the new work in the new middle aisle already started by me' (i.e. this was a further benefaction towards the nave), and the sum of 6s 8d to all of 120 other churches. And so Northleach church is today characterised by the fine clerestory that illuminates the inside of the church. Another woolman, William Bicknell, later built the Lady Chapel here.

St Peter, Winchcombe

This church was built in *c.*1465 in a style that was less ornate than the other 'wool churches' of the region.

THE CELYS, MERCHANTS OF THE CALAIS STAPLE

Merchants played a considerable role in the wool trade, as they were pivotal to the processes of gathering, transporting and selling wool abroad. The foreign market was important as its large demand for English wool ensured that prices were high, and so profits were maximised. The increasingly regulated supply of

42 Right Northleach church, rebuilt in the fifteenth century, described by William Camden in 1586 as 'a neat church'. The clerestory, just visible in front of the tower, was probably part of the 'new work' funded by the 'wolman' John Fortey

43 Below Extract from the will of the wool dealer John Fortey of Northleach, 'wolman', dated 24 June 1458: (commencing fourth word from right) '... Item I bequeath 300 pounds sterling for the completion and infilling of the new work of the aforementioned aisle already started by me. Item I bequeath 20 pence for the work on the nave of the cathedral church of St Mary in Worcester. Item I bequeath £40 sterling for work on the naves of 120 of the nearest churches to the aforesaid Northleach church namely to each of them 6s 8d ...'. The 'new middle aisle' is plainly a reference to the nave, as distinct from the aisles. *(NA reference PROB 11/4)*

wool to this market was aimed at maintaining these profits, and ensuring that both merchants and the Crown benefited greatly. The merchants were generally willing agents of the Crown in this, as this usually gave them royal protection, which was useful insurance when moving around the troubled realms of medieval north-western Europe.

There were numerous merchants engaged in the wool trade, the most important of which were based in London. Some that performed this role, such as Thomas Betson, were associated with wealthy landed families such as the Stonors. Others, such as the Celys, traded entirely independently, but specialising in wool, and establishing links with specific wool-growing areas. Profits were high for most of those involved in the wool trade, except perhaps sometimes for the wool growers themselves, especially when the king went too far in his efforts to exercise control. However, if you were a trader on the international scene and the sheep were your own, as in the case of the Stonors, then profits could indeed be maximised.

More commonly, however, the wool trade depended on true merchants, who dealt in their own money. The Cely family were such merchants and were based in London, but also had a place in the country in Essex (Bretts Place, near Aveley) just east of London. This family features prominently in any account of the later fifteenth-century wool trade, since a large collection of 247 of their letters and miscellaneous papers has survived for posterity. These constitute an important collection, as they throw much light on the organisation of a medieval English firm. The papers also illuminate the financial activities in general of the capitalistic merchant dealers, as well as their Flemish, Italian and Spanish counterparts.

The Celys specialised in the sale of Cotswold wool to the Low Countries, and so for the period from about 1474 to 1488 there is an unparalleled window onto the Cotswold medieval wool trade, as the passage of wool can be traced in detail from the Cotswolds, via London, and onwards to Calais. However, the letters do have many gaps, and are often only one side of the correspondence, so that the picture that emerges is still incomplete, though enough survives for a very good impression to be given of the wool business at this time. Besides the letters provide the only concrete evidence for many of the more intimate aspects of the trade, such as how credit was arranged and how shopping lists for foreign luxuries were mixed in with the principal business. In addition the fluctuating state of the trade in wool is apparent, and this reveals how the Cotswold sheep farmer could easily be severely affected by events on the Continent.

When the sequence of letters opens, two Cely brothers, Richard the elder (-1482) and John, are trading as merchants of the staple. Another merchant, William Maryon, simultaneously a stapler and grocer, was closely involved with the family both on a personal level (as godfather to Richard the younger) and a business level. These were the senior partners of the firm, who, due to their senior standing, were based in England, while the more junior members were expected to carry on the business abroad living in one of the hostelries licensed by the Company of the Staple. Being abroad involved a great deal of travelling about, whether crossing the English Channel repeatedly, or moving between the markets and fairs of the Low Countries, while being based in Calais. The Cely letters feature mainly George Cely in this position, and he was one of Richard Cely's sons. Another son, Richard, also played a prominent part, mainly based in London, and sometimes assisting his brother in Calais.

The elder Richard Cely had married Agnes from Adderbury on the edge of the Cotswolds, just south of Banbury in Oxfordshire, and it is possible that this westwards connection led to the development of the Cely family's interest in Cotswold wool. Adderbury, together with Witney, were manors on the eastern edge of the Cotswolds, which were part of the bishopric of Winchester estate

(Farmer 1995), which was itself heavily involved in wool production. The Cely family tended to do much of their dealing in the heart of the Cotswolds at Northleach, which was just 42km (26 miles) from Adderbury. Adderbury would no doubt have been a useful stopping-off point on the frequent treks from London to the Cotswold area and back (*45*). At Northleach Richard Cely the younger dealt with the local wool gatherers (referred to at the time as *woolmongers*) such as John Bushe (Hanham 1975, letter 20); and later his widow Alice, John Perys (Hanham 1975, letter 53) and Jenkin Taylor of Farmington, but most of his wool was bought off William Midwinter (*44*), who later married the widow Alice Bushe.

44 Brass memorial of wool dealers William Midwinter (d. 1501) and his wife Alice (d. *c.*1503)

The normal pattern of the trade in England was for a buyer to ride out to the Cotswolds looking for as much Cotswold wool or woolfells as could be found. For the Celys Northleach was the place they favoured for this purpose. The route travelled by Richard the younger on so many occasions is not known in detail, but taking April–September 1480 as an example it seems to have involved travelling at least 585 miles over only a six-month period, entirely on horse-back (45). In contrast, sometimes the wool dealer went in search of the wool staple merchant, as when in November 1479 Richard Cely the elder was entertaining William Midwinter at London, and arranged to take 40 sacks off him 'the weche ys in pyle in Norlache' (i.e. at Northleach; Hanham 1975 letter 67). The demand for wool from this region remained especially high into the 1480s. In April 1480 Richard Cely the younger visited Northleach and Westwell (Oxfordshire) to pack 29 sarplers of wool. At Westwell the farmers had pasturage for 1,200 sheep, and were busy enclosing the arable to increase their capacity for rearing sheep (Smith 1976). On 2 April 1482 Richard Cely the younger wrote to his brother, George in Calais, in response to a letter only written on 27 March, that he was intending to ride from London to the Cotswolds on the Tuesday of Easter week (Hanham 1975, 135, letter 148) looking particularly for woolfells, as wool was thought to be in short supply. The previous year's clip had presumably now been sold, whereas fells might have been available on a more irregular basis according to fatalities, for instance over the winter and during lambing. Easter, therefore, seems to have been a favourite time to ride to the Cotswolds in search of wool.

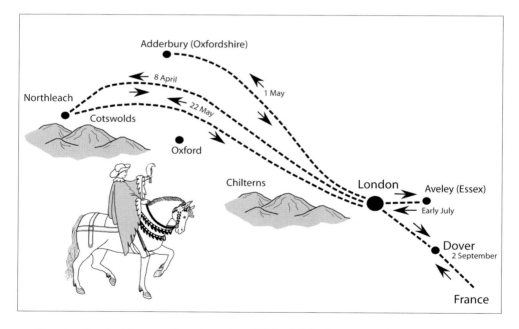

45 Map showing the itinerary of wool merchant Richard Cely the younger from spring to autumn 1480

However, on occasion the finding of wool that was for sale was generally difficult as the Italians also had a preference for Cotswold wool. They were favoured customers of the wool growers as they seem to have bought with ready cash, and if they had been busy they could sometimes corner the market, as in 1480:

> ... nor I haue not bogwyt thys yere a loke of woll, for the woll of Cottyswold ys bogwyt be Lombardys, werefor I haue the lese haste for to packe myn woll at London.
> (Hanham 1975, letter 107)

Sometimes shortages were not put down to any particular cause other than the general demand for Cotswold wool, so on 25 July 1481 Richard Cely the elder wrote to George Cely, who was either at Calais or Bruges:

> ... Also I fely be youre letter ye avyse me for to by woll in Cottyswolde. For sothe I schall haue of John Cely ys gaderyng xxx sacke, and of Wyll Medewynter of Norlache lx sacke, and I am avysyd for to by more, but woll in Cottyswolld ys at grete pryse: xiij s. iiij d. a tode, and gret rydyng for woll in Cottyswolde as was onny yere thys vij yere. ...
> (Hanham 1975, letter 122)

On other occasions the supply of wool was threatened in other ways, and disease was a concern, for instance in November 1481 news of sheep disease further north in England was noted in a letter announcing another expedition to the Cotswolds (Hanham 1975, letter 137). In 1482 Richard Cely the younger was seeking out some of the other local dealers himself rather than just relying on Midwinter, as he is recorded dealing with William Sygar of Campden, Margaret Caenes and Margaret Pynner of Chipping Norton, and Richard Coolys of Preston (Power 1933).

On average over the period 1478-88 the Celys shipped about 95 sacks a year, amounting to the wool of about 22,000 sheep per year, or about one-twentieth of the Gloucestershire production (Jones 1994, 93). Basically the wool merchants relied heavily on the storehouses of the middlemen in the Cotswolds, such as at Northleach, Chipping Norton, Chipping Campden, and Burford, all of which the Celys visited. It is likely that the merchant and woolmen networks were fairly stable parts of the trade, as they had been trading successfully for many years in this way, despite the efforts of the king to ruin the business through exorbitant taxation, and other interference (Jones 1994, 93). Though, paradoxically, his 'interest' in the trade may have ultimately been of benefit, as, of course, he tried to maximise his own profits as well.

The wool stapler made a written agreement with the woolman to buy so many sacks, paying the same price for both good and middle wool (the second grade of fleece), possibly sealing the deal in the porch of the local church (46). The wool was then sorted and packed by a professional packer (e.g. William Breton) and the sarplers sent to London by wagon. It is evident from the Cely letters that the

46 The porch of Northleach church (built in the early to mid-fifteenth century) where Richard Cely and other wool merchants may have sealed some of their wool deals

reputation of the wool merchant rested on the correct appraisal of wool quality, and that sometimes there were complaints from the end purchaser (Hanham 1985, 117). Therefore, reputable staplers such as the Celys would monitor the sorting and packing, as careful classification of the wool was essential. Evidently the qualities and types of wool were well known to the specialists, as sometimes wool was completely reclassified to another specific source as a result of previous inaccurate packing. The resulting bales (sarplers) at up to about 800lb each were too large for packhorses to carry, and they were usually conveyed at two to a wagon.

In London the wool was weighed at the Lead Hall (Leadenhall) in the presence of both the seller and the buyer, and carted to the wool quay for warehousing, if there was no awaiting ship. The buyer paid one-third of the price (4 *nails* per sarpler being rebated for the canvas and the turn of the weighing balance). The other two-thirds was usually paid in two instalments, the last perhaps a year after the date of the agreement. To make these payments the Celys would often borrow money off an English merchant adventurer in London, who in return received an obligation to be collected (in Flemish money) at a Flemish mart. The exchange rate would be detailed in the agreement for the loan. Sometimes, however, the woolmonger sought out the merchant and pressed them for overdue payments, such as when Richard Cely the younger in 1487 described how William Midwinter had arrived in London to collect a debt:

… I wndyrstonde be Adlyngton at Mydwyntter ys com. God ryd ws of hym. …
(Hanham 1975, 230, letter 230)

The 'postal' system between England and the Continent was surprisingly good when the correspondents took it in mind to use it, and letters could take as little as five days being couriered by hand. The letters suggest a world of uncertainty as political and economic influences beset the trade, and where the stakes were high, as the cargoes were so large and valuable. Despite this the business of making money was not always uppermost in the minds of the younger men, and especially in the case of George Cely who was stuck out at Calais most of the time. There was obviously time to relax when abroad, and the elder Richard was often found complaining that his letters were not being answered promptly enough. Clearly the father worried about the business, which was understandable, as large sums of money were bound up with each consignment of wool, and there were many opportunities for things to go wrong. Occasionally ships were lost to pirates, or sometimes seized by the authorities as a result of some political row. Cargoes could also be spoilt in transit, and sometimes had to be made good, though it is difficult to see how fleeces spoilt by seawater could be easily repaired, except by being dried out. The merchants had to be on their guard to watch out for unscrupulous mariners who would hide parts of cargoes, and the system of letters of transit (in effect delivery notes) were designed to overcome this. Plague and disease were widespread, and even serious fatalities from these were little commented on, so Richard the elder was obviously keen to hear that his sons were still safe, and able to receive the next delivery of wool or fells.

The news from Calais could sometimes be exasperating as Richard the elder wrote about his business and George Cely responded instead about the purchase of a new hawk in Calais. Admittedly this was a serious matter owing to the high associated cost and the matter of prestige. The pursuit of game with the hawk was a pleasure sought by any aspiring nobleman. Exotic goods were available in the markets, for instance, of Antwerp, and luxuries such as furs, which were indicators of status, were readily available. Sometimes these considerations took over from the wool business.

Once abroad the wool staplers, in the course of their business, regularly attended four marts of the Low Countries, to collect payment from their buyers, who had already visited them in Calais to purchase wool, and had made arrangements to repay by instalment. In this way the English merchants avoided having to carry large amounts of wool around the Low Country fairs, and trading together at Calais they could present a more unified pricing structure (i.e. high prices). Some of the main seasonal fairs for transacting this business were as follows (Hanham 1975, 250-1):

the *Passe* or Easter mart at Bergen-op-Zoom;
Sinksen (Whitsun) mart in the summer at Antwerp;

Bamis mart at Antwerp;

and the Cold mart at Bergen-op-Zoom.

The Celys did much of their foreign business with Gyesbryght van Wynsbarge, who was a merchant from Bruges, and the Dutch, who were becoming major wool buyers in this period.

The fairs endured for at least a month, sometimes being extended as a result of bad weather, so that the merchants could reach them. Payments tended to be made at the end of the fair, which meant that the English merchant could be kept waiting if he had arrived at its beginning. Presumably, therefore, the foreign merchant would tend to put in an appearance towards the end of the fair, if money was short.

The Cely letters also recall how the foreign buyers could be arbitrarily forced to buy old stock. The old wool was stock that had reached Calais by the end of February but remained unsold by 6 April (Power 1924; Hanham 1985, 135), some of which then had to be bought when buying new wool. Though for favoured customers special concessions were sometimes made, such as that the Leyden (Netherlands) merchants did not have to accept more than five grey or black woolfells per hundred.

Wool could be a very expensive commodity, and typically Richard Cely was contracting with Cotswold dealers, such as John Bushe, to buy large quantities, such as in 1476, when Bushe was to supply '40 sack of good cottys wolde wool, good wool and middle wool of the same price: the sack of both good and middle, 13 mark 20d' (£8 15s; Hanham 1985). This was at a time when the Celys were selling abroad at £12 13s 4d, and making about £1-2 per sack profit. Calais wool profits could, therefore, be considerable, and were about 10-25 per cent of the sale price. This compared to a price of £20 in Italy from an expenditure of £14 10s 6d per sack. As the Celys carried out about £2,000 of wool business in 1483-4, their annual profits would have been at least £200, and it has been calculated that each partner was making about £100 per annum (Hanham 1985, 396), the equivalent today of perhaps £500,000. Their expenses of keeping offices abroad and travelling regularly in search of wool would also have added to the costs of the trade. The possessions of the family in the later fifteenth century indicate that any surplus money was invested in land, and the purchase of lordships. However, cashflow could be a great problem: thus Richard Cely the younger wrote in 1480:

Ryught interly whelbelouyd and my syngeler good brother, I recomende me wnto you in as louyng whys as hartte con thynke. Plese hyt yow to wndyrstonde at the maky[ng] of thys howr father and mother, my godfather Maryon and whe aull wher at London in good heyll, thankyd be the good Loorde. Syr, I haue bene in Cottyssowlde and bohut for hus xxv^c pellys, pryse le C of xv^c: iij li., and of a M^l: heuery c iij li. iij s. iiij d., and I haue payd and a mwste pay vythin thys v days in parte of payment of thes fellys and for caryayge, xl li. and aboue, and I mwste pay to Wylliam Mydwynter at Bartyllmewys tyd xx li., and at Hallontyd xx li. for the forsayd fellys. Syr, I pray yow haue theys dayes in rememerans, my powr honeste lyes ther apon. ...

(Hanham 1975, letter 91)

At times, for instance, towards the end of the period covered by the Cely letters, political conditions disrupted the trade, and Lombards or Spaniards had to be engaged as bankers. In the few cases where interest charges can be worked out the usual rate seems to have been 2.5 per cent per month (an annual rate of 30 per cent).

But matters other than business sometimes occupied the thoughts of those on the English side of the business as well. In 1482 Richard the younger was seeking a wife and used his business trips to pursue this. On May Day 1482 he was shown on his outing from London an eligible young lady at matins in Northleach church, to whom he subsequently presented wine. He wrote to his brother George on 13 May 1482:

... The same day that I come to Norlache, on a Sonday befor mattens frome Burforde, Wylliam Mydwyntter wyllcwmyd me, and in howr comynycacyon he askyd me hefe I wher in any whay of maryayge. I towlde hyme nay, and he informeyd me that ther whos a yeunge genttyllwhoman hos father ys name ys Lemryke, and her mother ys deyd, and sche schawll dyspend be her moter xl li. a yer, as thay say in that contre, and her father ys the gretteste rewlar and rycheste mane in that conttre, and ther hawhe bene grete genttyllmen to se hyr and wholde hawhe hyr, etc. And hewyr matens wher done, Wylliam Mydwynter had meuyd thys mater to the gretteste mane abot the gentyllman Lemeryke, and he yeyd and informyd the forsayd of aull the matter, and the yewng gentyllwomane bothe; and the Sattyrday aftyr, Wylliam Mydwyntter whent to London, as aull wholl getherars wher sent for be wryt be the men of Pettyt, for inwynde and grete markyng, and thay hawhe day to cwm agen at Myhellmas. When I had packyd at Camden and Wylliam Mydwyntter departtyd, I came to Norlache ageyn to make a nende of packyng, and on the Sonday nexte aftyr, the same mane that Wylliam Mydwyntter brake fyrste to cam to me and telde me that he had brokyn to hys master acordyng to Mydwyntter desyryde hym, and he sayd hys master whos ryght whell plessyde ther whothe. And the same mane sayd to me hefe I whowllde tary May Day I schulde hawhe a syte of the yewnge gentyllwhoman, and I sayd I wholld tary wyth a good wyll, and the same day her father schuld a syttyn at Norlache for the Kyng, byt he sent whon of hys clarkys and rod hymselfe to Wynchecwme. And to mattens the same day come the yewnge gentyllwhoman and her mother-i-law, and I and Wylliam Bretten wher sayng mattens when thay com into chyrche, and when mattens vhos done thay whente to a kynnyswhoman off the yewnge genttyllwhoman; and I sent to them a pottell of whyte romnay, and thay toke hyt thankefully, for thay had cwm a myle a fote that mornyng; and when Mes whos done I come and whellcwmyd them, and kyssyd them, and thay thankyd me for the whyne, and prayd me to cwm to dyner wyth them, ... and thay made me promys them to drynke wyth them after dyner. And I sent them to dyner a galon whyne and thay sent me a heronsew roste, and aftyr dyner I com and dranke wyth them and toke Wylliam Bretten wyth me, and whe had ryught gode comynecacyon, and the person plesetheyde me whell as be the fyrst comynycacyon: sche ys yewnge, lytyll, and whery whellfauyrd and whytty, and the contre spekys myche good bye hyr. Syr, aull thys matter abydythe the cowmyng of her father to London, that whe may wndyrstonde what some he wyll departte with, and how he lykys me. He wyll be heyr wythin iij whekys. I pray send me a letter how ye thynke be thys matter. ...

(Hanham 1975, letter 165)

Richard was in the area to pack wool and was obviously mixing business and pleasure. However, he later married Anne Rawson, the daughter of a wealthy Yorkshire mercer who became sheriff of London, and benefited from her dowry to the sum of 500 marks (£323 6s 8d), an enormous sum for the day.

The Cely letters seem also to capture the transformation of a wool merchant into a general merchant or mercer. There was a clear trend towards staplers diversifying into mercering, and this is evident in the Cely purchase of a Breton fishing boat, which was refitted as their own small merchantman. William Marryon had joined with Richard and George in buying this, and as the *Margaret Cely* set sail in 1485 it was equipped with modern gunpowder weapons to repel any raiders. It seems to have been used by the Celys as a way of diversifying their business, as it carried wine, salt, and grain rather than wool.

In common with other wool merchants the Celys endowed their local church, which was the church of St Olave at Mark Lane in London. Both Richards are recorded as being principal benefactors of this church, though the evidence has not survived due to damage to the church in the Second World War. A monument was, however, recorded in the sixteenth century where Richard Cely and Robert Cely were described as 'principall builders and benefactors of this church' (Povah 1894). In a will of 1493 Richard asked to be buried in the chapel of St Stephen and 'in the tomb' where his parents were buried. Other memorials in the church recorded other wool merchants, and wool-packers of the fifteenth-sixteenth centuries (Povah 1894), demonstrating that this part of London was heavily involved in the wool trade.

TRADE WITH THE ITALIANS

The fourteenth-century tendency for the Italians to travel far and wide in pursuit of good wool had continued into the fifteenth century (47), when it was still generally acknowledged that some of the very best wool came from the Cotswolds. This then became the chief hunting ground for the Italian merchants. Southampton continued as the port of choice, and was now an impressive sight with its large gates and defensive walls (48). The records of the Southampton Weigh House, which list both the buyers and the sellers of wool being exported,

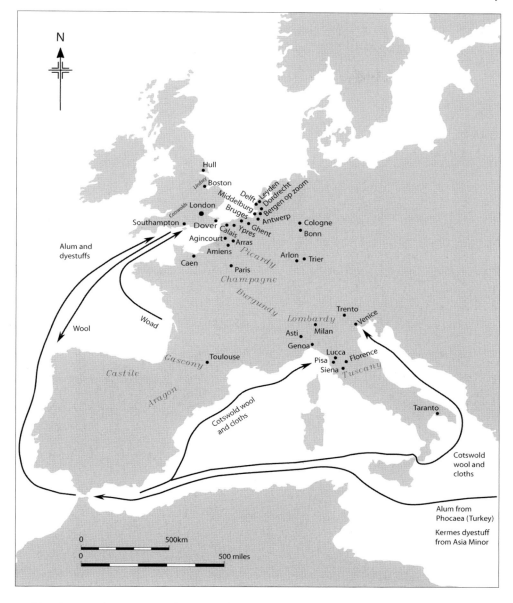

47 Plan showing the overseas trade routes of Southampton in the fifteenth century (after Platt 1973), and foreign places mentioned in the text

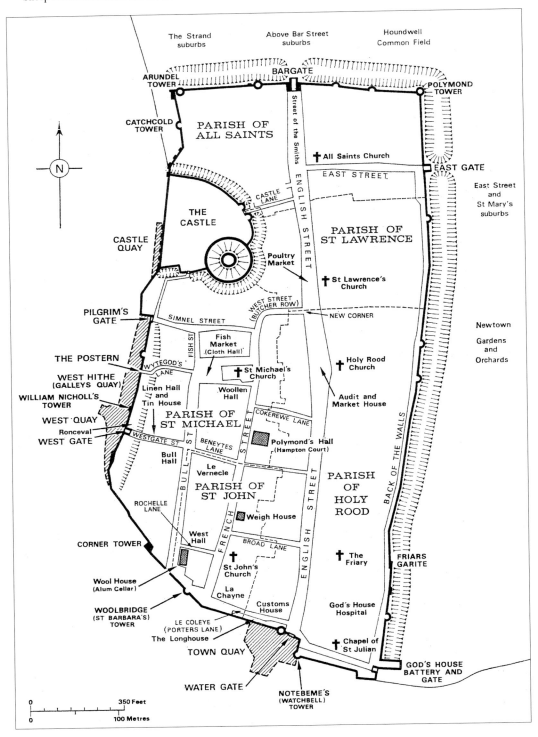

48 Plan of the port of Southampton in the late Middle Ages. (After Platt 1973)

show the prominence of the Cotswold woolmen. John Pynnock and William Fludgate of Burford, John Busshe and William Midwinter of Northleach, who also all supplied the Celys in London with much of their wool, all appear as clients of the Florentine and Venetian exporters (Ruddock 1951, 89). While the Italians let the locals deal in their imports, such as spices and exotically coloured pottery (49), in contrast they always dealt directly with their Cotswold wool suppliers. In turn the wool dealers were keen to do direct business with the Italians, as not only, as bankers, did they often have the ready cash, but they could often pay very high prices (Fryde 1983, 329).

The trade depended on close co-operation by the suppliers who would contract to bring the wool into Southampton via the main gate (50) by a certain day, as the Italian ships were infrequent though regular visitors. This meant that a lot of careful business arrangements had to be planned going far into the future. Italian dealers travelling in the Cotswolds would also send letters to agents in Southampton to expect wool, and sometimes these arrangements went awry, and the parties ended up in court. The latter occurred in 1429, when the Albertine buyer Serragli did not stick to his arrangements about the considerable consignment of 13 'bales' of fells (both sheep and lambs) bound by cart for Southampton, which he had collected together from Burford, Witney and other towns in the Cotswolds (*de Cotteswold*; Holmes 1960).

49 A fifteenth-century Florentine maiolica (tin glazed enamel) dish excavated in Southampton. *By courtesy of Southampton Museum of Archaeology*

50 Bargate, the main north gateway into medieval Southampton, where wool traders will have paid brokage (toll) fees

In other ways things did not always go to plan in this complex international trade. The Alberti were a particularly eminent Florentine family who had become papal bankers after the financial failures of other Italian firms in the 1340s (Holmes 1960). In the 1430s they also failed, leaving large debts across the Cotswolds which took years of international litigation to clear up. One bond for wool purchases for £666 13s 4d was owing to William Willey (Weoley) of Chipping Campden, and the document drawn up in Campden on 12 November 1435 still survives in the Medici archive in Italy. Despite going to a Florentine court in pursuit of the Alberti and winning, Willey was still not paid, and the debt was only redeemed ten years later when the Medici paid over the money as part of re-establishing the Florentine position in the English wool trade (Holmes 1960). Such cases must have had a diminishing effect on the wool trade, but the demand was so great that even such serious setbacks had little lasting effect.

The wool, after being carried long distances in bulging sarplers, would have been handed over at the wool beam in the Southampton Weigh House (*51*) to local agents of the Italian merchants. Storage prior to shipment was in the Wool House (*le Wollehous* of 1454; Burgess 1976), which still stands today, and is a large stone-built building at the end of Bugle Street (*52*). Members of the town porters' guild eventually carried the wool to the West Gate for loading onto the galleys. A visit to the nearby Customs House would have been necessary to verify any export licence or to pay customs dues, and part of the building used for this purpose survives today with the fanciful name of Canute's Palace (*53*).

51 The Weigh House in Southampton, where the king's weigh beam was kept. This tall thirteenth-century building with a fifteenth-century doorway and later alterations was gutted by Second World War bombing

52 The Wool House in Southampton, built in the late fourteenth century, which was used to store wool destined for export. The frontage has some eighteenth-century alterations

53 The fifteenth-century Southampton Customs House by the Water Gate, formerly a prosperous merchant's house of the late twelfth century and known today as 'Canute's Palace'. From this position next to the quayside officials would ensure that the heavy duties on exported English wool were collected

In the meantime the town's bakers must have been working overtime, as each time they set sail the Italians took on board many tons of biscuits for the journey (Ruddock 1951).

When the Venetians fitted out their galleys in the mid-fifteenth century they stipulated that Cotswold cloths and madder must be brought back to Italy, and not sold at ports on the way back (Brown 1864). Clearly the Cotswold cloths were held in the highest esteem, and had become one of the primary objectives of Italian trade with England in this period. In 1428 the firm of Sancasciano of Pisa was stocking six varieties of Cotswold cloth. In the second half of the fifteenth century Italian merchants dealing in Cotswold wool in Venice expected their profits to be as high as 47 per cent of the outlay in England, or 37 per cent of their total investment (Fryde 1976). This was higher than profits they could make on other commodities such as alum (at 26 per cent).

In 1442-4, which was a typical period of Italian trade, 27,414 sacks (approximately 4,500 tons) of English wool were exported, and alien duty was paid on 3,668 sacks (only 13 per cent). The English merchants envied these favourable conditions of trade, and so in 1456 there was a petition in the English parliament complaining that the Italians were roaming about the country buying up wool, cloth, tin and paying in ready cash (Fryde 1974, 328). Sometimes English merchants were tempted to export under the names of aliens, which was illegal. Accordingly, Thomas Canynges in 1456 was caught exporting 272½ sacks under the names of two Venetians.

The Italians were notorious for buying in bulk at high prices, so when the normal price for Cotswold wool was £8 per sack, the exceptionally wealthy Venetian Corner brothers still bought 19 sacks from the abbot of Cirencester in 1442-3 for £10 per sack. Another Venetian paid the same high price for wool from the abbots of Gloucester, Winchcombe and Oseney in the following year. In 1441-4 the Venetians, Lucchese and Lombards were regularly paying £9 a sack for the Cotswold wool, as this was backed by the high prices they could get in Italy which the English merchants were not able to reach (Fryde 1983). Complaints by the Celys in 1480 show that this situation long prevailed. However, the English may have exaggerated the impact of the alien traders, as the scale of the wool industry was so great that, despite the large amounts of wool the Italians handled, it was to remain a relatively small percentage of the overall export trade, except for a few exceptional years such as 1444-5 (53 per cent) or 1476-7 (69 per cent) where the wool supply seems to have been generally depleted (Fryde 1974, 329). In the later fifteenth century the Italians handled on average only around 10 per cent of the overall wool exports.

This competition seems to have been particularly fierce for the best wool, as general export figures do not bear out that the Italians were dominating the market. Anti-Italian sentiment was widespread again in the 1450s and official exploitation of this took place in 1458 when the Genoese were blamed for some pirates attacking two Bristol ships off Malta. Faced with a ban the Genoese paid £6,000 just to keep trading in England (Fryde 1983). So valuable was the trade that even this extortionate fine was no obstacle to its continuation.

The Italian trick of exporting wool without paying customs duties still continued, as long as the English king kept granting more special licences in return for large loans of cash. The loans to the king were a way of earning favour for other more profitable business rather than a profitable business in their own right. For instance, Gherardo Canigiani had a licence in 1473, in return for a loan worth £6,600, and part of the wool cargo was carried on behalf of the Medici of Florence. There were 711 sacks and 20 *nails* of wool, which had been bought at £6,795 16s 5d, and were packed and conveyed to the galleys for £952. The licence in this case saved £1,738 12s 3d. Some of this wool was bought off John Tame indicating its Cotswold provenance, but some of the Italians were not to be trusted as one of their number defaulted on the £311 16s 4d owed to John Tame (Holmes 1996, 279). Large quantities of wool were available in the Cotswolds at this time (Holmes 1996, 279), and this case shows also how the wool was still typically being paid for by instalments spread over several years (Holmes 1996, 280):

First bought of William Flodgate of Burford 45 sacks 28 nails of Cotswold wool at 9 marks a sack – sum £425

Whereof paid in hand in ready money	£215
Item payable the 15th day of May next coming	£105
Item payable the 15th day of March 1475	£105

The other Cotswold wool merchants named in this deal were:

Thomas Alan of Stow	62 sacks 4 nails
Thomas Jerveyse of Norton	45½ sacks 23 nails
William Saunders of Banbury	79 sacks 24 nails
John Tame of Fairford	96 sacks 40 nails
John Forte of Cirencester	43½ sacks 18 nails
Jane Lenarde and Richard Lombard of Campden	28 sacks 23 nails
Harry Bysshopp of Burford	35 sacks 6 nails
John Pynnok of Burford	58½ sacks 17 nails

Though Canigiani had broken with the Medici in 1473 his deals were still being referenced in Medici accounts in 1475. This transaction denotes a preference for Cotswold wool in these large-scale shipments. The wool was carried on a Genoese carrack and two Neapolitan galleys, 518 sacks having been purchased directly from Cotswold woolmen, and the rest being purchased from London merchants. The whole cargo was listed as from the Cotswolds, and so even the London-bought wool was from that locale. The London branch of the Cotswold wool trade must have been prolific judging by the activities of the Celys, but unfortunately it is less well known from surviving records than the Southampton branch.

The Venetians travelled in some style and their itinerary was set on departure, and with long spells in port of up to three months long. They protected themselves by having 30 crossbowmen per galley (Myers 1969, 1050). The tone of official despatches suggests that their trading partners in Flanders and England were natural allies, when any political difficulties arose. However, at the local level resentments festered about the Italian merchants, who were accused of buying up goods, and in particular wool and cloth, and storing them until the prices rose, and then partly reselling these back to the English (presumably at inflated prices in times of shortage). Their exclusive resorting with their own kind, and their freedom in importing and selling goods from abroad, was thought to be reducing opportunities for the English, whereas their engagement in 'easy occupations' (not ploughing or carting), was a particular cause for complaint. So in 1484 the king set about controlling the Italians more rigorously, ruling, for instance, that they had only eight months within which to sell their goods, and thereafter had to remove them, and they were also prevented from buying up and reselling English goods here, most especially wool and cloth (Myers 1969, 1052).

In 1499 the king paid Canigiani over £400 to cover his debts to Pynnock, Alan and Fortey (Holmes 1996, 283). Clearly this business was far from being free of risk, though the king on occasion appears to have been willing to act as a guarantor for his Italian merchants. Sometimes the debts were enormous, for John Fortey was at one time owed the sum of £884 13s 4d for wool supplied for shipment out of Southampton (Power 1926, 21).

A merchant's (possibly a stapler's) notebook of the second half of the fifteenth century (the *Noumbre of Weights*; see above) refers to the shipping of Cotswold wool at an average purchase price of £8 per sack (plus custom and subsidy) with freight on the Venetian galleys costing £2 (much more expensive than on a Genoese carrack). With the addition of all other expenses (e.g. transport to the port, handling, and customs at the alien rate in accordance with a statute issued in 1441) the final cost to the merchants was £14 10s 6d per sack, as against an expected final sale price of £20 in Venice. This compared very favourably for the seller with the contemporary sale price of £12 per sack in Calais. The expected profit in Italy was, therefore, about £5 10s per sack (Ruddock 1951, 197), the equivalent of 37 per cent return on the total investment, or 47 per cent of the original outlay in England up to the point of shipment. This was, by far, a much greater profit than could be made at Calais by the staplers (Fryde 1972, and 1983), and explains the avidity with which the Italian trade was pursued despite the huge financial backing that was necessary.

The English king himself sometimes indulged in this trade, especially since he would hardly tax himself, and stood to make maximum profits. For instance, Edward IV sent his ship *Mary de la Towre* from Southampton with a wool cargo (Power 1926, 21). A later cargo was sent from London with wool supplied by Heryot. Uzzano reckoned up the heavy costs of this trade from the wool grower to sale of the wool in Florence, and indicated a three- or four-fold increase in the price (Power 1926, 21). More often, however, the king sold his special licences directly to others to avoid any risks to his own finances, and it was a very useful way of paying off large debts (Power 1926, 21). These licences were sometimes granted to other members of the royal family for which the king was providing, notably Edward IV granted one to his mother in lieu of the £400 per annum he was supposed to be providing to her himself! His royal towns such as Southampton and Sandwich could also be beneficiaries in this way. Where the king owed money to staplers this was the obvious way to pay them back (e.g. to Heryot, Crosby, Stokker; Power 1926, 21). Such licences were transferable, and so became valuable tender in their own right.

But eventually the king fell out with the Italians, and towards the end of the fifteenth century the Italian ships began to be less frequent visitors. Instead English merchants hired ships to sail to the Mediterranean ports, including royal ships, emphasising the king's displeasure with the Italians. Wealthy London capitalists hired the royal ships, such as the *Sovereign* and the *Regent* and sent their goods to Southampton to be loaded. Gradually native Southampton merchants also joined in. The Venetians were singled out by being refused any wool, except if it was bound for Pisa and Florence (Ruddock 1951, 220). In 1490 a staple for English wool was set up in Pisa (Fryde 1983), as English ships were now regularly visiting. Troubles in Italy were also gradually making it less likely that its ships would make the journey, and the alum was also running out (Fryde 1983) making it less profitable for the Italians to make the trip to England. In this period the Cotswold wool was used for the most expensive Florentine cloth and so quality rather than quantity remained paramount (Postan 1973, 350). Licences were still being acquired occasionally in the early 1500s for export of wool. For instance, Brancino in 1510 gained a licence to ship out 100 sacks of wool, and various Cotswold woolmen were still regular visitors to Southampton, including Thomas Bushe, William Fludgate and the abbot of Cirencester's agent. However, cloth was now becoming a more important export cargo, including *cloths without grain* (Ruddock 1951, 237) which were probably going to be finished abroad.

Henry VIII granted the town corporation of Southampton in *c.*1515 a valuable licence to export 100 sacks of wool free of custom. Typically this licence was then purchased by Leonardo Frescobaldi for £296 13s 4d (Platt 1973). But Venetian ships ceased to arrive in England for wool in 1533 (Fryde 1974). Southampton's days as a major port were also numbered, as from the 1580s London merchants were effectively closing out provincial merchants (Platt 1973).

9

The sixteenth century

Where Cotswold's hillocks famed for weighty sheep ... with golden fleeces clothed
(Extract from William Camden's *Britannia* of 1586)

The Northleach wool dealers continued to trade at Southampton in the 1500s as in the previous century. So Thomas Bushe (*54* and *55*), the richest man in Gloucestershire in 1522, was recorded in the Southampton Weigh House accounts selling wool in 1525 (*56*). But the international situation was now changing radically, as the Italians eventually lost favour with the English king, and in 1542 the Venetian wool export licence was refused on the grounds that they were too friendly with the Pope (Chapman 1915).

In 1510–15 the average combined value of the cloth and wool exports was £104,000 per annum (80 per cent of all English exports), with London now handling 70 per cent of the trade and foreign merchants having up to 50 per cent of the business (Hoskins 1976, 178). London was taking a more dominant role in this trade and Southampton went into decline from the early sixteenth century, as London merchants stopped using it as a way of avoiding a hazardous trip through the Channel (Hoskins 1976, 180). There was also less demand from the Southampton hinterland for easy access to the high seas, as the local wool was instead, to some extent, being diverted to local spinners and weavers. Weaving was a way of supplementing incomes, especially when farm work was at a low ebb during the winter. Weavers were in demand given the buoyancy of cloth sales and so a wave of immigrant cloth workers from the Low Countries was generally to be welcomed (Lipson 1953, 61).

Though cloth was eclipsing wool in terms of international trade, it was still recognised that it was local wool that gave England its tremendous economic advantage (*33*). This was a period in which the public outcry against sheep farmers rose to a crescendo. Many contemporaries make reference to the clearance of the poor from land so that landlords could run large numbers of sheep without hindrance, as expressed in a popular ballad of *c.*1520:

54 *Left* Brass memorial in Northleach church of wool merchant Thomas Bushe (d. 1525) and his wife Joan (d. 1526)

55 *Below* Detail of the Thomas Bushe brass at Northleach church showing a sheep and a woolpack

Gret men makithe now a dayes
A shepecott in the churche.
... Towns pulled down to paster shepe: ...
(Tawney and Power 1924a, 19)

The Tudor explorer John Leland writing in 1536-9 (Smith 1964) observed for himself 'the great flokkes of sheepe' in the Cotswolds, but also noted here that 'in some places there groweth fair corn'. This sounds like a reference to the traditional sheep-corn husbandry of the Cotswolds, where sheep were also being carefully used to increase the fertility of the local arable fields.

But generally the decay of smaller farms was continuing apace as the engrossers sought to increase their pastures at the cost of arable (*AgHEW* IV 216). A national commission of enquiry into depopulation set up by Cardinal Wolsey started to bring prosecutions and the dismantling of enclosures was enforced where these had caused deprivation to others. However, it was difficult to win this war against enclosure, when both the main tenants and the landlords were jointly intent on this course. In 1533 it was stated in a new act of parliament that sheep were the cause of the decline in rural population, since 'great profit that cometh from sheep', and a limit of 2,400 sheep was set, subject to a penalty of 3s 4d for every sheep in excess of this number (lambs under one year old did not count, and, if the sheep were on private land, there was no limit anyway). But farmers got around this by assigning the maximum number of sheep to each member of the family. There was also a regulation that no more than two farms were to be held by any landlord, and informers were invited to police the system (*AgHEW* IV, 217).

There was a general awareness that some landowners were taking advantage of sheep and wool production to the detriment of other members of society and that prices were rising rapidly (Watson 1932, 372):

As divers ... subjects ... have ... invented ways and means how they might accumulate and gather together into few hands as well great multitudes of farms ... and ... sheep, putting such lands as they can get to pasture ... One of the greatest occasions that moveth ... those greedy and covetous people so to accumulate ... is onely the great profit that cometh of sheep ... that some have 24,000 ... a good sheep for victual that was to be sold for 2s 4d or 3s at the most is noe sold for 6s or 5s or 4s at the lest and a stone of clothing wool ... accustomed to be sold for 18d or 20d is now sold for 4s or 3s 4d at the least ...
(Extract from the 1533 Act)

The sites of many deserted medieval villages can be found in the Cotswolds today, and this does suggest that the widespread tendency to clear away weakened communities from the fourteenth century onwards, to make way for sheep, may have applied here. However, there is little proof, and the process of desertion may instead have followed a natural course, as the climate deteriorated slightly in this period and people, in response, sought shelter on more sheltered lowland sites. Overall this pattern contrasts with the trend in the adjacent Severn Vale to the west where desertions were less common (Roberts and Wrathmell 2000), and where the farming regime was quite different, and perhaps more immune to the pressures of the day.

One case that may illustrate the prevailing situation in the Cotswolds was that of the abbot of Hailes, who kept 900 sheep at Longborough and owned most of the parish. He was accused of harassing his tenants, who were not well off, but the value of his holding at £38 per annum was probably enough to have made any attempt to gain greater profits too much of a scandal for enclosure to be attempted. He certainly had the power to carry this through, as there would have been no other major interests to object (Cornwall 1988), but enclosure was not finally instigated at this time. In contrast, Sezincote was enclosed in 1486, and so occasionally enclosure was followed through in the Cotswolds as elsewhere.

The Depopulation Act of 1536 does not list Gloucestershire as a county affected by settlement desertion, and this tends to confirm that this was not an area where the loss of rural population was most extreme. However, it is clear from land values that enclosure was very advantageous to the landowner, since enclosed pasture was valued at 1s 6d to 3s per acre, and enclosed meadow at 3s to 5s in 1547-8 (Tate 1943, 21), and so there must have been plenty of pressure from the more business-minded to follow the enclosure course.

Some abbeys were returning to the direct farming of sheep and were again directly involved in foreign trade in the generation before the Dissolution, which suggests that the profitability of large estates was now returning. Oseney Abbey, for instance, took back pasture (*AgHEW* IV 313) and was dealing in wool at Burford, as well as returning to the practice of collecting wool (either in rent, by tithe or by purchase). Both Bruern and Oseney Abbeys were exporting to Calais, as well as Cirencester, Gloucester, Winchcombe, Hailes, Pershore and Evesham Abbeys in the early 1530s. In the early sixteenth century, 2,000 sheep were sheared at Barrington, which was the centre for the Llanthony Priory shearing, and this shows that the sheep numbers remained high. The letters of John Johnson who was a merchant of the staple (e.g. *Cal LPFD* XIX pt I, no. 43) show that dealing in Cotswold (*Cotsall*) wool was still substantial in the 1540s.

The Cotswold dealers were still delivering wool to Southampton, as the Weigh House Book records in 1525-26, when the payments by Thomas Bushe (56; SA ref. SC5/8/1), and Edmund Tame were recorded for the hire of the city's weights. Wool remained a source of wealth for nave reconstruction at Cirencester in the early sixteenth century, where merchants' marks are carried aloft in the roof space by angels (Verey 1970). The abbot of Cirencester Abbey also seems to have invested in two more fulling mills in 1535, having benefited presumably from the one he always had (Woodman 1978).

Sheep were, therefore, still fundamental to the local economy. Local wills of this period mention wool-combs. The customary tithe of the parson was very much involved with sheep, and ½d was levied for each ewe or lamb sold between 11 November and 3 May, 1d for each sheep sheared and ½d for each sheep from

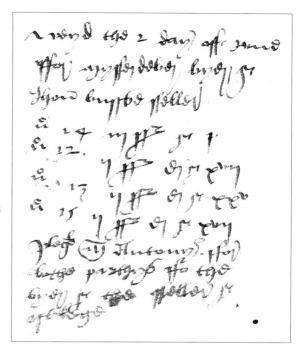

56 Southampton Weigh House accounts of 2 June 1525 showing Thomas Bushe of Northleach delivering four sarplers (nos 12-15) to the wool beam for weighing before handing them over to the buyer. For instance, the entry for Sarpler no. 13 'ii ss di xxv' records that this sarpler weighed 2.5 sack weights, and 25 *nails*, a total of 1085lb (493kg). *(SA reference SC5/1/33)*

another parish given pasture in Stanton and Snowshill. The parson also took the third lamb in every ten (though there was a provision for smaller flocks to contribute less). Nor did he lose out at the shearing with every tenth pound made from the sale of wool to be paid before St Michael's Day (29 September; Barnard 1927). It seems to have become common for sheep to graze outside their parish in the pursuit of decent pasture, and in 1551 the rector of Compton Abdale was claiming ½d for each stranger's sheep. The prevalence of sheep is understated in local records, as the sheep were looked after by a village shepherd and so had less chance to stray, unlike horses.

The wool business could still be transacted in the time-honoured way, where deals were struck for long-term fixed price contracts, and so, for instance, George Somerfield contracted in 1504 to sell all his Gloucestershire wool to Richard Tanty of Chipping Norton for the remainder of his life at the fixed price of 5s 8d per stone (Bowden 1962). This compared to a home sale price of £8, and a Calais price of nearly £14 for a sack of Cotswold wool in *c*.1527 (Munro 1978, table 10). Some wool merchant families had been upwardly mobile, but sometimes still held onto the source of their original wealth. So William Grevel, a lawyer and probably a descendant of the Chipping Campden wool merchant, still held pasture in Blockley in 1507 and left sheep to Llanthony Priory in his will (Dyer 1980). Other merchants extended their activities by managing sheep runs themselves, such as Thomas Bushe of Northleach who leased Withington in 1510 and Thomas Davys of Stow who leased Stapenhill pasture in Blockley in 1508.

As enclosures increased, sheep numbers were creeping up, whereas stints on the common had usually restricted tenants to 50–60 sheep per yardland holding, and so set a limit on the number of sheep in a parish. Cleeve tenants, for instance, were allowed 30 sheep per yardland, and on this basis John Lawrence in 1523 had 360 sheep on the Cleeve commons. There was a contemporary estimate of 4.5 million sheep in 1545 of which 1.5 million were kept on commons (Hoskins 1976, 83), but this is probably an underestimate. A more detailed estimate of 1547 (for potential state tax purposes) puts the number of sheep at 8.5 million.

A sheep poll tax was enacted in 1549 but repealed in the same year (Beresford 1953). This was a failed attempt to slow down the conversion of arable to pasture. It was proposed that the subsidy should be levied at a rate of 1½d per sheep or 2d per ewe on enclosed pasture, or 1d per sheep on commons and open fallow, which would imply that sheep were more valuable in the former case. But the tax when introduced was higher and more complicated, as well as highly unpopular. It relied on a local panel of the parish priest and some honest villagers to take the sheep census, but in most cases honesty proved extremely scarce. The panel, even if it could be got together, hardly ever reported finding any sheep! Surviving records suggest that in many cases only one sheep farmer per village was listed (Beresford 1954b), and he was presumably the most unpopular!

The selling of monastic properties at the Dissolution, so that the Crown could realise their worth rather than the Catholic Church, created a flurry of land deals in the middle of the century. In many cases the land and property would previously have been in monastic hands for long periods, and these estates were generally in good order as the monks were capable landlords, who often maximised their cash income, as well as supplying their own basic needs as much as possible. This was a time when more pressure was put on pastures as a result, it seems, of increasing numbers of sheep due to the demand for wool remaining high, especially as the home textile industry had got into its stride. Many of the new owners of former monastic lands were also intent on rearing more sheep and so retained the sheep while often releasing any arable on lease, just as the monasteries had done before them.

There was now more opportunity to buy land. Indeed, some of the commissioners for the suppression of the monasteries in Gloucestershire were themselves active dealers in wool, such as John Arnold who kept 420 sheep at Eastington near Northleach (Rhodes 2002). But there was also an admission from the sixteenth century that the quality of the wool was in decline and that Spanish wool was becoming a serious threat (Tawney and Power 1924a). At the same time it was commonly understood that sheep kept on enclosed pasture rather than the common produced much more wool, and this must have encouraged the movement towards enclosure.

Pasture for sheep was another of the assets seized by the Crown at the Dissolution and Stanton and Snowshill demonstrates how sought-after this was. These were former possessions of Winchcombe Abbey and were sold off, eventually coming into the hands of a Newbury (Berkshire) cloth maker, whose son sold off various parts (Barnard 1927) apparently to local landowners. Temple Guiting also saw much speculation about its sheep pastures in the sixteenth century. But pastures were now being put under pressure through overstocking, as evident from decreasing stints set during the sixteenth–seventeenth centuries, which were enforced locally through the manor courts.

The effects of the Dissolution could be spectacular as monastic buildings were transformed by their new owners. In 1546 William Stumpe, a clothier of Malmesbury, rented Oseney Abbey and employed 2,000 people to make cloth. A Burford cloth maker called Tuckar also attempted to buy Abingdon Abbey with its fulling mills intact (Lipson 1953, 76) probably for a similar scheme. At Cirencester Leland recorded 'a right goodly clothing mill' being set up within the abbey ruins (*Gloucestershire VCH* II), though the scale of the operation is not made explicit. At Gloucester Thomas Bell set up a cap-making workshop in the Blackfriars (Johnson 1985). Some of these larger initiatives, such as at Oseney, were in advance of their time, as they were more in keeping with a factory system, but the state was still too suspicious of such large undertakings to allow them to succeed. The Weavers' Act of 1555 was aimed at controlling this factory tendency, at least outside the towns, by insisting that clothiers should keep only one loom, and weavers no more than two (Lipson 1953, 78), though independent weavers took little notice.

At the outset of the sixteenth century unfinished broadcloths had been the mainstay of the West Country cloth industry, except for the famous scarlet cloth of Stroud (Ponting 1957, 37), and cloth exports increased enormously to 84,000 in the reign of Henry VIII. In the mid-sixteenth century cloth exports reached 122,000 (Finberg 1975, 86). Wool exports were ebbing away, but the best quality English wool had remained in demand. In some of the most eminent cloth-making centres of Flanders (e.g. Ghent and Brussels) there were still pronouncements that only English wool must be used. This was for the very highest quality products (Bridbury 1982, 95), and it is likely that lesser qualities of English wool were now simply priced out of the market by Spanish wool of medium quality which carried little tax.

The cloth industry was now being especially favoured by the authorities in the second half of the sixteenth century, though only in the towns, with the exception of the Stroud area (*Gloucestershire VCH* II, 157). The tendency to weave rather than till the land was countered by laws restricting the number of looms available and restricting the industry to specific towns and districts. However, rural growth in cloth manufacture carried on regardless of efforts by the authorities to control it. Cloth making was also subject to many bad practices and laws were passed in the mid-sixteenth century to try and raise standards.

A clothing statute of 1552 stated that broadcloth must be 7 quarters (1.6m) wide, 26-28 yards (23.8-25.6m) long and weigh 44lb (20kg). This was quite a heavy cloth which would be about the weight of a heavy overcoat today. These statutes were repeatedly varied! They were a government attempt to make up for the increasing decline of the medieval guilds. There was felt to be a need for apprenticing ('until a man grow unto the age of 24 he is for the most part, though not always wild, without judgement and not of sufficient experience to govern himself'). The better cloths, the 'reds' and 'whites' in Wiltshire, Gloucestershire and Somerset, were regulated, when wet, to conform with the dimensions stated in the statute of 1552, and, when dry, they were supposed to weigh at least 64lb (29kg) for 'whites' and 60lb (27.2kg) for 'reds'.

Always alert to a potential threat to the state, Cecil, confidant of Elizabeth I, wrote on the 'Export in cloth and wool' in c.1564 that cloth making was becoming a distraction, since he observed that the cultivation of the land was in decline and that the cloth worker was less manageable than his rustic equivalent. He suggested sending any out-of-work cloth makers to Ireland (Ponting 1957, 58-9). Similar fears of work running out might explain an Act of Parliament passed in 1577 which demanded than any male over six years old should wear a woollen cap made in England as part of their Sunday dress (Baddeley 1924).

The Cotswolds were now renowned for its broadcloth made at many places, and most especially on the fringes of the hills including at Dursley, Wootton under Edge, Bath, Trowbridge, Bradford-on-Avon, Cirencester and Malmesbury (Carus-Wilson 1952). The types of cloth were now no longer styled after towns but instead they are called 'Stroudwaters', 'Cotswolds' or 'Castle Combes', or generally referred to as 'Westerns'. The work had moved down the valleys, for example to Stroud or Chalford in the south Cotswolds. The clothier was becoming a prominent member of society, having started by parcelling out of wool to spin into yarn. They provided very low wages and often complained that some of the wool was stolen. The weight of the yarn was supposed to be much the same as the wool handed out, with the additional butter or oil added for carding being the equivalent of any waste that had been lost. The variability of the wool, combined with the variable quality and character of the spinning, in the end made it very difficult for the weaver to achieve consistency even in a single cloth (Ponting 1957, 39).

It was just as well that the Cotswold cloth makers were advancing, as conditions abroad for the English wool trader were deteriorating. In the mid-sixteenth century there was still some semblance of the profitable export licence trade. John Stephens, gentleman and woolman of Bourton-on-the-Hill, was granted a licence in 1552 to export (or resell in the home market, so revealing the precarious nature of the trade) 500 sarplers. However, the system when turned internally had no checks, and Stephens and his associates were eventually hauled into court for exceeding their quota by 3,500 sarplers in the Cotswolds! (Bowden 1962, 128).

In 1558 Calais was captured by the French, and so the wool staple moved to Bruges. The 1561 charter raised the export duty that had for so long been £2 to £3 for each sack up to 3,000, and 53s 4d for each sack above that. More troubles forced a move from Bruges in 1569, but this was inconvenient, and so the mart returned to Bruges in 1574. It was now so difficult to make profits that merchants were leaving the trade (Bowden 1962, 162). A change of direction was needed and the staplers were allowed to trade at home instead, though here they were unable to achieve a privileged position. They also failed to transfer their privileged position in wool export trade to cloth, as the Merchant Adventurers succeeded in excluding them in a monopoly of trade with the Netherlands in 1579 (Bowden 1962, 163). Competition with Spanish wool was also making trade in English wool abroad extremely difficult.

With the setbacks in the export trade becoming more common, the home market became more important. Here prices for fleeces remained good. A Northleach will put the value of 200 Cotswold sheep in 1560 at £40 (Anon. 1881, 319). The 1,000 sheep on Compton Common were profitable with one witness attesting that '9 score' sheep yielded 13 tods at 22s per tod, while another says 200 sheep give 16 tods at 24s per tod (cf Cely's 13s 4d per tod in 1480; Kosmala 1993). In the later sixteenth century William Fermor was dealing in wool equivalent to a flock of 18-27,000 sheep in the Cotswolds (*AgHEW* IV, 545), so there were still plenty of sheep here. Another inventory gives the price of sheep in 1584/5 as 4s 4d each with a tod of wool worth 16s (Havinden 1965, no. 129). But, despite wool being the essential ingredient for the advancing national cloth industry, the sheep farmer was still a figure to be criticised for his ceaseless pursuit of profit to the waste of the community. 'Gredy gentylmen whyche are shepemongers and grasyers' and 'catapillers of the commonweale' were phrases applied to the hated farmers seeking to take advantage of the rising price of wool in the second half of the sixteenth century (Seebohm 1927, 195).

The specialised buildings of the sheep farmer remained a characteristic of the farming scene. The rector of Bourton-on-the-Water still had a sheep-house near his new mansion in 1584, and the rector of Broadwell also had a sheep-house next to his barn (Jones 1994, 144-5), as these buildings continued to be regarded as essential to good sheep rearing. Another rural building referred to in this period is the *wooll house*, presumably a workshop judging by the contents of one belonging to a wealthy yeoman at Witney (Oxfordshire) in 1583, which included cards, scales and shears. Presumably this was a sheep farmer who also prepared wool for spinning (Havinden 1965, no. 107).

In parallel with the growing importance of cloth making the clothier became a more established figure. Some were foreigner cloth makers, who had been officially encouraged to emigrate to England, such as the de la Plaigne (Playne) family from Flanders, who were to play a major part in Cotswold industry for generations (Lewis 1996). They do not seem to have had the same social cachet as their predecessors, the wool merchants. In common with other successful traders they typically wanted to invest their profits in land, but in 1576 the established old gentry were obviously feeling threatened, so they secured a law limiting the buying of land by clothiers in Wiltshire, Somerset and Gloucestershire, and restricted them to 20 acres (Ponting 1957, 50). The newly enriched clothiers followed in the footsteps of the merchants of the previous century in another way, as they also spent some of their money on the local churches. As well as climbing socially the clothier was taking more control over his business. Whereas a local official known as the alnager was supposed to inspect the cloth before sealing them, this responsibility had often by the sixteenth century passed to the clothiers themselves for a substantial payment.

By the end of the sixteenth century the wool staplers had disappeared in the face of the rise of the Adventurers, and in this period Spanish wool was being imported, which was an ominous sign of things to come. At the same time the growth in sheep farming reached a natural peak and was soon to be followed by the return to corn growing which gathered pace from around 1600 (Beresford 1954b).

The Cotswold sheep was still going strong, however, and as usual was being celebrated for its wool in 1586, when it was described by William Camden (1551–1623) as a mainstay of the region:

> Upon these hills are fed large flocks of sheep, with the whitest wool, having long necks and square bodies, by reason, as is supposed, of hilly and short pasture; whose wool is much valued by foreign nations.
>
> (*Camden's, Britannia*, 1586)

10

The seventeenth century

By the end of the sixteenth century the Merchant Adventurers had taken over a monopoly of the undyed broadcloth trade and were involved by 1606 in the annual export of over 80,000 undyed broadcloths (Ponting 1957, 61). The early part of this century (1601-20) was one of economic revival, and the textile industry was one of the chief beneficiaries. However, the import of wool from Ireland and from Spain was undermining the value of English wool (*AgHEW* IV, 641). Fortunately, sheep were also now being appreciated for their meat at a time when corn prices were rising, and so farmers were presumably not so concerned with wool quality. Formerly (up to the late medieval period) the meat market had only been supplied with old or diseased animals, and, except for personal household consumption, even cattle had been fattened and killed only at the end of their useful working lives. As this new trend towards meat production gathered pace beef might well have completely eclipsed mutton, as cattle were easier to move long distances and the larger carcase size made supply more straightforward. However, the meat supply of large cities reached far into the surrounding country, and so, for instance, sheep farmers even in the Midlands were able to take advantage the London meat market.

Under King James in 1614 there was an attempt to eliminate foreign cloth competition by banning the export of English wool (Bowden 1962) on which some of the best foreign cloth producers depended. Various proclamations were made against the export of sheep and wool in 1603-25 and 1625-49. This created the perfect situation for wool smuggling to become rife; the best English wool could still command much better prices abroad, as some foreign cloth makers persisted in their traditional loyalty to English wool. The export ban was also a royal gesture of support to the new manufacturing class, and a sign of disapproval to the merchant class since the king no longer saw English wool as a keystone to his economic policy, as the medieval kings had. At the same time the government backed moves against the middlemen who were held responsible for the maintenance of unnecessarily high wool prices, and so the merchant staplers were even targeted for prosecution. This led to a compromise where the manufacturers were given the right to buy direct from the wool producer from June to Michaelmas (29 September), with wool dealing only being possible for the remainder of the year. But in 1624 the restrictions on middlemen dealers were lifted. Some would-be staplers were even trying to re-introduce the medieval practice of controlling the wool trade as a monopoly, as English kings could sometimes still be prevailed upon to bestow such exclusive privileges (Bowden 1962).

In the 1620s English hat makers in particular experimented with Spanish wool, and this resulted in new industry on the Somerset and Wiltshire border (Bowden 1956-7). Spanish wool was also widely used throughout Gloucestershire for the coloured cloths which now began replacing the undyed broadcloths as the main product (Ponting 1957, 57). Gloucestershire again shone, this time as a cloth-making region producing dyed broadcloths. The seventeenth century saw what amounted to the industrialisation of cloth production in the Cotswolds, and it became a major employer, particularly in the Stroud area, where, on average, 42 per cent of occupations were involved in cloth making in 1608 (Perry 1945). For instance, at North Nibley there were 5 clothiers, 58 weavers and 15 fullers out of a male population of 132, but this was the most extreme example of a settlement involved in cloth production (Perry 1945). Uley similarly had over half its adult males working as weavers (Finberg 1975). Sometimes specialist craft skills were threatened by innovations in machinery, as the industry looked for improved production methods. For instance, in the 1630s there were disputes about the introduction of gig mills for raising the nap just before shearing (Watson 1932, 374), but eventually the Stroudwater clothiers were successful in continuing these techniques with the support of the law.

Wool was not yet losing its value and it remained a source of some wealth to landed families, as the earl of Middlesex's estates in Warwickshire, Gloucestershire and Worcestershire in 1631 derived an income of over £1,500 per annum from fleeces alone, and another £1,000 from other sheep related business (Bowden 1962). However, there are indications that this situation was not maintained for much longer, and it was fortunate that the development of the mutton market went some way to soften this blow as the seventeenth century wore on. Cotswold sheep were being sold at Smithfield in London in 1622 and it is possible that, with the return to corn growing on a large scale, the Cotswold sheep were in favour still as they would still have been useful to the farmer for improving the fertility of the fields, as had been widely practised on the Cotswold Hills in the medieval period.

It is unlikely that there had yet been any diminution in the numbers of sheep as the following shows sheep from several neighbouring parishes being pastured together, presumably because pastures in their own parishes were full:

John Ardway of Broadway	100
Thomas Blissard of Laberton	70

Widow Alice Blissard	60
Young Richard Fisher of the Cross	30
Edmund Ray	20
James Hale	20
John Tisoe of Buckland	40
John Browne of Broadway	40
Thomas Bridge of Laberton	20
Total	400

The number of sheep pastured on Snowshill Hill remained similar into the 1640s (Barnard 1927). And presumably other commons, which have survived as wide open spaces till today, such as Cleeve Hill (57), also remained stocked with sheep.

In addition to cloth weaving the knitting of hose was now being organised as a local industry. In 1658 there is evidence that the local rector was acting as a middleman organising the production of hose on a large-scale at an average price of 2s a pair (Barnard 1927). Though by this period, as the wool trade became less prominent in the local economy, towns such as Winchcombe may well have diversified into other businesses, there were still in 1608 five shepherds listed in the town's working population of 153 heads of families (Donaldson 1978). Rather than wool and textiles going into decline there was instead a proliferation

57 Cleeve Hill, a large area of upland summer grazing for sheep in the Middle Ages

of other activities in town and country, which made it seem that these products were now less significant.

Costs associated with wool production would seem to have been increasing. Detailed accounts of an Oxfordshire sheep enterprise in 1625–30 indicate that the gathering of sufficient hay for the flock amounted to nearly half the wages bill for annual shepherding. Shearing was a lesser expense at 3s (3s 4d) per 100 sheep. The usual rate for winding the wool up was 4d per 20 fleeces.

By the mid-seventeenth century Spanish wool was becoming a popular choice for English cloth makers. English fleeces were becoming heavier as the sheep were now often being raised on the rich pastures of newly enclosed ground, and breeding by selection for size was now much easier. This gave rise to a longer, coarser wool as well as a larger sheep and this type of wool fortunately was suited to the newly growing production of worsted cloth. This was a new type of light-weight cloth where patterns could be introduced into the design. A substantial worsted industry grew up in eastern England, and it seems likely that this was in response to the new type of wool that was becoming increasingly common.

In the second half of the seventeenth century the companies of the wool staplers finally faded away. The cloth handlers at Blackwell Hall, who had links with manufacturers, dealers and customers, instead found they could exploit their position, and they themselves dealt in Spanish wool, which was now much in favour. But the advent of Spanish wool may not have been the disaster it seems at first sight. Rather the booming English cloth industry was out-stripping home supply of wool, and so foreign sources had to be exploited as well. Sheep remained a common sight in the Cotswolds. The vicar of Northleach church watching the numbers of lambs being born was very careful in 1682 to describe the tithes he expected from the villagers of nearby Eastington, where for each 30 lambs, he was entitled to take the third best from the first ten (i.e. after the owner had first picked two), then the eighth best from the next ten, and then the tenth from the remainder. If a sheep was sold that had been pastured locally, then he was paid 2d, or 1d for sheep belonging outside the parish (Jones 1994, 146). Wool also remained a feature of local markets, with Daniel Defoe recording 5,000 packs of wool being sold annually at Cirencester market (Bowden 1962).

The cloth industry was now such an important employer that sometimes it received special support from national government. Parliament in 1678 introduced a certification system for burial in wool with a fine for evasion, which was to be split between the informer and the poor (Delderfield 1967). It is difficult to believe that such legislation was necessary when it was estimated that two-thirds of English exports were woollen goods, and that half of Europe was popularly thought to be clothed by England in the later seventeenth century. Most of this was done with English wool, as the import of foreign wool was inconsiderable until the nineteenth century (Lipson 1953, 52). However, this was only possible because of the ban on exporting English wool abroad, and the availability of foreign wool which deflated the price and so made cheap raw materials available.

For English cloth producers quality of the wool seems to have become less of an issue, as there is less evidence than in earlier periods for specific types of wool being demanded. In the absence of guilds to set standards it is possible that the highest quality cloths were just not made any longer.

II

The eighteenth century and later

When sheep breeds were finally distinguished across the country the Cotswold sheep was defined as one of the long wools, a widespread type including several different breeds, and from the eighteenth century with a geographical distribution from the Cotswolds north-eastwards into Lincolnshire. This distribution was along the Jurassic ridge, the same area as had been associated with both the Cotswold and Lindsey sheep of the Middle Ages, whether they were specific breeds at that time or not. The Cotswold type of sheep was already distinctive, based on its thousands of years of development largely in isolation, where it had adapted naturally to the land and to particular farming methods, notably cotting and folding. Its thick fleece was probably due to regular exposure on the hills, and its large well-formed body may reflect a diet rich in calcium and other minerals from the natural pastures of the limestone uplands. The only known outside influence was that its medieval character required periodic infusions of Lindsey blood perhaps to maintain the wool quality at its best.

The Cotswold sheep of the first half of the eighteenth century was, therefore, probably still true to its medieval type when it was described in living memory as having been then 'a small light carcass, polled animal' with 'a fleece of fine wool of about 3lb', while by the later eighteenth century this long-woolled sheep had been 'improved' but 'not changed' (Marshall 1796). The eighteenth century is marked by many modern commentators as the period when there was a great deal of selective breeding of sheep, though it is also admitted that there is little detailed documentary evidence for this. Bakewell popularised the Leicester breed of sheep, and its widespread introduction generally increased the amount of long staple wool available across the country (Bowden 1956-7). However, Cotswold breeders may not have persisted with the Leicester, as at least one writer in the early nineteenth century reckoned that too much breeding with Leicesters reduced the size of the sheep, as well as reducing the quality and quantity of wool (Marshall 1818). These adverse developments were sometimes even addressed by resort to pure-bred Cotswold rams suggesting that some of the original breed were retained (Elwes 1893).

The impact of this period on the Cotswold is, therefore, controversial, as some suggest that crossing with Leicesters altered the sheep out of all recognition, while others contend that the undoubted interest in breeding had little effect on the Cotswold. George Turner observed in 1794 that 'the fashionable Leicestershire sheep have been occasionally introduced into this district, and … have been found to improve the breed in shape and disposition to fatten'. The Cotswold longwool by the end of the eighteenth century was yielding 8lb of wool (Marshall 1796).

The trend towards enclosures was now given greater impetus across the Gloucestershire Cotswolds, as elsewhere in England, through a new parliamentary mechanism and the pace of change was increased as agricultural improvements swept across the countryside. This was generally accompanied by an increase in arable as the uplands were now being ploughed up. Where sheep were retained, wool prices show a preference for sheep kept on pasture rather than those grazing on fallow fields (Smith 1747), and folding on the arable was now generally going out of favour.

But the Cotswold wool was certainly no longer as desirable, and in 1767 the Herefordshire wool was three times its value, showing how far Cotswold wool had declined. However, it was not only the sheep that were changing, as some of the smaller towns such as Tetbury and Minchinhampton, that had been holding their own as wool and yarn markets, were now on the verge of decline as the more local industries gave way to the larger factories. This economic decline of the Cotswolds was to continue throughout the next century and this, combined with the natural remoteness of much of the region, has largely been responsible for maintaining its traditional rural character, reflected in the Cotswolds of today.

THE NINETEENTH CENTURY

Farming in the nineteenth century was a very different business than it had been in the Middle Ages. In the continuing absence of cheap fertilisers there was a natural tendency to adopt a mixed arable and pastoral regime if possible. Enclosure allowed profits to increase, though the farmer was at the mercy of world markets as transport improved. Yet there were opportunities for both arable and pastoral farming to thrive. The number of improved Cotswold (Leicester Cotswold cross) sheep at Eastington increased from 400 to 1,500 in around 1807, and 500 sheep a year were sold for meat (Rudge 1807). A similar post-enclosure pattern occurred at Aldsworth where 200 sheep became 1,800, and yet the fleeces increased in weight from eight to five to the tod, i.e. up to 5½lb each (Rudge as cited in *Gloucestershire VCH* II). New ways of managing had clearly led to a far heavier fleece in the local sheep (*58*).

The new improved Cotswold had the economic advantage that they matured and put on weight twice as fast as before. Further crossing with the Hampshire Down sheep produced a better quality sheep (the Oxford Down) in terms of meat and also finer wool, and it remained hardy (Copus 1989, 48). In 1875 it was reckoned that there were 453,881 sheep in Gloucestershire (*VCH* II, 244) out of a total sheep population of about 17 million in England and Wales (1866 census; Beresford 1954b), and here the Oxford Down was the most common type (*ibid* 249). The Cotswold now began to lose out, except that it was a popular choice for foreign breeders across the world, and especially in New Zealand (Read 1865). Its apparent resistance to scrapie, a serious disease, kept it in some demand. In response to this interest in pure-bred stock the Cotswold Sheep Society was founded in around 1892 and Robert Garne of Aldsworth was its first president, his family's records of a Cotswold flock going back to the late eighteenth century (Gibbings 1995).

58 Painting by Richard Whitford of prize-winning mid-nineteenth-century Cotswold sheep with William Lane of Broadfield Farm, near Northleach and his shepherd. *By courtesy of Iona Antiques, London*

THE TWENTIETH CENTURY

The Cotswold breed continued in its general decline in numbers and, with industrial innovation making long wool unnecessary for worsteds and then the collapse of corn prices which meant that the breed's last advantage as a means of fertilising poor arable was diminished, the breed became largely redundant. By the 1960s there were only about 200 left, at a time when sheep numbers in England were about 20 million (Garner and Ingram 1973). In 1966 the Cotswold Breed Society was re-established, and as a result the good qualities of the breed can still be appreciated today (Gibbings 1995).

The Cotswold sheep has, therefore, survived (59 and 66) and today the ram and ewe yield a fleece of about 22lb (10kg) and 13lb (6kg) respectively (Gibbings 1995). The wool is also quite fine (mid-40s on the Bradford Count system) with a staple length of about 10in (250mm), as well as being heavy. Contemporary modern craft spinners have a high regard for it, perhaps reflecting to some extent the high esteem it has been held by earlier generations of wool workers across Europe.

59 Cotswold ewe with lambs, one sitting on the ewe's back. © *Shaun Gibbings*

12

A hidden past

An archaeological approach is useful for seeking out some tangible links with the sheep farmers and wool dealers of the Middle Ages. The most famous of these have already been alluded to, specifically the 'wool churches' and the memorial brasses that survive, such as at Northleach church. But it is also possible to trace more subtle evidence of the medieval wool trade in the wider landscape.

Much of the openness of the higher ground in the Cotswolds has now gone with the advent of enclosures, but it still survives in a few places such as on Cleeve Hill (57) and Minchinhampton Common (13). These areas still represent the type of terrain that the sheep were once grazed on in the summer. Where the shepherd or farmer kept a sheep-house, these buildings have also occasionally survived after conversion to another use reflecting the high quality of the original constructions. It is usually claimed that the picturesque buildings of Arlington Row in Bibury incorporate such remains, for instance. Slight earthworks might otherwise mark the site of derelict sheep-houses at a less favourable location, as at Stanton (29). Large barns, that are usually regarded as exclusively for grain storage, should sometimes perhaps in the Cotswolds be viewed as being at least partially for wool storage, for instance at Frocester or at Stanway (18), on the Gloucester Abbey and Tewkesbury Abbey estates respectively. But it is the surviving sheepwashes which provide some of the best evidence, as their numbers reveal how extensive sheep farming was in the region into the nineteenth century.

SHEEPWASHES

Washing the sheep was an ancient country practice, and it arose because the wool attracted a better price if dirt had already been removed, besides having the additional advantages that it made the shearers' job more pleasant and it improved the keeping quality of the fleece, as long as it was thoroughly dried before storage. During washing, substances in the sheep's wool helped produce a natural detergent which made the washing very effective. It was often said that the water became soapier as more and more sheep passed through (Ryder 1983b).

It is likely that convenient places on streams had always been used for this purpose, and so the medieval shearing centres, such as Blockley and Sherborne, probably functioned in this way by selecting a convenient length of stream. In these cases some of the workers often stood in the water, for example at Uley. At some time, and certainly by the early nineteenth century, it became common to use a purpose-made structure, usually in, or just to one side of a stream, or even at a spring, if the water could be dammed back to provide a useful supply. This type of purpose-made sheepwash, such as on Cleeve Hill Common (60), is now the most widespread surviving structure that offers a tangible link back to the rich history and tradition of sheep farming in the Cotswold in earlier times. Several of these sites have recently been restored, including the Cleeve Hill sheepwash (61).

Sheepwashes have been given little attention by previous commentators on the history of the region. Research into these sites was aided by the Ordnance Survey, whose surveyors were instructed in 1906 to record this type of site on new mapping. The first systematic attempt to survey these sites was as recent as the mid-1990s, when 40 sheepwashes were located mainly in the north Cotswolds (Garrett and Hodgkins 1995), and were tentatively dated to the eighteenth or

60 Cleeve Hill sheepwash in use in the early twentieth century

61 Cleeve Hill sheepwash today (restored). The water supply was from a spring-fed reservoir further up the hill

nineteenth century. Most recently, sheepwashes have formed the subject of a survey undertaken across the whole of the Cotswolds AONB in 2001-2, covering an area of 2038km² (790 square miles) and 282 parishes. This located a total of 69 sheepwash sites of the traditional type (*62*), as distinct from sheep-dip sites which are a later introduction associated with the chemical disinfection of the sheep (Hurst *et al* 2002).

The purpose-made washes are, so far, known to be only 100-150 years old, having generally been in regular use until the early twentieth century, though some may be on much earlier sites. By the nineteenth century machinery was being installed that could wash the wool better after shearing. So the Cotswold sheepwashes, the last of them used in the 1950s, are now usually in a much decayed state. If enough remains they can still sometimes be recognised by their particular design, which comprised five basic elements (*63*):

a) a water supply – this could be either running water, i.e. the sheepwash was built directly in the stream-bed, or a head of water collected in a reservoir above the wash site, or even just a good spout of water from a spring;

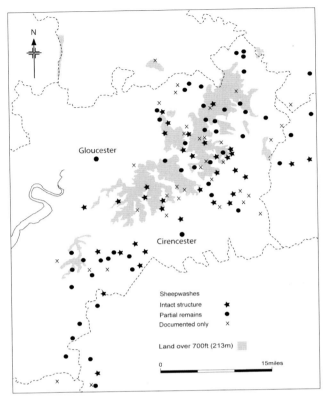

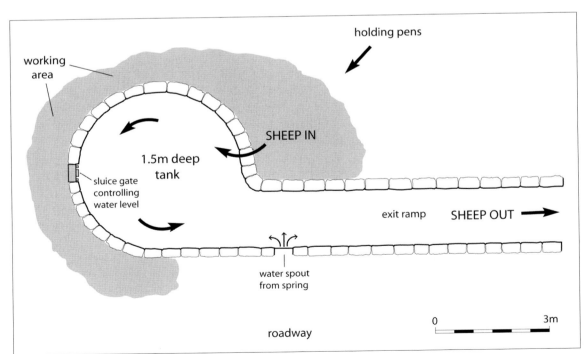

62 Left Distribution of sheepwashes in the Cotswolds. (After Hurst *et al* 2002)

63 Below Component parts of a typical sheepwash based on the Cutsdean sheepwash. *Illustrated by Carolyn Hunt*

b) the wash tank – this was usually about 10m² in volume, and about 1.5m deep. The water was often delivered into the tank by a water-spout set above the water level in the tank;

c) throwing position – this was often marked by a large flat stone and was the point at which the sheep was cast into the water. It was best to assist the sheep into the water backwards (William Firkin pers comm), as this meant that it had less idea what was in store and so struggled less. The shepherds used their crooks to manoeuvre the sheep under the spout and to ensure they were well soused;

d) exit ramp – the sheep were able to clamber out of the tank on their own along a shallow ramp, which was often quite narrow, as if to allow only one sheep out at a time;

e) drying area – a mown meadow next to the sheepwash would have been ideal as a place for the sheep to dry out for a day or two before shearing.

It is possible that structures of this general type were constructed for entirely different uses, such as flax retting, though the presence of an exit ramp is a good indication of a design primarily for washing sheep. Though with the sheep washing only taking place over a short period each year, even the purpose-made sheepwash was potentially put to other uses during the rest of the year.

Distribution

Sheepwashes can be found all over the Cotswolds (62) and in fact they are a regular rural feature found across much of England, though they often go unrecognised. However, the Cotswolds has a far greater concentration of this type of site generally, with one local concentration in the valleys of the rivers Coln, Leach and Windrush (north Cotswolds), and another at the head of the River Avon (south Cotswolds). The latter includes areas where there was no easy source of running water and so sheep farmers must have gone to a lot of trouble sometimes to wash their sheep regardless. Such a distribution shows the extent of the agricultural specialisation that had been achieved in parts of the Cotswolds.

Typology

Many of the sheepwashes were fine stone structures built from ashlar blocks. Unfortunately this type of construction technique cannot be easily dated, though in some cases repairs have been carried out with bricks which can be dated to the nineteenth century, or later. Shapes of the sheepwashes vary, probably indicating how localised the designs were. The two commonest types are distinguished in ground plan, their pool being either rectangular (41 per cent), or curved (mainly circular; 34 per cent) in shape, Kingham (64) being an example of the former and Prescott (65) of the latter.

Antiquity of sheepwash sites

Early place-name evidence indicates a sheepwash site at Shipston-on-Stour

64 Kingham sheepwash situated on the leat of a mill and on the edge of the village. An example of the rectangular type; the exit ramp is missing

65 Prescott sheepwash, remotely situated on a hillside. An example of the circular type, it was supplied with water from a spring-fed reservoir further up the hill

(Mawer 1924, 63) which has pre-medieval origins. So clearly, regular sites for this purpose can go back a very long way and some of the sites known from later times could have had a long history of use, of which there is no surviving documentary record. Place-name evidence certainly indicates that sheep washing sites were widespread in medieval times; for example the *Wassepole* (washpool) at Chastleton listed amongst the properties of Oseney Abbey in *c.*1220 and the *Wassemere* at Charlbury, referred to in the Eynsham Abbey chartulary dated 1363 (Gelling 1953). Other place-name evidence for sheepwashes in Gloucestershire largely dates from the seventeenth century onwards, such as *le Washebrooke* at Painswick (Smith 1964). Many of these places remain unassociated with any surviving washing structure, and it is most likely that the local stream served this purpose without any modification being necessary.

13

Postscript

Historical evidence is necessary in some abundance before much can be learnt about the past. Fortunately throughout a long period when the Cotswolds played a major part in the success of the English economy in the Middle Ages, the growing and selling of its wool has been well documented, not only in this country but also in parts of continental Europe, and sufficient records have survived to enable a fairly detailed account of its history to be constructed. Without these records it would have been impossible to assert for Cotswold wool in particular, and English wool in general, such a major role in history, or to understand the way in which a whole trade was conducted. It is the historical records alone, and, therefore, the merchants themselves, that have allowed the story of Cotswold wool to be told.

Fortunately some eminent historians, such as E. Power and E.M. Carus-Wilson, followed by E.B. Fryde and J.H. Munro, began to tease out this thread of history and much original research was done on this subject. Important primary sources such as the Southampton port books were studied in detail in order to extract detailed annual returns, so at least the extent of the foreign trade could be accurately gauged. Many incidental references in more local documents have provided a confirmation of the extent that sheep were farmed in the Cotswolds to justify the numerous references in the port books and in foreign documents. To be able in the fifteenth century to follow the actions – and indeed the footsteps – of the Celys, as they harness together both the local and international trade to their interests, so that the whole complex system by which Cotswold wool reached the weavers of Flanders was revealed, is quite frankly amazing.

If the archaeologist, relying on buried evidence alone, had attempted the theme of medieval economic history without this bounty of records, it is unlikely there would have been any, even basic, clue as to the importance of medieval English wool, and of some wools, like the Cotswold, in particular. An archaeological approach may be of some use when an industry gives rise to large features such as quarries, or to large amounts of waste products such as in the case of iron making, but it is of little use for detailed investigation of even the

66 Cotswold ewes and lambs at the Shakespeare Countryside Museum at Mary Arden's House, near Stratford-on-Avon, where Shakespeare's father periodically dealt in Cotswold wool. © *Cotswold Sheep Society*

most basic themes such as food supply, or the supply of perishable raw materials such as wool, or cloth.

The physical fabric of the past, therefore, remains very elusive, and, but for the efforts of historians, it is unlikely much would have ever come to light to illuminate the role of wool in English history, and to identify the special significance of certain areas, such as the Cotswolds. Fortunately as well, in this case, those interested in ancient breeds have also recognised the special character of the Cotswold sheep (*66*), and so through their efforts this type of sheep, with its long and distinguished history, can still be seen in a few places today.

Glossary of terms

Alum

Alum was used for fixing dyes, and was mainly sourced in north Africa, Asia Minor and the Black Sea, though the most famous source was Phocaea (now on the west coast of Turkey), which had been exploited by the Greeks in earlier days. Extraction of the alum was a long process, which involved long roasting of the rock and watering for four months, before boiling, after which it set solid into a colourless crystalline mass.

Brasil

A red dye brought from tropical regions. It was prepared from the wood of an East Indian tree (*Caesalpina Sappau*) and the best quality came from Ceylon.

Broadcloth

The first horizontal looms were narrow, but in the mid-thirteenth century the broadloom was invented in Flanders, which was 2-3m in width and accommodated two weavers. The cloth, manufactured from short fibred wool, was then heavily fulled so that the weave was no longer evident and to produce a silky texture (Lockett 1974). A broadcloth measured 24 x 1¾yds (21.9 x 1.6m; Szarmach *et al* 1998) and about 4⅓ broadcloths could be produced from a single sack of wool, with the wool of about 50 sheep going into each cloth, and two cloths being about the equivalent monetary value of one sack of wool (Carus-Wilson 1954).

In the early sixteenth century a cloth at Coventry weighed around 90lb or more (Carus-Wilson 1954), whilst a standard Flemish late medieval broadcloth of 32 x 2¾yds contained 40lb of wool and took about 12 days, in addition to pre-weaving labour of at least 12 days. An annual output of about 20 broadcloths per loom was possible (Munro 1988).

Canvas

Canvas was used for packing wool into sarplers, the large bales used for long-distance transport, and the best canvas and thread came from Arras in north France.

Carding

By the fourteenth century wool-combs were superseded for shorter staple wool by hand cards made with nails, and later with wires. Important improvements were also made to carding in the seventeenth century, when finer cards meant finer spinning and finer cloth, so much so that a pound of wool made twice as much cloth as before (Kerridge 1972, 22). Mechanical methods of carding were developed using a cylinder by Richard Arkwright for the cotton industry in the eighteenth century, and then transferred to wool production (Ponting 1957, 95).

Combing

This was the older method of preparing the wool for spinning, while carding with wire brushes was only introduced in the twelfth century to provide a more efficient method of working with short-fibred wools. Carded short staple wool went for woollens, and combed long staple wool went for worsteds.

Dyeing

This was usually carried out on the woven cloth rather than the unwoven wool, except in the case of worsted cloth. The cloth was first scoured with fuller's earth or urine to clean it and finally washed in cold water before dyeing. Where the dyers were working other than with woad, the dyeing involved boiling the cloth for long periods and alkaline water was essential (Munro 1988).

The accounts of a cloth maker in Ypres, who was using Cotswold wool in 1501 to make five black cloths, gives a detailed break-down of the costs involved as follows:

Cost of one sack of fine Cotswold wool	£22.60
Tax	£0.10
For each cloth the costs were as follows:	
Raw material and tax	£4.54
Wool preparation	£0.24
Spinning, weaving, fulling, tentering	£2.29
Dyeing in black:	
Alum	£0.23
Blue dyeing in woad (wool)	£0.76
Red dyeing in madder (cloth)	£0.55
Assistant's wage	negligible!
Shearing and finishing	£0.14
Total per cloth	£8.76

Clearly the bulk of the cost lay in the purchase of the wool, but the costs of fulling and the dyeing were also quite major investments (Munro 1983, 52, table 3.12).

Dyer's Rocket or Weld (*Reseda luteola*)

This produced a yellow colour which was not commonly used on its own. It was used with woad to produce greens such as Lincoln Green.

Dyer's Greenweed (*Genista tinctoria*)

This produced a yellow colour.

Ell

One yard in length.

Fells

These were sheepskins with the wool still attached and 240 woolfells were considered the equivalent of a sack of wool for taxation purposes (Origo 1957, 71). The Celys bought Cotswold fells at £3 per 120 in 1478 (Hanham 1985, 162), and on one occasion paid freight of 20d per 100 for these (Power 1933, fn 148). Summer fells were often from the butchers in London. The wool was generally longer than if it had been sheared and there was the advantage that the leather could be sold on, especially for glove making. However, they could be a much more difficult commodity to transport in good condition (Hanham 1985, 149).

Folding

This was the practice of keeping the sheep in open wattle pens, which were gradually moved across a harvested arable field to ensure it was evenly manured. After enclosure the practice was changed to folding on turnips and other fodder crops, though with the same purpose of improving the land for a subsequent corn crop.

Fuller's earth

A non-plastic clay used in the final washing of the felted cloth to remove soap and oil (Kerridge 1972, 21). It is found in the Cotswolds between the Great and Inferior Oolites.

Fulling

This is the process of felting cloth in order to matt the short fibres together by shrinkage in order to strengthen the fabric. It originally involved a process of washing underfoot for three days in a vat of soap and fuller's earth (kaolinite; hydrous aluminium silicate) to remove oil added before spinning, with subsequent tentering to remove wrinkles (Szarmach *et al* 1998) and then shearing. Mechanisation of fulling was introduced into Normandy by 1086, into England by the twelfth century, and was arguably the most important mechanical advance in cloth production until the modern industrial revolution. This put Flanders at a disadvantage, as Flanders did not have convenient water-power, but there were some urban water-powered mills there from at least the sixteenth century. Mechanical fulling provided a considerable cost saving (Szarmach *et al* 1998), as two fullers treading the cloth had taken three to five days, while the fulling mill was probably two-three times faster (Munro 1988). A Flemish fuller in around 1400 processed 30-35 cloths per annum, while the average weaver produced 20 broadcloths per annum (Munro 1994, 30).

Gig mill

In the fifteenth century the water-powered gig mill was introduced using teasels set on a roller (Kerridge 1972, 22), which was a mechanical means of raising the nap of a cloth.

Hitching

A method of folding involving feeding on turnips with the sheep in a temporary wattle enclosure moved every day about a field in order to increase its fertility.

Hogg, or hoggaster

Hoggs are sheep between weaning at four months and a first shearing. The term is still used today and, when qualified with other terms, it can also be applied to older sheep (National Sheep Association 1998). However, some modern commentators (e.g. Bischoff 1983) assign the medieval usage of the term to sheep after a first shearing.

Kermes

Imported from Asia Minor, Spain and Portugal this was the most expensive dye-stuff in medieval Europe, and was produced from insects (Carus-Wilson 1954). It was fixed with alum, and was otherwise known as 'grain' (*granum*). It could account for 60 per cent of the cost of the finished cloth at a time when material and labour costs for cloth were on average 4-22 per cent of the final price. In mid-fifteenth century Flanders *kermes* cost 29-times the most common red dye-stuff which was madder. The brilliant red scarlet woollen cloth made with *kermes* was, accordingly, the most expensive made, and was comparable with high-quality silk (Munro 1979, table 3.15). It was the main source of the medieval scarlet that was worn by kings. It seems likely that the finest English wools, such as Cotswold, would often have been used with this product.

Lokes (locks)

Loose pieces of fleece wool.

Madder (*Rubia tinctoria*)

Madder, made from a European herb, was the most commonly used dye-stuff for a fast red colour and had to be fixed with alum (Munro 1983, 53). *Kermes* and later cochineal (used with tin) eventually replaced it. If used with woad, it produced a purple colour (Lockett 1974).

Mordant

This was necessary to fix dyes and to make them fast. The most widely used mordants were alum or cream of tartar (Munro 1983, 53). These chemicals also helped to cleanse the cloth of any remaining oil or grease, which had been added during earlier stages of processing, and had not already been removed by scouring and fulling.

Nail (*clou* or clove)

This English unit of weight was 7lb (half a stone), and there were 52 nails to the sack. The Calais nail was half this weight, and there were 90 to a Calais sack-weight.

New draperies

The 'new draperies' were worsted cloths made from long combing wool.

Potash

This was universally used as a mordant with woad and supplied from north Germany and the Baltic.

Refuse

This was poor quality wool, which was often packed separately.

Sack

The English sack of wool weighed 364lb (26 stones or 166kg). The 1275 Grant of Custom to the king equated a sack of wool to 300 woolfells ('which make one sack'), but in the fifteenth century 240 fells was accepted as the equivalent to a sack. Sack weights seemed to have varied abroad with a fifteenth-century Calais sack weighing 315lb (Munro 1978, 151). For export the wool was wrapped in canvas and the preferred weight of this sarpler was then around 800-1,000lb (up to 454kg).

Sarpler

This was a bale of a set size but not of a uniform weight. In the later fifteenth century the sarpler was usually 2-2¾ sack-weights, and was, therefore, 728-1,000lb in weight. The sarpler bale was made using canvas; for instance Richard Cely the elder in 1480 ordered 600yds of canvas from Arras with the specification that it was to be at least 1¾yds wide. At this time it was expected that 12yds of canvas would cover a sarpler at a cost of 4s, and in the weighing an allowance of 28lb was made for the canvas covering (Hanham 1985). The bale was tied with ears in each corner and bore the merchant's mark and a unique sort reference, and information on the wool source and quality – see examples on the memorial brasses at Northleach church (3 and 67). The method of gathering each corner presumably helped with carrying by providing something to hold onto. They were transported by wagon, with usually two being the normal load in the fifteenth century, costing about 18s 9d per load (or about 2 per cent of the average buying price) from the Cotswolds to London (Hanham 1985, 119).

Scarlets

This was generally a full grained cloth, which had low shearing fees but high dyeing fees. The term could, confusingly, apparently be used of cloth not yet dyed scarlet.

Scouring

This was the process of cleaning the newly woven cloth prior to dyeing and chiefly involved immersion in urine (Ponting 1957, 15).

Shearing (cloth)

The process of cropping the raised surface of the cloth with shears just after fulling. It was intended to produce a smooth surface like silk and allowed dyes to have the maximum effect. Often the cloth was dyed before being given a final shearing (Munro 1988).

Shearing (sheep)

The fleece was shorn as it was about to be naturally discarded, when an undercoat was left on to protect the animal. The age of a sheep was often stated on the basis of how often it had been shorn, with the first shearing usually being at 15 months (Stuart 1995). Shearers were expected to shear 70 sheep per day in the seventeenth century (Ryder 1983b).

Sheep-cote (sheep-house)

This was a specialised building for sheep, which was found on many larger estates, where several could be in use. Characteristically they were long and narrow in plan, and often 100ft (31m) or upwards in length (AgHEW III, 879). They were used for keeping the sheep in at night, and for storing sheep fodder and equipment, often while the flocks were grazing on the higher, more remote, ground. They were important for lambing, and were usually associated with pens and yards.

Spinning

This was still done in the classical fashion using a spindle and a distaff until the early Middle Ages. In the late twelfth and thirteenth centuries, the spinning wheel was developed which increased production of yarn from c.110m to 350m per hour. By c.1467 a better wheel permitted warp to be made this way as well and this improved the quality of work in fine woollens. Spinning, whatever the method, was the most costly stage of cloth manufacture. The Medici's sixteenth-century account books state that it accounted for 47 per cent of pre-finishing costs, compared to wool preparation at 20 per cent, weaving at 28 per cent and fulling and tentering at 5 per cent (Munro 1988).

Stamfords

This was a high-quality type of cloth made originally in Stamford in Lincolnshire, and then widely imitated (Bridbury 1982).

Staple

This was a merchant organisation, where the merchants acted together in a continuous mart set up by the state to force trade in a particular direction. The English Crown favoured this for wool, since an organised system meant that customs were less easy to evade and those in charge of the trade could be scrutinised (Lockett 1974), and held responsible to the extent that they could be expelled and ruined if found guilty of maladministration. It also became a prime mechanism for the political manipulation of foreign trade in the interests of England.

Tar

This was used together with grease for smearing on sheep to protect them and applied in the autumn for protection during the winter (Ryder 1983b). Only about seven sheep a day could be coated as it had to be done carefully by hand.

Teasel (Fuller's Teasel, *Dipsacus sativus*)

This introduced species of teasel was used to raise the nap prior to shearing the cloth. In contrast to the native teasel the Fuller's Teasel has bracts spread out below the head rather than pointing up and its prickles have fine hooks. Its hooks were particularly elastic, which was essential for the manufacture of highest quality cloth. It was first imported from the Continent in the medieval period, but eventually grown in Gloucestershire, where it was best grown on fertile clay and fetched 2d per 1,000 in 1327 (Brill 1968, 78). The nineteenth-century evidence suggests that 1,500–2,000 teasels would be used up in the production of a single cloth.

Tentering

This was carried out after fulling but before shearing. It restored quite a lot of the cloth area, which had been lost by shrinkage during fulling, as well as giving the cloth an even length and width.

Tod(d)

A *tod* was 28lb of wool.

Washing

This was usually done in May or June (Lockett 1974). The medieval washers were expected to do 20 sheep per day each (Stuart 1995).

Weaving

The horizontal treadle loom was introduced in the eleventh/twelfth century, replacing the warp-weighted upright loom and this could produce long cloths. It achieved a tight weave, and increased productivity being about three-times faster than the upright loom (Munro 1988).

Wether

A castrated ram. These were kept for the quality and quantity of their wool.

Winding

This term applies to the folding up of the fleeces, once shorn, so they could be packed. Feasting traditionally followed the packing (as depicted by Shakespeare in *The Winter's Tale*, Act IV, Scenes 2 to 3).

Woad (*Isatis tinctoria*)

This dye-stuff produced a blue colour, and also black. Woad was the most commonly used dye-stuff, and it was produced, like madder, in both England and Flanders. Amiens was the main source from the latter area and close trading links were developed with the ports of London, Norwich and Bristol, where the balls of woad were imported. However, Picardy and Toulouse (Languedoc) also came to specialise in its production. It was grown in England, for instance around Wotton-under-Edge which was noted for its dye-houses, and it still persists wild around Tewkesbury (Brill 1968, 79).

To use the woad was mixed with potash in water and first allowed to ferment for three days. Blue-dyed cloths were generally the cheapest of all the coloured cloths. If re-dyed with red or weld-yellow then browns to greens were possible, or black was possible if the blue cloth was re-dyed with madder (Munro 1983).

Woolfells – see fells

Woollens

Woollen yarn was made from short-stapled wool, and after weaving the woollen cloths needed fulling (Szarmach *et al* 1998), as this forced the short fibres together, and produced a stronger cloth.

Woolmen

These were the local dealers in wool, who collected wool locally and sometimes were sheep owners themselves. They would have required extensive storage facilities and worked by contracting to deliver so much wool at a set time in London, or other ports.

Wool-packers

These had their own separate organisation from the staplers, the *Fellowship of Wolpackers of London*, and were sworn in before the Exchequer in order to regulate the trade and try to prevent fraudulent practices. It was their job not only to pack, but to value the wool, and to safeguard the buyer from various abuses. To reduce the opportunity for fraud the wool was to be packed where it was grown. They often travelled around with the local dealers sampling the wool on the farm, and then selecting it on behalf of the wool merchants. It was tempting for them to deliberately underestimate the quality, and buy cheaply for themselves, but this practice was banned in 1473.

Worsted

This was a fine light cloth made from a tightly twisted long-woolled yarn, which was coarse and strong. It was named after Worsted near Norwich, where some Flemish weavers had settled. It was hardly fulled at all so that the pattern of the weave remained evident (Lockett 1974), and so could be made in areas that had no swift flowing streams suitable for fulling.

Appendix: Medieval wool merchants and dealers of the Cotswolds

BRASSES AT NORTHLEACH CHURCH

William Bicknell (-1500)

William Bicknell built the chapel on the south side of Northleach church (*Gloucestershire VCH* IX, 140). Only fragments of his memorial brass survive.

Thomas Bushe (-1525)

A Northleach brass memorial to Thomas and Joan Bushe (d. 1526) is an elaborate example with two canopies over the figures incorporating a figurative image of his name and the arms to confirm his status as a merchant of the Calais Staple (54). He bequeathed to his wife £400, his two daughters £266 and his four sons £500 in all, together with land in Oxfordshire, Wiltshire, Gloucestershire and Berkshire (all wool-growing areas), as well as a farm at Taynton let to a London merchant and member of the Calais staple (NA reference PROB 11/21). He was now a grazier as well as a wool dealer and merchant, as perhaps represented respectively by the ram and woolpack (sown down the middle) at his feet. He leased the bishop of Worcester's estate at Withington. His wife, Joan, like his mother Alice Bushe (later Midwinter), is given the symbols of the wool trade showing that she was a wool dealer in her own right. His son John was also a woolman and merchant of the Calais Staple (*Gloucestershire VCH* IX, 128).

In about 1510 Thomas Bushe had been trading with *Brancino de Marini* a merchant of Southampton, whose main export was cloth. In 1522 he was the richest man in Gloucestershire outside Gloucester, his goods being worth £800 (*Gloucestershire VCH* IX, 128), and in the 1520s he was still actively travelling to Southampton to complete sales on wool (56).

John Fortey (-1458)

The brass memorial to John Fortey in Northleach church shows him with one foot on a sheep and another on a woolpack (35). He is particularly attributed with being the sponsor of the new fifteenth-century nave and the spectacular clerestory in the church (Monk 1935), which is based on a now missing part of the inscription which went as follows: 'and after his disese the rofe made' (Jones 1994, 94). He was described as a 'wolman' in his will (NA ref PROB 11/4), and he bequeathed

£300 'to finish and complete the work he had started in the new middle aisle', as well as £40 shared equally between 120 other churches around Northleach to be spent on the naves 'that the parishioners of the same may remember him in their prayers'. A sum of £15 was also to be used to pay for a chaplain over a period of three years. He left 20d for the fabric of the nave of Worcester Priory church, and 20s to each of the four orders of friars of Gloucester and 4d to every prisoner in Gloucester Castle. He also gave £200 for the making of linen and woollen clothing for the most needy and 20s to each of 40 poor reputable girls ('of good and decent conversation') for their marriage. Amongst other good causes the repair of roads and bridges was to be carried out using any residue. The bequests mentioned in this will amount to over £600, and this excludes the value of any of at least three tenements in Northleach. One of his executors was a John Fortey, dyer of Cirencester (Power 1933, fn 78), who engaged in an action against Simon Nory of Florence brought in 1460, presumably to seek repayment of debts owed to John Fortey at the time of his death.

Thomas Fortey (-1447)

The brass memorial to Thomas Fortey in Northleach church shows him with a woolpack at his feet alongside Agnes his wife. His son was John Fortey (-1458).

William Midwinter (-1501) and Alice (-c.1503)

A brass memorial in Northleach church is presumed to commemorate William Midwinter as the merchant's mark has an inscribed 'M' (44). The scale of his business is reflected by its value of £753 5s 11d with the Celys alone in 1487 (Power 1933). He became the bailiff of Northleach in 1493, and in 1501 he left £600 and lands in Northleach when he died. In addition he made bequests to 21 local churches (Jones 1994, 94). The emblems of his trade, the sheep and the woolpack, are seen at his feet on his brass (67). His wife Alice, the widow of John Bushe, was a wool dealer in her own right being mentioned as such in the Cely correspondence, and in her will of 1502 she made bequests to ten churches 'where I have been most accustomed to buy wools' (Monk 1935, 59).

67 Detail of William Midwinter memorial brass dated *c.*1500 in Northleach church showing a sheep and woolpack at his feet

John Taylour (-1509)

John Taylour was described in his will as of Farmington and his wife was Joan (d. 1510). As in the case of the Midwinter and Bushe families, he is shown with both a sheep and a woolpack at his feet to indicate that he was both merchant and a flock-master (36). The brass had clearly been made at the end of the fifteenth century, and has one of the clearest representations of a medieval Cotswold sheep (3).

Unknown woolman

This is a high-quality full-size brass to an unknown woolman and wife of c.1400 (32). The only clue to his identity is an inscribed 'T' on the belt.

BRASSES IN OTHER COTSWOLD CHURCHES

John Camber (-1497)

John Camber was a merchant of Worcester, who seems to have been a Cotswold wool merchant as he provided funds for extensive elaboration of the church at Sevenhampton, where his brass memorial survives (Verey 1982).

William Grevel (-1401) and his wife

William Grevel and his wife are shown in Chipping Campden church on a brass considered generally to be the finest brass to a wool merchant (19); and comparable to brasses in the Lincolnshire wolds (Norris 1965). In 1367 he bought a property in the town for 10 marks and built a new house. The bay window of his new house strongly promotes the perpendicular architecture that was later to transform the local church (Jones 1994, 97). He was a privileged member of the trading towns of Coventry and London, and had married the sister and heiress of Sir Philip Thornbury. His dealings are little known, though in 1383-5 he bought £133 worth of wool from the bishop of Worcester's clip at Blockley. He and a John Grenell (i.e. Grevel), both of 'Campedene', wool merchants, together with many other wool merchants mainly from Lincolnshire, were indicted for wrong-doing on 16 October 1395 (CPR 1391-6).

In his will he bequeathed 100 marks (£66 13s 4d) 'to the building of the nave and body of the church' (Verey 1982), and the money for four chaplains to say mass for his soul for ten years (Rushen 1899). A descendant bought Warwick Castle in 1605, and acquired the earldom of Warwick in the eighteenth century.

Philip Marner (-1587)

Cirencester church has his memorial brass of 1587 (Johnson 1985).

Robert Pagge (-1440)

The Lady Chapel floor in Cirencester church has the incomplete remains of several fifteenth-century brasses of merchants and Robert Page and wife are shown with a merchant's mark on a woolpack set within a shield (Norris 1965). He was commemorated as a builder of churches and roads.

Reginald Spycer (-1442)

Commemorated on a brass in Cirencester church.

John Tame (-1500)

John Tame was a wealthy wool stapler merchant who rebuilt Fairford church in about 1490-1500 (Hoskins 1976, 159). He had built up a large textile business in Cirencester, and ran large flocks of sheep around the town. When prosecuted in 1455-60 he was described as 'alias merchant, alias gentleman, alias woolman, alias yeoman' (Power 1933). He was one of several Cotswold woolmen selling large amounts of wool to *Gherardo Canigiani* in 1475 for export via Southampton on a

Genoese carrack and two Neapolitan galleys (Ruddock 1951, 90). In 1478-9 he was the fourth largest shipper of goods out of the port of London (Hanham 1985, 245). He left over £200 in fine articles for the local church, and his son, Edmund Tame, later became High Sheriff of Gloucestershire (Lipson 1953, 77).

John Townsend (-1458)

John Townsend is possibly commemorated by the surviving wool merchant brass at Lechlade church. He was a Lechlade wool merchant (*Gloucestershire VCH* VII, 115), whose deals included contracting to supply two alien merchants in 1452 with wool worth £1,078 (Hoskins 1955).

William Weoley (*alias* Welley; -1450)

This was a wool merchant in Chipping Campden following on from William Grevel. William Weoley took up a case against the Florentines in 1442 following their defaulting on a debt of £1,180 for wool he had sold to the *Albertini* company of Florence.

John Younge (-1451)

His memorial brass is in Chipping Norton church, and he was a woolman (Taylor and Tomlinson 1987).

OTHER WOOL MERCHANTS AND WOOLMEN

Thomas Adynet (-1409)

He was probably a woolman of Northleach who had land in several parishes and loaned money to the king. In 1397 he had lent the Crown 50 marks (*Gloucestershire VCH* IX, 127-8).

Thomas Alen

Thomas Alen of Stow-on-the-Wold was one of several Cotswold woolmen supplying the Italian merchant Canigiani at Southampton in 1475 (see John Tame above; Ruddock 1951, 90).

Thomas Arnold

When prosecuted in 1455-60 he was described as 'of Cirencester gentleman, alias clothman, alias woolman, alias chapman' (Power 1933).

John Ashfield

Traditionally this Chipping Norton wool merchant has been regarded as the rebuilder of the parish church in around 1485.

Thomas Betson (-1486)

Thomas Betson was a merchant of the Staple of Calais and associated in business in 1476-80 with a gentry family from Oxfordshire, the Stonors, who seem to have been an early example of large-scale sheep graziers. He bought fells from Whyte of Broadway, John Elmes of Henley-on-Thames, and from Robert Turbot of Lamberton (Laverton; Power 1924). One July he shipped 2,348 fells from Northleach (Massingham 1938). He is mentioned in both the Stonor and Cely letters.

Henry Bishop

Henry Bishop of Burford was one of several Cotswold woolmen supplying the Italian merchant Canigiani at Southampton in 1475 (see John Tame above; Ruddock 1951, 90), and was responsible for the fine set of almshouses beside Burford church.

William Bradway (-1488)

This Chipping Campden wool merchant left 100 marks (£66 13s 4d) for building the nave of the church in 1488 (Powell 1992), perhaps helping to finish the major rebuilding of the period (Jones 1994, 98). He seems to have belonged to a family with wool business connections in the town, as a John Bradway was acting on behalf of Richard Leynard of Chipping Campden in around 1500 in an effort to recover a wool debt owing to them both.

Bryddok

Bryddock (Power 1933, 366, fn 34) was involved in suing the widow of the Florentine factor of the Medici Company, Canigiani, for £884 13s 4d worth of wool with which they had supplied him at Southampton.

John Bushe (-1477)

John Bushe lived in Northleach, and dealt with the Celys. His widow Alice, who died c. 1503, married William Midwinter the main Cotswold supplier of the Celys' wool export business in 1478-92. His son Thomas Bushe, who died in 1525, and grandson John were both merchants of the Calais Staple.

Robert Calf

The Woolstaplers Hall in Chipping Campden was built for Robert Calf in the late fourteenth century (Verey 1970).

The Cely family

The wool dealing of this family over two generations shows how a London merchant specialised in the Cotswold wool trade with Flanders.

William Chester

William Chester of Stow-on-the-Wold was a merchant stapler who provided the local fifteenth-century almshouses, and his father before him had donated the market cross (Johnson 1994).

John Eryngton (or Hervyngton)

John Eryngton was a *wollemonger* of Chipping Campden in the 1430s (Rushen 1899, 21).

William Fludgate

He was a woolman associated with Burford, who traded in Cotswold wool with the Italians at Southampton from at least 1475 until the early 1500s (Ruddock 1951, 89).

The Garstang family

The Garstang family were wool merchants who were responsible for a chantry chapel in Cirencester church c. 1430-60. Hugh Garstang died 1464 (Baddeley 1924).

John Hakeburne

As abbot of Cirencester Abbey (1504-22) his arms had the heads of three Cotswold rams, suggesting a keen interest in wool dealing.

Ralph Hammond

He was probably a Northleach woolman, as his executor was trying to recover a £136 debt from a London merchant in 1354 (*Gloucestershire VCH* IX, 127).

Thomas Jerveys

Thomas Jerveys of Chipping Norton was one of several Cotswold woolmen supplying the Italian merchant Canigiani at Southampton in 1475 (see John Tame above; Ruddock 1951, 90).

John Lenard

One John Lenard of Chipping Campden was selling wool to John de Ponte in 1457 (Power 1933, fn 92). When prosecuted in 1455–60 he was described as 'dyer, wolleman, yoman, alias merchaunt' (Power 1933).

Richard Lennard

One Richard Lennard of Chipping Campden was one of several Cotswold woolmen supplying the Italian merchant Canigiani at Southampton in 1475 (see John Tame above; Ruddock 1951, 90).

John de Ludlow

Though unproven there seems to be a possibility that the Welsh Marcher family of de Ludlow, who built up tremendous wealth from wool in the Welsh borders, may have had some link with Chipping Campden in the late thirteenth century when a family of this name is mentioned there.

John Perys

John Perys was a woolman of Northleach mentioned in the Cely letters in January 1479 as being as good a source of quality wool as William Midwinter (Hanham 1985, 119).

John Pynnock (-1486)

John Pynnock of Burford was certainly involved in the wool trade, and built the south transept chapel of his local parish church. He is named in Southampton records as trading with the Italians in Cotswold wool in 1475 (Ruddock 1951, 89).

Richard Wenman

He was a wool dealer who was prominent at Witney.

Henry Woolmonger

Henry Woolmonger (*Gloucestershire VCH* VII, 115) was a wool dealer in Lechlade in the late thirteenth century.

Further reading

THE COTSWOLD SHEEP

The main sources for the early history of the Cotswold sheep are early literary allusions, and eighteenth-century and later regional agricultural histories (e.g. Marshall 1796, and 1818; Rudge 1807), and the earliest breed description was by Harmer (1892). The Cotswold wool, however, has a much longer history being mentioned, for instance, in the records of wool dealers from the medieval period onwards, though much of this evidence is very scattered. A general survey of the history of the Cotswold wool trade was provided in 1978 by Marian Woodman, and Lyn Gibbings produced a most accessible introduction to the Cotswold sheep breed in 1995.

An archaeological study of horned and polled sheep by Armitage and Goodall (1977), focusing heavily on the Cotswold sheep and combining a comparison with their medieval images, was a pioneering attempt to understand about earlier types of sheep, though this work seems to have largely gone unnoticed. Subsequent archaeological recording of sheep bones building on the data collected by Armitage and Goodall has not been consistently practised.

EARLY SHEEP FARMING IN THE COTSWOLDS

This chapter relies mainly on archaeological data, where Ryder pioneered the detailed study of sheep remains from the 1960s onwards, in an era when numerous sites were being excavated. Ryder wrote extensively on the subject culminating in *Sheep and Man* in 1983 which was a worldwide study of sheep from antiquity onwards. Archaeological finds of wool in Britain became a focus for defining local types of sheep and attempting to determine when the medium longwool and true longwool emerged (e.g. Ryder 1983a, and 1984). Place-name evidence (EPNS volumes various counties) sometimes provides evidence for the significance of early sheep farming.

COTSWOLD WOOL IN THE MIDDLE AGES

This chapter charts medieval sheep farming practice based on the contemporary writing of Walter of Henley (Oschinsky 1971). The practical processes of trading wool, and of spinning and weaving are only described in general terms to provide a background for later chapters. For more information about early sheep farming see Seebohm (1927) and Trow-Smith (1957), and on medieval textile manufacturing techniques see Salzman (1931).

THE ELEVENTH AND TWELFTH CENTURIES

This chapter features some of the results of the published research by E. Carus-Wilson (1952) on the first appearance of fulling mills in the historical record, together with the first more detailed references to large flocks being kept, such as by Caen Abbey (Chibnall 1982).

THE THIRTEENTH CENTURY

Important framework studies were carried out by E. Power (1933) and T.H. Lloyd (1977), and these have since been supplemented by notable local historical studies, such as by C. Dyer (1980) and Aldred and Dyer (1991). Individuals come more to the fore as a result of lay subsidy lists and more is now revealed about occupations either through personal names or the definition of local services owed by the tenants of manors, for instance in Minchinhampton (Watson 1932). The foreign merchant also now makes a stronger appearance whose role is instrumental in stimulating the wool trade especially of the monasteries as evidenced in the Pegolotti list (Cunningham 1910; Lloyd 1973). Detailed analysis of the bishopric of Worcester estate by C. Dyer (1980) shows the complexities of medieval sheep rearing with flock movements over large geographical areas in order to exploit the Cotswolds upland pastures. Further studies of monastic estates have been carried out, for instance by Vose (1953) who showed some specialisation in wool production on the Worcester Priory estate.

Archaeological investigation has revealed a medieval Cotswold upland settlement at Upton, where historical research in parallel by R. Hilton and P. Rahtz (1966) has suggested a local economy based on sheep.

THE FOURTEENTH CENTURY

E.B. Fryde (1983) and J.H. Munro (1994) have provided much of the national financial and taxation background to the wool export trade for this section, and E.M. Carus-Wilson and O. Coleman (1963) charted the export performance of English wool and cloth. The great deals struck by the king to maximise mercantile profit from wool in pursuit of war with France have been addressed by Fryde (1952 and 1964), and the contribution made by the Italians has been similarly well served by historians such as A.A. Ruddock (1951), G. Holmes (1960), and E.B. Fryde (1974). Additional substance has been given to the latter topic by the archaeological investigations of the important medieval port of Southampton, which was combined with complementary historical study by C. Platt (1973). Contemporary records of the wool dealings of one Italian family, the *Datini*, survive and have been researched by Origo (1957). One of the chief consumers of Cotswold wool was the Florentine textile industry and Thompson (1931) charts the rise of its wool guild (the *Arte della Lana*) to a peak of production in the fourteenth-early fifteenth centuries.

C. Dyer (1980, 1987, 1988) again supplies important local detail of the fortunes of Cotswold settlement, and C. Dyer's 1995 study of sheep-cotes in the Cotswolds marks an important contribution to drawing out the local significance of sheep rearing across the region. During this period published original sources such as the tax lists for Gloucestershire (Franklin 1993) introduce whole communities for the first time.

It was during this period that the activity of cloth making began to eclipse wool exporting. The general survey of this industry by A.R. Bridbury (1982) provides a broad background, against which more local studies, such as by R. Perry (1945) and K. Ponting (1957), can be placed. More and more Cotswold wool was presumably now being directed towards cloth makers locally rather than being exported in a raw state, though records of this internal trade are more difficult to come by.

THE FIFTEENTH CENTURY

R. Hilton (1957), and C. Dyer (1980) provide accounts about the economic activities on large monastic estates with Cotswold interests, the latter charting the rise of the sheep grazier. E. Power (1926 and 1933) and T.H. Lloyd (1977) continue to provide a broader picture, while an intimate insight into the wool trade is provided by the surviving letters of the Celys and the Stonors, the former transcribed and studied revealingly by A. Hanham (1975 and 1985). The Italian trade in wool and cloth continued and has received much attention from historians such as A.A. Ruddock (1951), G.A. Holmes (1960 and 1996), and E.B. Fryde (1974). Numerous commentators meanwhile have alluded to the outward sign of prosperity in the legacy of rebuilt churches from this period, which has been attributed to the piety of the wool merchants, as documented in several well-known instances.

THE SIXTEENTH CENTURY

Now several contemporary commentators speak for themselves and local records, such as from the Weigh House in Southampton, have survived, as testimony to individual wool deals involving Cotswold woolmen travelling to Southampton to hand over wool (Southampton Archives). K.G. Ponting (1957) and P.J. Bowden (1962) have published broad surveys relating to this period, when weavers were establishing new centres in the south Cotswolds, and wool exports continued to decline.

THE SEVENTEENTH CENTURY AND LATER

From this period agricultural writers provide a contemporary viewpoint on sheep breeds and wool quality, as there was an increasing concern about boosting carcase size and wool yields in the eighteenth century (e.g. Marshall 1796). The Cotswold breed was rapidly losing favour with farmers. It just survived into the twentieth century through the efforts of Cotswold Sheep Society, and, only after a renewed effort by the Society in the 1960s, has the breed come to enjoy some revival because of its special qualities (Gibbings 1995).

A HIDDEN PAST

Few traces of the medieval wool trade heritage are to be found in the Cotswolds today. Some rural features, however, still survive as a tangible link with traditional sheep farming, and pioneering studies have been carried out, both in documentary research and fieldwork, by C. Dyer (1995) to examine sheep-cotes and their role. The first field survey of sheepwashes, recalling this ancient practice, was only carried out in the mid-1990s (Garrett and Hodgkins 1995), and this was supplemented by further, mainly documentary, research by Hurst *et al* (2002).

Other information

PLACE TO VISIT

Cotswold Farm Park,
Near Guiting Power,
Cheltenham,
Gloucestershire
GL54 5UG

www.cotswoldfarmpark.co.uk
E-mail: info@cotswoldfarmpark.co.uk

KEY ORGANISATIONS

Cotswold Sheep Society
www.cotswoldsheep.org
E-mail: info@cotswoldsheep.org

Rare Breeds Survival Trust,
National Agricultural Centre,
Kenilworth,
Warwickshire
CV8 2LG

Bibliography

Albarella, U., and Davis, S.J.M., 1994 *The Saxon and medieval animal bones excavated 1985-1989 from West Cotton, Northamptonshire. Ancient Monuments Lab Rep,* 17/94

Aldred, D., and Dyer, C., 1991 'A medieval Cotswold village: Roel, Gloucestershire' in *Bristol Gloucestershire Archaeol Soc,* 109, 139-170

Anon., 1881 *Gloucestershire Notes and Queries*

Applebaum, S., 1958 'Agriculture in Roman Britain' in *Ag Hist Rev,* XI(ii), 66-86

Arano, L.C., 1976 *The medieval health handbook: Tacuinum sanitatis.* New York

Armitage, P.L., 1983 'The early history of English longwool sheep' in *The Ark,* March 1983, 90-7

—, and Goodall, J.A., 1977 'Medieval horned and polled sheep: the archaeological and iconographic evidence' in *Antiq J,* 57(1), 73-89

Aston, M., and Viner, L., 1984 'The study of deserted villages in Gloucestershire' in Savile, A. (ed.), *Archaeology in Gloucestershire,* 276-93. Gloucester

Ayres, K., and Clark, K.M., 1999 'Birdlip Quarry' in Mudd *et al,* 449-62

Baddeley, W. St C., 1907 *A Cotteswold manor being the history of Painswick*

—, 1924 *A history of Cirencester*

Baker, A.R.B., 1973 'Changes in the later Middle Ages', in Darby, H.C. (ed), *A new historical geography of England,* 186-247

Barnard, E.A.B., 1927 *Stanton and Snowshill, Gloucestershire.* Cambridge

Beresford, M.W., 1953 'The poll tax and census of sheep, 1549' in *Ag Hist Rev,* I, 9-15

—, 1954a *The lost villages of England*

—, 1954b 'The poll tax and census of sheep, 1549' in *Ag Hist Rev,* 2, 15-29

—, 1971 'A review of historical research (to 1968)', in Beresford, M. and Hurst, J.G., *Deserted medieval villages,* 3-75

Bischoff, J.P., 1983 '"I cannot do't without counters": fleece weights and sheep breeds in late thirteenth and early fourteenth century England' in *Agric Hist,* 57.2, 143-60

Blair, J., 1994 *Anglo-Saxon Oxfordshire.* Stroud

Bond, J., 1973 'The estates of Evesham Abbey: a preliminary survey of their topography' in *Vale of Evesham Hist Soc Res Papers,* 4, 1-61

Bolton, J.L., 1980 *The medieval English economy 1150-1500*

Bowden, P.J., 1956-7 'Wool supply and the woollen industry' in *Ec Hist Rev 2 ser,* IX, 44-50

—, 1962 *The wool trade in Tudor and Stuart England*

—, 1967 'Agricultural prices, farm profits and rents' in Finberg, H.P.R. (ed.), *AgHEW 1500-1640,* IV, 593-695. Cambridge

Bravender, J., 1850 'Farming of Gloucestershire' in *J Royal Agric Soc England,* 11, 116-177

Bridbury, A.R., 1982 *Medieval English clothmaking; an economic survey*

Brill, E., 1968 *Old Cotswold.* Newton Abbot

—, 1973 *Life and tradition on the Cotswolds*

Brown, R., 1864 *Calendar of state papers and manuscripts relating to English affairs existing in archives and collections of Venice and in other libraries of northern Italy, vol 1, 1202-1509*

Burgess, L.A., 1976 *The Southampton terrier of 1454.* Southampton Records Ser, XV

Camden, W., 1586 *Camden's Britannia: a facsimile of the 1695 edition, published by Edmund Gibson.* Newton Abbot (published 1971)

Campbell, B., 1997 'Economic rent and the intensification of English agriculture 1086-1350', in Astill, G. and Langdon, J. *Medieval farming and technology: the impact of agricultural change in northwest Europe,* 225-50

Carus-Wilson, E.M., 1933 'The overseas trade of Bristol, in Power, E. and Postan, M.M. (eds), *Studies in English trade in the fifteenth century,* 183-246

—, 1941 'An industrial revolution of the thirteenth century' in *Ec Hist Rev,* XI, 39-60

—, 1950 'Trends in the export of English woollens in the fourteenth century', *Ec Hist Rev 2 ser,* III, 162-79

—, 1952 'The woollen industry' in Postan, M.M. and Miller, E. (eds), *The Cambridge economic history of Europe, vol II: trade and industry in the Middle Ages,* 614-92

—, 1954 *Medieval merchant venturers: collected studies*

—, 1959 'Evidences of industrial growth on some fifteenth-century manors' in *Ec Hist Rev 2 ser,* XII.2, 190-205

—, and Coleman, O., 1963 *England's export trade 1275-1547.* Oxford

Chapman, A.B., 1915 *The Black Book of Southampton, III, 1497-1620.* Southampton

Chibnall, M., 1982 *Charters and custumals of the Abbey of Holy Trinity Caen*

Clark, G., 1947 'Sheep and swine in the husbandry of prehistoric Europe' in *Antiquity,* XXI, 122-36

Coleman, O., 1960 *The brokage book of Southampton 1443-4*

Copus, A.K., 1989 'Changing markets and the development of sheep breeds in southern England 1750-1900' in *Ag Hist Rev,* 37.1, 36-51

Cornwall, J.C.K., 1988 *Wealth and society in early sixteenth century England*

Cram, C.L., 1973 'The animal bones', in Brodribb, A.C.C., Hands, A.R. and Walker, D.R., *Excavations at Shakenoak Farm, near Wilcote, Oxfordshire, part IV; site C.* Privately printed

Cunningham, W., 1910 *The growth of English industry and commerce.* Cambridge

Defoe, D., 1725 *A tour thro' the whole island of Great Britain,* vol 2 (2001 edition edited by McVeagh, J.)

Delderfield, E.R., 1967 *The Cotswold countryside and its characters.* Newton Abbot

DoE, undated *List of buildings of special architectural or historic interest: parish of Chipping Campden*

Donaldson, D.N., 1978 *A portrait of Winchcombe*

—, 2001 *Winchcombe: a history of the Cotswold borough.* Charlbury

Donkin, R.A., 1958 'Cistercian sheep-farming and wool-sales in the thirteenth century', *Ag Hist Rev,* VI(i), 2-8

—, 1973 Changes in the early Middle Ages', in Darby, H.C. (ed.), *A new historical geography of England,* 75-135

Dreghorn, W., 1967 *Geology explained in the Severn Vale and Cotswolds.* Newton Abbot

Drinkwater, J.F., 1982 'The wool textile industry of Gallia Belgica and the Secundinii of Igel; questions and hypotheses' in *Textile Hist,* 13(1), 111-28

Dyer, C., 1980 *Lords and peasants in a changing society: the estates of the Bishopric of Worcester, 680-1540.* Cambridge

—, 1982 'Deserted medieval villages in the west Midlands' in *Ec Hist Rev,* 35(1), 19-34

—, 1987 'The rise and fall of a medieval village: Little Aston (in Aston Blank), Gloucestershire' in *Trans Bristol Gloucestershire Archaeol Soc,* 105, 165-81

—, 1988 'Farming techniques: the west Midlands', in Hallam, H.E. (ed.), *AgHEW 1042-1350,* II, 369-98. Cambridge

—, 1989 *Standards of living in the later Middle Ages: social change in England c1200-1520*

—, 1991a 'Farming practice and techniques: the west Midlands', in Thirsk, J. (ed.), *AgHEW 1348-1500,* III, 222-238. Cambridge

—, 1991b 'The occupation of the land: the west Midlands', in Thirsk, J. (ed.), *AgHEW 1348-1500*, III, 77-92. Cambridge

—, 1995 'Sheepcotes: evidence for medieval sheep farming', in *Med Archaeol*, 39, 136-66

—, 2002a 'Villages and non-villages in the medieval Cotswolds' in *Trans Bristol Gloucestershire Archaeol Soc*, 120, 11-35

—, 2002b *Making a living in the Middle Ages: the people of Britain 850-1520*

Elwes, H.J., 1893 'Cotswold sheep: their, origin, history and present position' in *Cotswold Sheep Society Flock Book*, vol 2

Evans, A.K.B., 1998 'Historical evidence for the Anglo-Saxon church and medieval abbey', in Wilkinson, D.J. and McWhirr, A.D., *Cirencester Anglo-Saxon church and medieval abbey*. Cirencester excavations IV

Farmer, D.L., 1988 Prices and wages, in Hallam, H.E. (ed), *AgHEW 1042-1350*, II. Cambridge

—, 1991 'Marketing the produce of the countryside, 1200-1500' in Thirsk, J. (ed.), *AgHEW 1348-1500*, III, 324-430. Cambridge

—, 1995 'Woodland and pasture sales on the Winchester manors in the thirteenth century: disposing of a surplus, or producing for the market?' in Britnell, R.H. and Campbell, B.M.S. (eds), *A commercialising economy: England 1086 to c1300*, 102-31. Manchester

Fell, B.H., and Mackenzie, K.R., 1994 *The Houses of Parliament* (revised by Natzler, D.L.)

Finberg, H.P.R., 1955a *Roman and Saxon Withington*. University of Leicester Department of Local History Occasional Paper 8

—, 1955b *The making of the English landscape: Gloucestershire*

—, 1957a 'Some early Gloucestershire estates', in Finberg, H.P.R. (ed.), *Gloucestershire studies*, 1-16. Leicester

—, 1957b 'The genesis of Gloucestershire towns' in Finberg, H.P.R (ed.), *Gloucestershire studies*, 52-88. Leicester

—, 1957c 'Winchcombe Abbey and the manor of Sherborne', Finberg, H.P.R. (ed.), *Gloucestershire studies*, 89-113. Leicester

—, 1964 *Lucerna: studies of some problems in the early history of England*

—, 1975 *The Gloucestershire landscape*

Finberg, J., 1977 *The Cotswolds*

Fox, F.F., and Taylor, J. (eds), 1889 *Some account of the Guild of Weavers in Bristol*. Privately printed

Fox, H.S.A., 1989 'The people of the wolds' in Aston, M., Austin, D. and Dyer, C. (eds), *The rural settlement of medieval England*, 77-104

Franklin, P., 1993 *The taxpayers of medieval Gloucestershire: an analysis of the 1327 Lay Subsidy Poll with a new edition of its text*. Stroud

Fryde, E.B., 1952 'Edward III's wool monopoly of 1337: a fourteenth century royal trading venture', in Fryde, E.B. 1983

—, 1964 'The wool accounts of William de la Pole', in Fryde, E.B. 1983

—, 1972 'Anglo-Italian commerce in the fifteenth century: some evidence about profits and the balance of trade', in Fryde, E.B. 1983

—, 1974 'Italian maritime trade with medieval England (c.1270-c.1530)' in Fryde, E.B. 1983

—, 1976 'The English cloth industry and the trade with the Mediterranean c1370-c1480' in Fryde, E.B. 1983

—, 1983 *Studies in medieval trade and finance*. St Anthony York, 25

—, 1991 'Peasant rebellion and peasant discontents', *AgHEW*, III, 744-819

Garner, F.H., and Ingram, M.W., 1973 'Farming and industry: past and present', in Hadfield, C. and Hadfield, A.M. (eds), *The Cotswolds: a new study*. Newton Abbot

Garrett, J.V., and Hodgkins, T., 1995 'Stone built sheepwashes in Gloucestershire' in *Gloucestershire History*, 8, 11-14

Gelling, M., 1953 *The place-names of Oxfordshire*, EPNS, XXIII. Cambridge

George, R.H., 1926 'The contribution of Flanders to the conquest of England 1065-1086' in *Revue Belge de philologie et d'histoire*, 5, 81-97

Gerrard, C., 1994 'Cirencester: a medium sized market town in the medieval period' in Darvill, T. and Gerrard, C., *Cirencester: town and landscape. An urban archaeological assessment*, 98-118. Stroud

Gibbings, L.V. (ed.), 1995 *The Cotswold Sheep*. Ashford

Given-Wilson, C., 1996 *An illustrated history of late medieval England*. Manchester

Graham, R., 1907 'Ecclesiastical history' in *The Victoria History of the Counties of England. A history of Gloucestershire*, II, 1-126

Grundy, G.B., 1935-6 *Saxon charters and field names in Gloucestershire*

Haigh, G., 1947 *The history of Winchcombe Abbey*

Hallam, H.E., 1988 'Population movements in England, 1086-1350' in Hallam, H.E. (ed.), *AgHEW 1042-1350*, II. Cambridge

Hanham, A., 1975 *The Cely letters 1472-1488*, Early English Text Society, 273. Oxford

—, 1985 *The Celys and their world: an English merchant family of the fifteenth century*. Cambridge

Harmer, W.S., 1892 'Cotswold sheep: their origin, history and present position' in *Cotswold Sheep Society Flock Book*, 1

Hart, W.H., 1867 *Historia et cartularium monasterii sancti petri Gloucestriae*, III

Harvey, B., 1977 *Westminster Abbey and its estates in the Middle Ages*. Oxford

Harvey, P.D.A., 1965 *A medieval Oxfordshire village: Cuxham 1240-1400*. Oxford

Havinden, M.A. (ed), 1965 *Household and farm inventories in Oxfordshire 1550-1590*

Harwood, W., 2000 'The trade of Southampton 1448-9', *Hampshire Field Club and Archaeol Soc*, 55, 142-68

Hilton, R.H., 1957 'Winchcombe Abbey and the manor of Sherborne' in Finberg, H.P.R. (ed.), *Gloucestershire studies*, 89-113

—, 1966 *A medieval society: the west Midlands at the end of the thirteenth century*

—, and Rahtz, P.A., 1966 'Upton, Gloucestershire, 1959-1964', *Trans Bristol Gloucestershire Archaeol Soc*, 85, 79-146

Hodgson, E., 1976 *A history of Tetbury*. Dursley

Holmes, G.A., 1960 'Florentine merchants in England, 1346-1436', *Ec Hist Rev*, XIII(2), 193-208

Holmes, G., 1996 'Lorenzo de Medici's London branch', in Britnell, R. and Hatcher, J. (eds), *Progress and problems in medieval England*, 273-85. Cambridge

Holt, H.F., 1871 'The Tames of Fairford', *J Brit Archaeol Assoc*, 27, 110-48

Holt, R., 1985 'Gloucester in the century after the Black Death', *Trans Bristol Gloucestershire Archaeol Soc*, 103, 149-61

Hooke, D., 1978 'Early Cotswold woodland', *J Hist Geogr*, 4, 333-41

—, 1998 *The landscape of Anglo-Saxon England*. Leicester

Hoshino, H., 1983 'The rise of the Florentine woollen industry in the fourteenth century', in Harte, N.B. and Ponting, K.G. *Cloth and clothing in medieval Europe: essays in memory of Professor E.M. Carus-Wilson*, Pasold Studies in Textile History, 2, 184-204

Hoskins, W.G., 1955 *Sheep farming in Saxon and medieval England*, The Wool Education Society

—, 1976 *The age of plunder: King Henry's England 1500-1547*

Hurst, J.D., Robson-Glyde, S., and Lockett, N., 2002 *Sheepwashes in the Cotswolds AONB: map-based survey and conditional assessment*. Unpublished internal Worcestershire County Archaeol Rep, 940

Jackson, J.W., 1961 'The animal bones', in Clifford, E.M., *Bagendon, a Belgic oppidum: a record of the excavations 1954-56*, 268-71. Cambridge

Johnson, J., 1985 *Tudor Gloucestershire*. Gloucester

—, 1994 *Stow-on-the-Wold*

Jones, A., 1994 *The Cotswolds*. Chichester

Jones, A.H.M., 1960 'The cloth industry under the Roman Empire', in *Ec Hist Rev*, XIII(2), 183-92

Kerridge, E., 1972 'Wool growing and wool textiles in medieval and early modern times', in Jenkins, J.G. (ed), *The wool textile industry of Great Britain*, 19-33

King, A., 1988 'Villas and animal bones', in Branigan, K. and Miles, D. (eds), *The economies of Romano-British villas*, 51-9. University of Sheffield

Kingsford, C.L., 1919 *The Stonor letters and papers 1290-1483*, Camden Society 3 ser, XXIX

—, 1923 *Supplementary Stonor letters and papers (1314-1482)*, Camden Society 3 ser, XXXIV

Kosmala, K., 1993 *Compton Abdale in the Cotswolds*. Winchcombe

Langdon, J., 1997 'Was England a technological backwater in the Middle Ages?' in Astill, G. and Langdon, J. (eds), *Medieval farming and technology: the impact of agricultural change in northwest Europe*, 275-91

Latimer, J., 1903 *The history of the Society of Merchant Venturers in Bristol*. Privately printed

Lees, B.A., 1935 *Records of the Templars in England in the twelfth century: the inquest of 1185 with illustrative charters and documents*, Records of social and economic history, IX

Levitan, B., 1993 'Vertebrate remains' in Woodward, A. and Leech, P., *The Uley shrines: excavation of a ritual complex on West Hill, Uley, Gloucestershire, 1977-9*, English Heritage Archaeol Rep, 17

Levitan, B., and King, A., 1986 'Animal bones' in McWhirr, A., *Houses in Roman Cirencester*, Cirencester excavations III, 133-52

Lewis, J., 1996 *The Cotswolds: life and traditions*

Lipson, E., 1953 *A short history of wool and its manufacture (mainly in England)*

Lloyd, T.H., 1973 *The movement of wool prices in medieval England*, Economic History Review supplement 6

—, 1977 *The English wool trade in the Middle Ages*. Cambridge

—, 1982 *Alien merchants in England in the High Middle Ages*. Brighton

Locker, A., 2000 'Animal bone', in Lawson, A.J., *Potterne 1982-5: animal husbandry in later prehistoric Wiltshire*, Wessex Archaeological rep, 17

Lockett, A., 1974 *The wool trade*

Luccock, J., 1809 *An essay on wool, containing a particular account of the English fleece*

Lumby, J.R. (ed), 1895 *Chronicon Henrici Knighton Rolls Series*, II, 58-65

Macray, W.D., 1863 *Chronicon abbatiae de Evesham ad annum 1418*

McWhirr, A., 1981 *Roman Gloucestershire*. Gloucester

Madge, S.J., 1903 *Abstracts of inquisitiones post mortem for Gloucestershire 1236-1300*

Mallet, M.E., 1967 *The Florentine galleys in the fifteenth century*. Oxford

Maltby, M., 1998 'The animal bones from Roman 'small towns' in the Cotswolds', in Timby, J.R., *Excavations at Kingscote and Wycomb, Gloucestershire*, 421-8

Maltby, M., 2002 'The animal bone', in Enright, D. and Watts, M., 'A Romano-British and medieval settlement at Stoke Road, Bishop's Cleeve, Gloucestershire', *Bristol Gloucestershire Archaeol Rep*, 1, 44-9

Manning, W.H., 1972 'The method of manufacture of Romano-British woolcombs', *Ant J*, 52, 333-5

Marshall, W., 1796 *The rural economy of Gloucestershire: vol II* (reprinted 1979)

—, 1818 *The review and abstract of the county reports to the Board of Agriculture, vol 2: western department*

Mate, M., 1997 'Agricultural technology in southeast England 1348-1530', in Astill, G. and Langdon, J., *Medieval farming and technology: the impact of agricultural change in northwest Europe*, 251-74

Mason, E. (ed.), 1980 *The Beauchamp cartulary charters 1100-1268*, Publication of the Pipe Roll Soc new ser, 43

Massingham, H.J., 1938 *Shepherd's country – a record of the crafts and people of the hills*

Mawer, A., 1924 *The chief elements used in English place-names*. Cambridge

—, and Stenton, F.M., 1927 *The place-names of Worcestershire*. Cambridge

Mazzaoui, M.F., 1981 *The Italian cotton industry in the later Middle Ages 1100-1600*. Cambridge

Miller, E., 1965 'The fortunes of the English textile industry during the thirteenth century', *Ec Hist Rev 2 ser*, 18, 64-82

—, 1991 'Land and people', in Thirsk, J. (ed.), *AgHEW*, III, 1-33. Cambridge

Monk, W.J., 1935 *Northleach and around*

Morgan, N.T., 1985 'Animal bones', in Blockley, K., *Marshfield: Ironmongers Piece excavations 1982-3: an Iron Age and Romano-British settlement in the south Cotswolds*, BAR Brit Ser, 141, 330-52

Mudd, A., William, R.J. and Lupton, A., 1999 *Excavations alongside Roman Ermin Street, Gloucestershire and Wiltshire: the archaeology of the A419/A417 Swindon to Gloucester road scheme*, Oxford Archaeological Unit

Munro, J.H., 1978 'Wool price schedules and the qualities of English wools in the later Middle Ages', *Textile History*, 9, 118-69

—, 1979 *Bullionism and the bill of exchange in England, 1272-1663: a study*

—, 1983 'The medieval scarlet and the economics of sartorial splendour', in Harte, N.B. and Ponting, K.G. (eds), *Cloth and clothing in medieval Europe: essays in memory of Professor E.M. Carus-Wilson*, Pasold Studies in Textile History, 2, 13-70

—, 1988 'Textile technology of the Middle Ages', in Strayer, J.R. (ed.), *The dictionary of the Middle Ages*, 693-711. New York

—, 1994 *Textiles, towns and trade: essays in the economic history of late-medieval England and the Low Countries*

Myers, A.R. (ed.), 1969 *English historical documents, vol IV: 1327-1485*

National Sheep Association, 1998 *British sheep* (9th edition)

Noddle, B., 1979 'Animal bones' in Gracie, H.S. and Price, E.G., 'Frocester Court Roman villa. Second report 1968-77', *Trans Bristol Gloucestershire Archaeol Soc*, 97, 51-60

—, 2000 'Large vertebrate remains' in Price, E., *Frocester: a Romano-British settlement, its antecedents and successors*, Gloucester and District Archaeol Research Group

Norris, M., 1965 *Brass rubbing*

Oschinsky, D., 1971 *Walter of Henley and other treatises on estate management and accounting*. Oxford

Origo, I., 1957 *The merchant of Prato*

Pantin, W.A., 1933 *Documents illustrating the activities of the general and provincial chapters of the English Black Monks 1215-1540, II*, Camden Soc 3 ser, 47

Patterson, R.B., 1998 *The original acta of St Peter's Abbey*. Gloucester

Perkins, V.R., 1899 'Documents relating to the Cistercian monastery of St Mary, Kingswood', *Trans Bristol Gloucestershire Archaeol Soc*, 22, 179-256

Perry, R., 1945 'The Gloucestershire woollen industry 1100-1690', *Trans Bristol Gloucestershire Archaeol Soc*, 66, 49-137

—, 1986 *Wotton-under-Edge; times past-time present*. Wotton under Edge

Phillimore, W.P.W. (ed.), 1894-5 'Merchants' marks', *Gloucestershire notes and queries*, VI, 10-12

Platt, C., 1973 *Medieval Southampton: the port and trading community AD 1000-1600*

Platt, C., Coleman-Smith, R., and Hurst, J.G., 1975 'The pottery: introduction', in Platt, C. and Coleman-Smith, R., *Excavations in medieval Southampton 1953-1969, vol 2 (The finds)*, 16-31

Ponting, K.G., 1957 *A history of the West of England cloth industry*

Postan, M.M., 1973 *Medieval trade and finance*. Cambridge

Povah, A., 1894 *The annals of the parishes of St Olave Hart Street and Allhallows Staining in the City of London*

Powell, G., 1992 'A note on Chipping Campden', in Bishop, L., *The general accounts of the churchwardens of Chipping Campden 1626 to 1907*, Campden Record Ser

Power, E., 1924 *Medieval people*

—, 1926 *The English wool trade in the reign of Edward IV*

—, 1933 'The wool trade in the fifteenth century', in Power, E. and Postan, M.M. (eds), *Studies in English trade in the fifteenth century*, 39-90

—, 1941 *The wool trade in English medieval history*

Pritchard, F.A., 1984 'Late Saxon textiles from the City of London' in *Med Archaeol*, 28, 46-71

Rahtz, P., 1969 'Upton, Gloucestershire, 1964-68', *Trans Bristol Gloucestershire Archaeol Soc*, 88, 74-126

—, and Hirst, S., 1976 *Bordesley Abbey*, BAR Brit Ser, 23

Read, J.M., 1865 *The Cotteswold sheep*. Cirencester (reprinted from the *Agricultural Gazette*)

Reece, R., 1976 'From Corinion to Cirencester: models and misconceptions', in McWhirr, A. (ed.), *Studies in the archaeology and history of Cirencester*, BAR Brit Ser, 30, 61-80

Rhodes, J., 2002 *A calendar of the registers of the Priory of Llanthony by Gloucester, 1457-1466, 1501-1525*, Bristol and Gloucestershire Archaeol Soc

Richmond, I.A., 1955 'Note on *Tapete Britannicum*' in Caputo, G. and Goodchild, R., 'Diocletian's price-edict at Ptolemais' (Cyrenaica), *J Roman Studies*, 45, 114

Roberts, B.K. and Wrathmell, S., 2000 *An atlas of rural settlement in England*

Rogers, J.E.T., 1866 *A history of agriculture and prices in England, vol 1: 1259-1400*. Oxford

—, 1882 *A history of agriculture and prices in England, vol 2: 1401-1582*. Oxford

Ross, C.D., 1964 *The cartulary of Cirencester Abbey*

Rothwell, H. (ed.), 1975 *English historical documents vol III: 1189-1327*

Royce, D., 1892 *Landboc sive registrum monasterii beatae Mariae virginis et sancti Cenhelmi de Winchelcumba in comitatu Gloucestrensi, ordinis sancti Benedicti*, I

Ruddock, A.A., 1951 *Italian merchants and shipping in Southampton 1270-1600*, Southampton Record Ser (new ser), 1

Rudge, T., 1807 *General view of the agriculture of the County of Gloucester*

Rushen, P.C., 1899 *The history and antiquities of Chipping Campden in the County of Gloucester*

Ryder, M.L., 1964 The history of sheep breeds in Britain, *Ag Hist Rev*, XII (i), 1-12, and 65-82

—, 1981a 'British medieval sheep and their wool types' in Crossley, D.W. (ed.), *Medieval industry*, CBA Res Rep, 40, 16-28

—, 1981b 'Wools from Vindolanda', *J Archaeol Sci*, 8, 99-103

—, 1983a 'The history of sheep in Britain: wool remains throw light on past fleece changes', *Popular Archaeology*, April 1983, 4(1), 16-19

—, 1983b *Sheep and man*

—, 1984a 'Sheep representations, written records and wool measurements', in Clutton-Brock, J. and Grigson, C., *Animals and archaeology: early herders and their flocks*, BAR Int Ser, 202, 69-82

—, 1984b 'Medieval sheep and wool types', *Ag Hist Rev*, 32

—, 1993 'The textile fibres and the sheep figurines', *Britannia*, XXIV, 204-7

Salzman, L.F., 1931 *English trade in the Middle Ages*

Sayles, G., 1931 'The "English Company" and a merchant's oath' in *Speculum*, 6.2, 177-205

Scaife, R., 1999 'Pollen analysis of the Churn valley river channel', in Mudd *et al*, 502-10

Scott, R., 1959 'Medieval agriculture' in *Wiltshire VCH IV*

Seebohm, M.E., 1927 *The evolution of the English farm*

Sherborne, J.W., 1971 *The port of Bristol in the Middle Ages*

Sherborne muniments, 1900 *Calendar of the charters, rolls and other documents, as contained in the muniment room at Sherborne House in Gloucestershire*. Privately printed

Sherwood, J., and Pevsner, N., 1974 *The buildings of England: Oxfordshire*

Shilson, J.W., 1944 'Weighing wool in the Middle Ages' in *Antiquity*, 70, 72-77

Smith, A.H., 1964 *The place-names of Gloucestershire, Part I*, EPNS, XXXIII. Cambridge

Smith, B., 1976 *The Cotswolds*

Smith, B.S., and Ralph, E., 1996 *A history of Bristol and Gloucestershire*

Smith, J., 1747 *Chronicon rusticum-commerciale; or memoirs of wool* (reprinted 1968)

Smith, L.T., 1964 *The itinerary of John Leland in or about the years 1536-1539*

Snooks, G.D., 1995 'The dynamic role of the market in the Anglo-Norman economy and beyond, 1086-1300' in Britnell, R.H. and Campbell, B.M.S. (eds), *A commercialising economy: England 1086 to c1300*, 27-54. Manchester

Stephenson, M.J., 1988 'Wool yields in the medieval economy', *Ec Hist Rev 2 ser*, 41.3, 368-91

Stuart, R., 1995 *Shepherds and sheep 1580-1660*

Sutton, A.F., 2002 'The Merchant Adventurers of England: their origins and the Mercers' Company of London', *Historical Research*, 75(187), 25-46

Swynnerton, C., 1923 'Some early court rolls of the manors of Stonehouse, King's Stanley, Woodchester, and Achards' in *Trans Bristol Gloucestershire Archaeol Soc*, 45, 203-52

Szarmach, P.E., Tavormina, M.T. and Rosenthal, J.T. (eds), 1998 *Medieval England: an encyclopaedia*

Tate, W.E., 1943 'Gloucestershire enclosure acts and awards', *Trans Bristol Gloucestershire Archaeol Soc*, 66, 1-70

Tawney, R.H., and Power, E. (eds), 1924a *Tudor economic documents, vol 3: pamphlets, memoranda and literary extracts*

—, (eds), 1924b *Tudor economic documents, vol 2: commerce, finance and the Poor Law*

Taylor, A., 1993 'A Roman lead coffin with pipeclay figurines from Arrington, Cambridgeshire', *Britannia*, XXIV, 191-225

—, and Green, M., 1992 'Arrington' in *Current Archaeology*, 130, 420-22

Taylor, P., and Tomlinson, M., 1987 *Wool on the back: travel the old pack horse routes*

Thawley, C., 1982 'The animal remains', in Wacher, J.S. and McWhirr, A.D., *Early Roman occupation at Cirencester*, Cirencester excavations I, 211-227

Thoen, E., 1997 'The birth of Flemish husbandry: agricultural technology in medieval Flanders', in Astill, G. and Langdon, J., *Medieval farming and technology: the impact of agricultural change in northwest Europe*, 69-85

Thomas, J.F.H., 1955 *Sheep* (revised edition)

Thompson, J.W., 1928 *Economic and social history of the Middle Ages (300-1300)*

—, 1931 *Economic and social history of Europe in the later Middle Ages (1300-1530)*

Toynbee, J., 1964 *Art in Britain under the Romans*. Oxford

Toynbee, J.M.C., 1973 *Animals in Roman life and art*

Trow-Smith, R., 1957 *A history of British livestock husbandry to 1700*

Turner, G., 1794 'General view of the agriculture of the County of Gloucester with observations on the means of its improvement' in W. Marshall, *The review and abstract of the county reports to the Board of Agriculture first published 1809*, 394-418 (reprinted 1969)

van Uyten, R., 1983 'Cloth in medieval literature of western Europe' in Harte, N.B. and Ponting, K.G., *Cloth and clothing in medieval Europe: essays in memory of Professor E.M. Carus-Wilson*, Pasold Studies in Textile History, 2

van Werveke, H., 1971 'The Low Countries', in Postan, M.M., Rich, E. and Miller, E., *The Cambridge economic history of Europe, III, Economic organisation and policies in the Middle Ages*, 340-60

Verey, D., 1970 *The buildings of England: Gloucestershire, the Cotswolds*

—, 1982 *Cotswold churches*. Gloucester

Vose, E.K., 1953 *The estates of Worcester Cathedral Priory in the later Middle Ages*, unpublished typescript dated 1990 (Special Collections, University of Birmingham library)

Watson, C.E., 1932 'The Minchinhampton custumal and its place in the story of the manor', *Trans Bristol Gloucestershire Archaeol Soc*, 54, 203-384

Whitfield, C., 1958 *A history of Chipping Campden and Captain Robert Dover's Olympick Games*. Eton

Whitlock, R., 1965 *A short history of farming in Britain*

Wild, J.P., 2002 'The textile industries of Roman Britain', *Britannia*, XXXIII, 1-42

Willard, J.F., 1926 *Inland transportation in England during the fourteenth century*

Williams, C.H. (ed.), 1967 *English historical documents vol V: 1485-1558*

Wilson, J.M., 1919 *The Liber Albus of the Priory of Worcester: parts I and II, 1301-1339*

Woodman, M., 1978 *Cotswolds to Calais: the golden age of Cotswold wool*. Gloucester

Wright, T. (ed.), 1861 *Political poems and songs*, Rolls Ser

Yealland, S., and Higgs, E.S., 1966 'The economy', in Hilton, and Rahtz, 139-43

Index

Places are generally in Gloucestershire, unless otherwise stated

If you are interested in purchasing other books published by Tempus,
or in case you have difficulty finding any Tempus books in your local bookshop,
you can also place orders directly through our website

www.tempus-publishing.com